The Post-Soviet Economy

The Post-Soviet Economy

Soviet and Western Perspectives

Edited by
Anders Åslund

Pinter Publishers
London

First published in Great Britain in 1992 by
Pinter Publishers Limited
25 Floral Street, London WC2E 9DS

British Library Cataloguing in Publication Data

A CIP catalogue record for this book is available from the
British Library.

ISBN 1-85567-039-9

Typeset in New Baskerville by Koinonia Ltd, Manchester
Printed and bound in Great Britain by Biddles Ltd,
Guildford and King's Lynn

Contents

Tables

Contributors

Sergei Aleksashenko, Dr, Department of Economic Reform, Scientific-Industrial Union, Moscow; worked previously in the Reform Commission of the USSR Council of Ministers and participated in the Shatalin group that drew up the 500-day programme in August 1990.

Anders Åslund, Professor, Director, Stockholm Institute of Soviet and East European Economics, Stockholm School of Economics; author of *Gorbachev's Struggle for Economic Reform* (Pinter, 1989 and 1991); adviser to the Russian government.

Alexander Bim, Dr, Deputy Director, Institute of the Market, the USSR Academy of Sciences, Moscow. Author of *Reforma khozyaistvennogo upravleniya: zadachi, opyt, problemy* (Moscow, 1989).

Stuart Brown, Assistant Professor, Department of Economics, Georgetown University, Washington, DC; specializes in regional and foreign trade issues in the USSR.

Boris Fedorov, Professor, European Bank for Reconstruction and Development (EBRD, London) and Institute of the Study of Economic Policy (Moscow); former Russian Minister of Finance; participated in the Shatalin group that drew up the 500-day programme in August 1990; specializes in financial and monetary issues.

Leonid Grigoriev, Dr, Head of Department of Privatization, Institute of the Study of Economic Policy (Moscow); Russian Deputy Minister of Finance and Economics; participated in the Shatalin group that drew up the 500-day programme in August 1990.

Ardo Hansson, Associate Professor, Department of Economics, University of British Columbia, and visiting fellow at WIDER (World Institute for Development Economics Research, UN, Helsinki); working on transition and macroeconomic stabilization in formerly socialist countries.

Grigorii Khanin, Dr, visiting fellow, Stockholm Institute of Soviet and East European Economics, and Novosibirsk; author of original reassessments of the growth of the Soviet national income, *Dinamika ekonomicheskogo razvitiya SSSR* (Novosibirsk, 1991).

Vladimir Kosmarskii, Head of Department, Institute of Employment and All-Union Centre for the Study of Public Opinion, USSR Academy of Sciences, Moscow; Russian Deputy Minister of Labour.

Susanne Oxenstierna, Dr, Swedish Institute for Social Research, University of Stockholm; author of *From Labour Shortage to Unemployment? The Soviet Labour Market in the 1980s* (Almqvist & Wicksell, 1990).

Jeffrey D. Sachs, Galen I. Stone Professor of International Trade, Harvard University; former or current adviser on economic policy for a dozen governments, notably Poland and Russia; co-author of the programme 'Window of Opportunity' or 'Grand Bargain' for the USSR in July 1991.

Pekka Sutela, senior specialist on the Soviet economy, Bank of Finland, Helsinki, and Associate Professor, University of Helsinki; author of *Economic Thought and Economic Reform in the Soviet Union* (Cambridge University Press, 1991).

Acknowledgements

This book is based on a selection of papers presented at a conference on the Soviet economy in crisis and transition, held at the Stockholm School of Economics, 11–12 June 1991, and organized by the Stockholm Institute of Soviet and East European Economics. It was a small research conference with about 40 participants, facilitating intense discussion. The participants represented a wide range of views and a large number of nationalities. The papers included in this volume have been revised and edited under the impact of the lively discussion.

Hence gratitude should be expressed not only to the authors, but also to the active participants (in alphabetic order): Hans Aage, Annika Alexius, Carlos Asilis, Erik Berglöf, Igor Birman, Wlodzimierz Brus, Pawel Dembinski, Hilde Grönblad, Philip Hanson, Manuel Hinds, Hans-Hermann Höhmann, Konstantin Kagalovsky, Sten Luthman, Ivan Major, Pavel Pelikan, Marian Radetzky, Per Ronnås, Peter Semneby, Aleksandr Shokhin, Örjan Sjöberg, Michael Sohlman, Ulf Stange, Joakim Stymne, Ann-Mari Sätre-Åhlander, Albina Tretyakova, Aleksei Ulyukaev, Kristian Uppenberg, Yevgenii Yasin and Gennadii Zoteev.

Vanita Singh Mukerji and Marion Cutting have provided editorial assistance; Gun Malmquist and Eva Gentzschein have offered secretarial services and Birgitta Högfeldt functioned as conference secretary.

Both the conference and consecutive work on this book have been financed by the Swedish Royal Academy of Sciences and the Stockholm Institute of Soviet and East European Economics. In particular, I should like to express my appreciation of the unfailing support from the board of our Institute, including Göran Ennerfelt, Michael Sohlman, Rune Barnéus, Katarina Brodin, Staffan Burenstam Linder and Gunnar Lund.

Regardless of the many people who have kindly assisted in the production of this book, the ultimate responsibility for any remaining errors must fall upon me.

Anders Åslund
Stockholm, September 1991

Introduction

Anders Åslund

When this book was conceived, it was obvious that the Soviet economy was in a severe economic crisis and it was plain that the existing policies could not be pursued for much longer. But it was by no means clear which direction the Soviet leadership would take, or indeed what kind of countries would arise out of the Soviet Union. Uncertainty is a great challenge to scholarship. When organizing the conference on the Soviet economy in crisis and transition, we tried to take a multitude of uncertainties into consideration. What kind of turning-point was the country approaching? Our hope was not to predict what would happen but to help to uncover the essential aspects of the Soviet economy that will remain relevant whatever happens in the political sphere.

Another ambition has been to involve primarily young economists, who have matured but who are looking at the swiftly changing Soviet scene with reasonably fresh eyes. Moreover, we wanted to have a fair mixture of views and nationalities. Thus, it is intentional that half the authors in this book are Soviet citizens and half are Westerners, though we have tried to contrast Soviet and Western views only to a limited extent. After all, individual variations are far greater. We have not tried to pursue a clear line of reasoning, but rather to reflect different perspectives. Although the views differ widely, there is a clear pattern. While most of the Western authors argue in favour of a swift change based on the Polish model of a comprehensive change of economic system, the Soviet participants tended to be more favourably inclined towards more gradual change. The Soviets tended to nurture greater hope that the state would be able to mitigate the effects of the necessary shocks. However, there was hardly any disagreement on such major points as the need for a fully-fledged market economy and massive privatization. The disputes focused upon how the transition to a market economy should occur.

The book is organized in four parts. Our goal has been to cover key topics that will remain relevant. Part 1 discusses the state of the Soviet economy. In Part 2, macroeconomic stabilization policies and foreign trade issues come to the fore. Relations between the republics and the centre of the union are also such important problems from an economic point of view that Part 3 of the book is devoted to them. Finally, Part 4 discusses how the Soviet Union – or its future separate parts – may face the future.

When discussing the Soviet economy, it seems necessary to start with an overall assessment. Who could be better for this task than Grigorii Khanin, an independent economist from Novosibirsk who has long pursued his own research into the murky Soviet statistics and arrived at a far more pessimistic assessment than any serious researcher had done before him. Today, however, it appears that Khanin's research has been more accurate than even his friends believed, and it seems as if in some cases he has been excessively optimistic. The appropriate title of Khanin's paper is 'The Soviet Economy – from Crisis to Catastrophe'. Who today can deny that this is what is happening in the USSR? Still, Khanin's theses were controversial at the conference many of his Soviet colleagues argued that he had exaggerated the size of the actual economic decline.

If any true systemic change is to take place, the population must be prepared to accept it. As a senior researcher at the All-union Centre for the Study of Public Opinion, Vladimir Kosmarskii has been among the pioneers in the field of opinion research. His paper analyses public attitudes to the transition to a market economy. It contains a multitude of statistical materials that have not been published in the West before. One of the most conclusive results is that a deep sense of economic crisis prevails and that people realize that no swift improvement is likely, which is an important precondition of radical change. At the same time, however, the population are not prepared to undertake any sacrifices in order to help their governments, clarifying the poor legitimacy of the Soviet government and most republican governments in 1990. The market economy has been widely accepted and privatization has also gained a majority support. However, scrutiny revealed that the support for privatization was shallow, and that most people have opted for some kind of collective ownership of at least larger enterprises. The attitude to unemployment has undergone a fast change, from extremely negative to ever-greater acceptance. In most polls, the regional differences are palpable: Estonia is the most reformist and Central Asia the least. Generally, public attitudes appear to be in a state of flux. The number of uncertain respondents is large; the shifts in public opinion are huge; the revealed attitudes vary greatly in response to how a question is put.

Susanne Oxenstierna has undertaken a rigorous investigation into trends in employment and unemployment: unemployment is inevitably one of the least attractive consequences of a transition to a market economy, particularly at an early stage. Oxenstierna sorts out the differences between Soviet and Western concepts with clarity, as well as scrutinizing multiple kinds of Soviet statistics. Although there are significant margins in the final assessments, it is clear that Soviet unemployment is rather limited by Western standards, while it is equally obvious that it is already increasing and that it is likely to be boosted in the transition to a market economy.

The second part of the book is devoted to macroeconomic stabilization and foreign trade. Ardo Hansson has taken on the task of assessing the risk of hyperinflation in the Soviet Union. He does so by systematically discussing what types of hyperinflationary shocks there are and what propagation mechanisms may exist. His paper has the great merit of drawing on a wide literature on extreme inflationary pressures and stabilizations and he compares the results with the Soviet situation. Hansson also perceives what special Soviet features may be of significance. His conclusion is that the Soviet situation is very serious, although hyperinflation cannot be taken for granted. So it is vital to introduce a comprehensive stabilization programme and Hansson suggests its basic features.

Pekka Sutela continues by discussing the role of the external sector during the transition. His paper follows naturally after Hansson's, focusing on the meaning and importance of various forms of convertibility and foreign-exchange regimes. Sutela also considers arguments in favour of a gradual or a swift opening of an economy to the world economy. While he is basically in favour of the swift liberalization of foreign trade, he argues that there are special Soviet features, such as the enormous size of the country, that make the need for the swift liberalization of foreign trade less than in Poland, for instance.

In his paper, the former Russian Minister of Finance, Boris Fedorov, discusses the same issues that Hansson and Sutela have elaborated. Still, his paper is rather different because of its perspective. On the one hand, Fedorov wants to underline the paucity of the economic knowledge of Soviet policy-makers and economists. On the other hand, he criticizes Western economists for not realizing how special the Soviet Union is. Many concrete suggestions are to be found in this paper. In conclusion, Fedorov does not end up all that far from the positions of Hansson and Sutela, though, with his emphasis on Soviet peculiarities, he is distinctly more cautious and in favour of a more gradual approach.

The third part of this book investigates the difficult issues of federation, confederation or community. Its two papers discuss the same issues but from somewhat different perspectives. Sergei Aleksashenko contrasts the Soviet situation with the basic choices and clarifies what they imply. He pays particular attention to monetary and fiscal questions. He discards as not very viable the popular option of a weak confederation. For economic reasons, he would prefer the maintenance of a single monetary system, but he recognizes that such an option is hardly politically possible. Thus his paper ends without any apparent hope for any reasonable solution, which appears wise a couple of months and a number of declarations of independence later.

Stuart Brown's approach is rather different. He tries to establish in what field there is a Western economic theory that may be applicable to the economic relations between the republics and the centre. After having pinpointed relevant theory, he assesses its implications for the federal crisis of the USSR. Much of his paper is concerned with the multiple aspects of fiscal federalism. Another approach is club theory, suggesting how different, complementary interests may lead to collusion. A third perspective is offered by the application of the game theory to interrepublic bargaining. The manifold approaches appear to open up the problems and Brown's conclusions appear distinctly more optimistic than Aleksashenko's, although they do not play down the complexities.

My own paper, which opens the fourth part of the book, is a critique of the most significant Soviet reform plans. It draws on lessons from the transition process in Eastern Europe. A major focus of this paper is the importance of democratization for successful systemic change in a formerly socialist country. It is a truism that the relations between the centre and the republics are a vital problem that raises political obstacles. Surprisingly, however, many problems seem to be a result of a lack of intellectual comprehension. Much of the ensuing heated debate concerned my discarding of gradualism to systemic change as a lack of understanding, which several Soviet economists particularly perceived as flawed.

Alexander Bim focuses on the role of the state in the transition to a market economy. Bim argues in favour of a social-democratic strategy, which allows the state to play a substantial role, while he sounds several warnings against too liberal strategies. In essence, however, his is an advocacy against ideology as such and in favour of pragmatism. He argues that the state will play a substantial role so that it can provide such a social security system that people will be prepared to accept reforms.

A common assumption is that public ownership prevails in communist states. Leonid Grigoriev strips us of that illusion. He claims there are ulterior or hidden property rights to most kinds of so-called public property. Any privatization implies that certain parts of the actual owners – the Nomenklatura – will lose property. Therefore they first fight against privatization and later on adjust through Nomenklatura privatizations. Grigoriev looks at different forms of property and suggests that a successful strategy of privatization should be based on 'divide and rule'. Reformers need to form alliances with certain parts of the Nomenklatura.

This conference was held at the time when a group of Soviet and American economists and political scientists sat in Cambridge, Massachusetts, and elaborated what has come to be known as 'the grand bargain' or a window of opportunity: a plan for swift systemic change in the USSR in sincere collaboration with the West. Jeffrey Sachs came over and presented the ideas as they then stood. His oral presentation has been recorded and adapted, though some of the oral style has been retained. His presentation undoubtedly aroused the most intense debate. A multitude of diverse opinions were aired. Many questions probed into whether the conditionality was sufficiently strict. Without trying to sum up the general attitude to these proposals, the sheer tension in the atmosphere made it evident that they were considered vitally important for the future debate over systemic change and stabilization in the Soviet Union or its future parts.

While I write these lines, the failed coup has already occurred in the Soviet Union and the Baltic republics have gained international recognition. Rather than introducing indications in the various articles on where future developments may go in the light of today, I think it is more appropriate to maintain the integral reasoning from June–August 1991. This is not only a picture of a time. It is also an assessment of what it is possible to accomplish in a certain kind of economic and political situation. The reader is probably better helped by a book comprised of articles with common assumptions.

Anders Åslund
Stockholm, September 1991

PART I
THE STATE OF THE
SOVIET ECONOMY

1

The Soviet Economy – from Crisis to Catastrophe[1]

Grigorii Khanin

The aim of this paper is to analyse the state of the Soviet economy in the period starting from the middle of 1990, when it sharply deteriorated. My main goal is to present as complete a picture of the economic situation as possible. Considerably less room will be dedicated to explaining the reasons for the deterioration of the state of the economy. I will predominantly deal with the immediate reasons, leaving aside the deeper reasons which are connected to the history of Soviet society and the course of perestroika.[2]

Because official Soviet estimates on the dynamics of macroeconomic indicators are unreliable, I have corrected them, taking into account how they differ from my own alternative estimates (see Khanin, 1991a). Moreover, serious new problems with the statistics have arisen, especially those on the most recent stage of Soviet economic development. Statistics on physical indicators became less reliable because the monitoring of truthfulness in statistics had become less rigid, while the incentives to distort them remained in effect (for example, for the sake of increasing the wage fund). The quantity of physical indicators published in monthly and quarterly reports decreased. Analysis of the budgetary situation has become more difficult because of the elimination of a unified USSR state budget (as a result of the establishment of sovereignty for the union republics). Also, complete data about the size and degree of fulfilment of the budgets of the union republics and the extra-budgetary allocations that had been formed anew in 1991 are lacking. For these reasons, my analysis will make use of fragmentary data published in the press.

In this paper I differentiate between two types of grave economic states: crisis and catastrophe. A crisis in an economy (as in medicine) is a temporary state of decline, which ends with recuperation. The prerequisites of recuperation are laid during the period of the crisis. In a catastrophe, by contrast, a self-destructive mechanism is operating, impeding the revival of the economy. Such a self-destructive socioeconomic mechanism became rooted during the years of totalitarian regime in the USSR. In order to revive the economy, this self-destructive mechanism must be destroyed. A catastrophe is characterized by chaos in the economy, when it becomes impossible to provide for the most elementary needs of the population. Before this stage of economic decline has been reached, even in the presence of the self-destructive mechanism, the situation can still be considered an economic crisis.

Economic crisis

An economic crisis in the USSR began in the third quarter of 1988 when the national income fell by 1 per cent compared to the same period in 1988 (Khanin, 1990). By now it has been going on for three years, thus nearing the length of the deepest and longest-lasting crises in a market economy. At the end of 1988, the crisis was on the scale of the Soviet crisis at the beginning of the 1980s (a 2 per cent fall in national income per year in 1981–82). Meanwhile, the old state and economic structures and methods of governing were gradually losing their grip, while fundamentally new and competent people did not appear on the scene. In a more normal political situation the crisis would have become protracted and deep, but would only have turned into an economic catastrophe after the passing of many years. Therefore, I would argue that the sharp political struggle of the perestroika period gave the crisis its catastrophic nature.

The crisis began to turn into an economic catastrophe in the second half of 1990. According to data from Goskomstat (the USSR State Committee on Statistics) the national income fell by 3.5 per cent in the third quarter of 1990 compared to the same period in 1989. Considering that the real change in the national income had been overestimated by 5-6 per cent for many years by Goskomstat, the decline in the national income was 8.5–9.5 per cent. In the fourth quarter of 1990, Goskomstat's figures showed that the national income had fallen by 8.5 per cent. If we correct this for hidden inflation, this gives a decline by 13.5–14.5 per cent for the year.[3]

Data on the dynamics of the production of electrical power and railroad transportation, which I have used as an indicator of the quarterly change in production in past years, indicate a significantly smaller drop (3–5 per cent). Several possible explanations for this can be found in the particularities of economic development during the second half of 1990 and the first quarter of 1991. Particularly noticeable was the drop of production in construction, which uses a small share of electricity (and in the first quarter of 1991 a drop was also noticeable in agriculture, which also represents a small share of electricity use). Second, railroad transport not only carries the output of the given period, but also the stocks of output, which implies a time-lag between the fall in production and a fall of transports. Third, an important factor in the fall in national income for this period has been the drop in foreign trade turnover, which is linked in part to the production of electricity and railroad transport. On the other hand, it is quite likely that precisely in this period, when the monitoring of truthfulness in book-keeping was abandoned, that over-reporting of the production of energy and railroad transportation began to rise sharply.

Foreign currency crisis

In addition to the general reasons, the onset of economic catastrophe was hastened by four separate and more concrete reasons: the foreign-currency crisis, the fall in the production of raw materials, a fall in the supply of labour and a deterioration of fixed capital. The foreign-currency crisis turned out to be exceptionally perceptible for the Soviet economy because over the 1970s and 1980s the USSR's dependence on foreign economic ties had grown dramatically. In the speeches of Soviet state officials this 'condition' had received the apt name of 'the imports plague' (*importnaya chuma*). Evidence of industry's tremendous dependence, for example, on imports from East European countries can be seen in how deliveries from this region were needed in the enterprises of the Ministry for Machine Tools to produce almost 45 per cent of output, the Ministry of Agricultural Machinery 38 per cent, and the Ministry of Metallurgy 30 per cent (Otdel, 1991, p. 73).

When imports were cut back sharply, cuts should have been made in production for the branches of the economy dependent on imports, as well as in the volume of retail trade turnover and investment. After the sharp drop in world fuel prices in the mid-1980s, the Soviet Union succeeded in maintaining (and even somewhat increasing) its volume of imports by expanding fuel exports and sharply increasing its foreign debt, but only temporarily. It would have been impossible to maintain such a high volume of fuel production and, consequently, of fuel exports. On the other hand, credit payments should have increased and confidence in the USSR as a borrower should have decreased.

The fall in the production and exports of oil, oil products and coal began in 1989 and took on huge proportions in the first quarter of 1991. If the absolute drop in oil exports we saw in the first quarter is repeated in each remaining quarter, then oil exports for 1991 will fall to 60 m. tons compared to 144 m. tons in 1988, oil products to 20 m. tons from 61 m. tons, and coal to 20 m. tons from 39 m. tons (*Narodnoe khozyaistvo*, 1989; 'Ekonomika SSSR', 1991). Exports of several other types of raw materials are dwindling, such as timber (to 8 from 20 m. cubic metres) and cotton fibre (ibid.).

The decrease in exports is partly due to decreased fuel production. But this is not the whole explanation for the fall in fuel exports, especially of oil and oil products. With the decreased production, domestic consumption of oil and oil products should have been cut back, thus liberating them for much-needed export. Thus, when the national income had plummeted by 35 per cent between 1988 and 1991, and the use of oil and oil products per unit of national income could not have risen by more than 5 per cent per year, its domestic consumption should have been decreased by at least 20 per cent or by 80 m. tons (in 1988, domestic consumption was 402 m. tons). Since production had decreased for this period by 90 m. tons, oil and oil products exports should have been cut back by a maximum of 10 m. tons, instead of the actual 125 m. tons.

What is more surprising is that despite this obvious abundance of oil within the country, there is still not enough to go round. Another explanation may be that actual production was less than the production figures show, because of the widespread and growing practice of over-reporting (*pripiski*). A third, partial explanation may be the growing losses in transportation and storage.

Because of reduced fuel exports, the growing expense of servicing the foreign debt, and the limited amount of gold in the currency reserve, by the end of 1989 a number of foreign trade organizations had begun to cease making payments on their loan obligations. This came as a complete surprise to the majority of Western economists and bankers, who had believed in the CIA estimates suggesting large Soviet currency reserves in gold. The Soviet failure to meet its payments exposed the scale of the CIA underestimation. Analysis of the methods used to assess the size of Soviet reserves and production of gold shows that these methods suffer from very serious shortcomings. (One of them, for example, assumes that the productivity of analogous Soviet and American machinery and equipment is the same, which is absurd.)

My own estimate of annual gold production in recent years is a volume of no more than 180-200 tons, instead of the 270-350 tons one commonly sees in Western literature.[4] My estimate is based on different kinds of sources, including fragmentary data (employment figures in the state gold-mining enterprises, the ratio of the number employed in state v. *artel'* (miners' coop) goldmining, and the ratio of labour productivity in state v. artel' goldmining).[5]

An even smaller amount of annual gold production (125-175 tons) was estimated in the summer of 1990 by the Shearman and Lehman company (Commission of the European Communities, 1990, p. 163). But this seems too low to me; at this level, the Soviet gold reserves would have already been exhausted and the sales of gold on the world market would have sharply decreased, neither of which has happened. Calculating that the CIA has exaggerated the quantity of gold mined over the past ten years by at least 100 tons a year, the current gold reserves of the USSR can be estimated at a maximum of 500 tons instead of the figure of more than 2,000 tons calculated by the CIA.[6] Such limited gold reserves can well explain why Soviet organizations on a massive scale did not make their foreign payments in 1990. A related, but very important confirmation of the exceptionally small size of the Soviet gold reserves came in the autumn of 1990 when the USSR refused to supply information (beyond the minimal requirements) about the scale of production and reserves to the commission of the four international economic organizations which was studying the condition of the Soviet economy in connection with proposals to extend economic aid (IMF et al., 1991, pp. 278–9).

As a result of the apparent inability of the USSR to meet its payments, in 1990 Western banks stopped offering credits to the USSR without government guarantees, that is, under the normal conditions. Credits were promised to the USSR in the order of 15 billion dollars (Commission of the European Communities, 1990, p. 25) by a number of different Western countries in the autumn of 1990, but by the end of 1990 even they abruptly stopped granting credits.

It became necessary to cut imports radically because of a combination of factors: in 1990, reserves of gold were markedly reduced; foreign currency reserves fell sharply from 14.7 to 5.1 billion dollars over the same year (IMF et al., 1990); the payments due on the foreign debt peaked in 1991 and exportable goods sharply decreased. Even the transition to a system of settling accounts with the CMEA countries in world prices and convertible currency, which was very advantageous to the USSR, could not alleviate the situation. Imports to the USSR started ebbing in the second half of 1990, and in the first quarter of 1991 they were reduced by 45.1 per cent compared to the same period in 1990 ('Ekonomika SSSR', 1991). To illustrate this, I can say that if the cut-backs in imports are to remain at the level of the first quarter of 1991, it will mean that imports of rolled ferrous metals will practically cease and imports of tea will be nearly cut in half compared to 1989 (ibid).

Diminishing raw materials and supplies

For the first time during times of peace, the production of raw materials and supplies shrank significantly in the USSR. Beside fuels, we are talking about ferrous and non-ferrous metals, timber, raw materials for the chemical industry, agricultural raw materials and so on. Reductions were highly noticeable in the second half of 1990, and in the first quarter of 1991 they took on huge proportions. For example, production fell by 13–15 per cent in animal husbandry output, commercial timber, a number of non-ferrous metals, chemical fibres and threads, and potash. On top of dwindling domestic production of raw materials, an even greater reduction in imports took place. Though due to reduced exports, domestic consumption of some supplies (such as fuel) shrank less than production. However, cases like this were the exception, and, moreover, even domestic consumption was significantly lowered. Considering the high (and growing) material-intensity of the Soviet economy, the decrease in raw materials and supplies (after former stockpiles had been drained) should have quickly led to the reduced production of final output. Reports in the Soviet press told of increasingly frequent cut-backs and even of stoppages in production due to shortages of raw materials, supplies and semi-finished products.

Decreasing employment

Limited labour resources are becoming a problem. In the material-production branches (except for construction) an absolute reduction in the number employed began as early as 1987. In 1990 alone, the number employed in state industrial enterprises shrank by 2 per cent ('Soobshchenie Goskomstata', 1991a). Employment in agriculture is decreasing rapidly. From 1989 to 1991 the number of people working on collective farms (*kolkhozy*) and state farms (*sovkhozy*) has dropped by 15 per cent (*Sovetskaya Rossiya*, 19 June 1991, p. 2).

Disaggregated employment figures illustrate the situation even more dramatically. Employment is falling much more in areas with a more highly-qualified work force (the RSFSR and the Baltic republics) and among the working ages in the countryside where in many regions of the country the work force is already mainly made up of old people and inveterate drunkards. Thus in the RSFSR the number of men aged between 16 and 29 in the countryside shrank from 4.8 million in 1979 to 3.8 million in 1989, or by 20 per cent. Out of these, the number between the ages of 15–19 dropped from 2 million to 1.2 million, or by 40 per cent (*Molodezh SSSR*, 1990, p. 7). The availability of labour in the countryside in many regions has become so poor that now nearly all major agricultural undertakings (such as sowing or harvest) require the help of people from the cities. With perestroika came a diminished respect for authority and this was enough to seriously threaten the 1990 harvest. In a number of areas, they had to declare a state of emergency for the harvest time (which had little result, since few people took any notice of it).

Deteriorating fixed capital

Over the past two years, a qualitative deterioration has taken place in the economy's supply of fixed productive capital. Aged and worn fixed capital began to be a problem by the middle of the 1960s, taking on threatening proportions by the end of the 1980s. Thus, according to official reports, the percentage of fixed capital in industrial production that is obsolete grew from 36 per cent in 1980 to 48 per cent in 1989 (*Narodnoe khozyaistvo*, 1990, p. 353). The actual degree of depreciation is significantly greater, since the replacement value of the most out-dated and worn capital, by my estimates, has been seriously underestimated and thus its share of the overall value of the productive capital is too low.

However, the state of fixed capital assets as a whole deteriorated less than other production factors, because of the over-accumulation which went on for many decades. As S. M. Nikitin (a department head at IMEMO, the Academy of Science's Institute for the World Economy and International Relations) once put it: 'It's not machines we lack, it's wisdom.'[7]

But priorities have changed over the last two years. The Soviet leadership has sought to improve the population's sinking standard of living and to cut the budget deficit while refusing to make any serious cuts in military spending. Instead, efforts have been at the cost of sharp reductions of investment in fixed productive capital starting in 1990. In addition, even the lowered plan targets in investment were significantly under-fulfilled because of deplorable work by builders and the shortage of material resources. As a result, the amount of production capacity put into operation has shrunk drastically. Now this amount appears to be much lower than the amount of productive capital which should be taken out of service. For instance, over the past 30 years, 10–11 m. kilowatts of electrical power generating capacity were put into operation every year. In 1989 this was 3.3 m. kW, and in 1990, 5.1 m. kW (*Narodnoe khozyaistvo*, 1990, p. 545). Thus the volume of production capacity and of fixed capital is undergoing a noticeable absolute decrease.

From crisis to catastrophe

Any one of these reasons would have been sufficient to put the economy in serious difficulties. But together they have made the situation critical. The economic crisis turned into a virtual catastrophe in the first quarter of 1991, when the national income of the USSR shrank by 10 per cent according to Goskomstat ('Ekonomika SSSR', 1991). Correcting for hidden inflation of 5–6 per cent, the real fall was probably 15–16 per cent. This fall was especially dramatic in agriculture (13 per cent officially) and in construction, where the situation is worst of all (even the high-priority construction of housing went down by 27 per cent officially) (ibid).

Everything indicates that the situation will continue to decline in the remaining months of 1991. So far, industry is still functioning, though at lower volumes, using the material resources left over from previous years. But even these are running out. Unemployment and stoppages in many enterprises are likely to increase.[8] According to the CPSU Central Committee's department for socioeconomic policy: 'In light industry alone, over 400, or one-third of factories could stop production, and around one million people would be out of work' (Otdel, 1991, p. 74). It is possible that the giants of Soviet industry such as the *ZIL* and *Rostsel'mash* enterprises, with tens of thousands of employees, might have to stop production (ibid). *Gossnab* (the USSR State Committee for Material and Technical Supply) estimates that in the chemical and timber complex alone, output would shrink to less than half (ibid, p. 73). It is possible that these estimates are somewhat exaggerated, but they accurately express the trend.

Agriculture – traditionally the weakest sector of the Soviet economy – is now facing grave difficulties. Already it is clear that agriculture will work under very difficult conditions in 1991. Because of the decrease in the autumn ploughing and in the sowing of the winter crops in 1990, the volume of springtime field work in the country as a whole should rise by 25 per cent, and in certain regions it should double or triple (*Izvestiya*, 18 March 1991). Incidentally, on the eve of the sowing campaign in 1990, it turned out that there was a severe shortage of mineral fertilizers, pesticides, fuel, seeds, spare parts, agricultural equipment, and auto and agricultural machine drivers. Because of this, a significant reduction of the area sown is expected (ibid). Nor can we expect a repetition of last year's huge, but only partially reaped, harvest although the weather forecasters do predict an unprecedented harvest.

The combination of reduced area under crops and lowered yield will surely bring a significantly lower harvest. Considering the large losses in the harvesting process and over-reporting (for grains academician Vladimir Tikhonov estimated last year's actual yield at 165 m. tons instead of the official figure of 218 m. tons)[9] (*Moskovskie novosti*, 1990, No. 34, p. 10), the actual yield could be much lower. This could lead to a state of semi-famine in the cities and in many agricultural regions in the immediate future. Government sources estimate the 1991 grain harvest at 185-195 m. tons, or 23-33 m. tons less than in 1990 (*Izvestiya*, 11 June 1991, p. 3). This harvest is within the range of the average annual grain crop in the twelfth five-year plan (191.1 m. tons for the first four years of the twelfth five-year plan) (*Narodnoe khozyaistvo*, 1989, p. 420). Despite this, it will be more difficult to supply the population and non-private livestock husbandry with grain compared to past years because the *kolkhozy* and *sovkhozy* have become less willing to surrender their grain to the state at prices far below market value, and because there is not enough foreign currency to purchase grain abroad. Feed preparation in 1991 has been lagging far behind 1990 levels (*Izvestiya*, 8 July 1991, p. 1).

The strikes, especially the miners' strike, that took place in March and April 1991 inflicted serious harm on the economy. The production of coal in March dropped by 18 per cent, and, of this, coking coal dropped by 33 per cent ('Ekonomika SSSR', 1991).

All this allows us to assert that the second, third and fourth quarters of 1991 will give worse results than the first. For the year as a whole, the drop in the national income can hardly be less than 20 per cent.[10] Taking into account the drop in national income by about 15 per cent over the previous two years[11] (Khanin, 1991b), this gives a fall in the national income by 32 per cent: that is, about in the range of the American depression of 1929–32 (*Statistical Abstracts*, 1960, p. 304). Moreover, a serious lack of food is possible by the end of 1991, something the USA did not experience, (nor did they live in such a general state of shortage).

Deepening budget crisis

The breakdown of the system of finance and credit began as a consequence of misguided economic policy, and has become even more acute because of the economic crisis. The peak of this breakdown came in 1991. The union budget is in a critical condition. Because many union republics refused to meet their obligations and because of the general economic crisis, the union budget deficit – 26.7 billion roubles in the first quarter, or 106 billion roubles, if we extrapolate for the year – was as much as 56 per cent of expenditures(!) ('Ekonomika SSSR', 1991).

Regarding the budgets of the union republics, I can mention the situation in the RSFSR. For the first quarter, the RSFSR budget deficit reached some 30 billion roubles, or 120 billion, extrapolating for the whole year (*Izvestiya*, 19 April 1991). I believe the situation in the remaining republics may be even worse. I have sought to determine the approximate deficit for all the union republic budgets together using the shares of the RSFSR in the outlays of the other union republic budgets for 1989 (54 per cent) (*Gosudarstvennyi byudzhet SSSR*, 1990, p. 22). Based on this share, the total deficit for the budgets of the union republics (excluding the RSFSR), appears to be 222 billion roubles. Thus, the total budget deficit should be 328 billion roubles.[12]

Changes made in 1990 in the USSR's financial system meant that a whole range of outlays that were formerly budget expenditures are now paid from different allocations such as the pension fund, the stabilization fund and several others. Thus it is important to check what is included in the state budget when making comparisons with past budgets and budget deficits. Since there is no evidence that pensions are being withheld this year, it is obvious that the established amounts are being disbursed from the pension fund. The stabilization fund (earmarked for financing centralized capital investment, subsidies to unprofitable enterprises and so on) received only 359 m. roubles for the first quarter, while the amount set for the year was 114 billion roubles (*Izvestiya*, 12 April 1990).[13] There were no projected outlays from this fund. I can only assume that the situation of other funds is similar to the stabilization funds: less incoming money than projected, while outlays are similarly smaller too. Thus the set size of the deficit should remain the same, even after taking these new allocations into account.

To determine how large the deficit is in relation to the gross national product, we would have to know its size in current prices for the first quarter. Since this has not been published, we must make our own rough estimate. The GNP was approximately 1,001 billion roubles in 1990 prices (Zoteev, 1991, p. 53). Prices on investment goods grew in the first quarter of 1991 by 44 per cent compared to 1990.[14] The official rise in retail prices of goods and services was 26 per cent ('Ekonomika SSSR', 1991). Taking into account the relationship between the volumes of retail-trade turnover and the sales of paid services on the one hand, and of state capital investments on the other (148 and 39.6 billion roubles respectively in the first quarter of 1991) we get a general rise in prices in the economy of 1.3 times (for the lack of other data, determined only by these two elements).

The final results of the 2 April price rises in retail prices on goods and services are still unknown. Official sources estimate a rise of 1.7 times the old level but this is clearly on the low side, since it underestimates the rise in 'regulated' and free prices. I would say that the level of retail prices is about twice the old price level.[15] If at the same time the retail trade turnover for goods and services is to decline by 15 per cent, then in the next three quarters of the year the GNP will grow by 377.4 billion roubles (=148 x 3 x 0.85). This would mean the GNP would be 1,577 billion roubles for the year (taking into account the 10 per cent decrease in the national income in the first quarter of 1991), while the deficit of the consolidated

USSR budget would be 20.4 per cent.[16] Obviously the quarters to come will affect the size of the deficit. On the one hand, the retail price rises made on 2 April were aimed to reduce the deficit. Sergei Aleksashenko (1991) estimates a reduction of 50 billion roubles for the year, and a reduction of 38 billion for the remaining three quarters of this year. On the other hand, due to the accelerating decline in the national income, receipts to the consolidated budget will decrease even more, and this will bring larger gains from the rise of prices.[17] This colossal budget deficit has arisen despite the fact that planned outlays have decreased sharply and the population is experiencing a tremendous deterioration in their standard of living.[18] As Yegor Gaidar (1991, p. 11) has aptly noted, at similar levels of deficit as a part of GNP – 23.6 per cent and 14.4 per cent – *coups d'état* took place in Argentina and Chile.

There were several reasons for the seven to eightfold increase in the planned budget deficit of 25-30 billion roubles. There was an absurd proposal about achieving 'some growth' in the gross national product (and consequently in the ordinary receipts to the state budget from domestic production and turnover). Imports of consumer goods dropped dramatically (imports which had been facilitating the huge budget income). The amount of incoming money from the new sales tax was seriously overestimated (instead of the 80-100 billion roubles that were planned, 13 billion roubles will be received). Tax discipline had softened, a usual occurrence when a state's administration is in turmoil.

A dangerous new manifestation of the crisis of the financial and credit system is the rapid increase in defaulted loans on short-term bank loans and mutual accounts between enterprises and economic organizations. On 1 March 1991 these totalled 46 billion roubles, an increase of 61 per cent over the year – while the growth of the gross national product in current prices was slightly more than 20 per cent ('Ekonomika SSSR', 1991, p. 17). The system of commercial banks that was created in all haste is now in dire straits because of the poor economic standing of its borrowers, under-qualified personnel, poor monitoring and numerous abuses. Many of these banks could go bankrupt at any time, thus putting their founders and depositors in a bad position (*Wall Street Journal*, 6 June 1991, p. 1).

Sky-rocketing inflation

The budget deficit has grown – between three and four times compared to 1990, depending on how the 1990 deficit is estimated (at 60 billion roubles, in the official data, or at 80 billion, in the view of independent economists). The population's money incomes are increasing ever more rapidly (by 24 per cent in the first quarter of 1991 compared to 16.9 per cent in 1990). Meanwhile, the volume of production and the import of consumer goods is shrinking. All of this has reinforced inflation instead of curbing it, as the October 1990 government programme had set out to do. Even the official index of retail prices expresses this tendency, despite the fact that it underestimates the real scale of inflation. In the first quarter of 1991, the price level rose by 25 per cent compared to the same period in 1990; while in 1990, the figure had been 5 per cent (calculated as an average of monthly data). As a result of the 2 April rises in retail prices and the transition to contractual and 'regulated' retail prices, the price level went up even further. It is already clear that it has risen by more than 100 per cent.

As in other countries with a weakened regime and an economy in shambles, an inflationary spiral is developing in the Soviet Union. Blue-collar and white-collar workers in many sectors of the economy are demanding wage rises twice or three times their current wage (the miners have already been promised this). From the second half of the year a new rise in agricultural purchasing prices is planned. Thus we are talking about a rise in prices this year by several hundred per cent, or a transition from inflation to hyperinflation. In an economy with a significant share of stable prices (before 2 April) inflation has expressed itself in the breakdown of the consumer market. Nearly all kinds of consumer goods have become shortage items, the gap between the prices in state trade and on the black market has grown sharply, and stocks in trade have fallen to critical levels.

Inflation has manifested itself most dramatically in the extraordinary drop over the last few months in the exchange rate of the rouble to the dollar at foreign currency auctions: from 21.6 roubles to the dollar on 14 December 1990 to 35.1 on 28 February 1991 (*Ekonomika i zhizn'*, various issues). The fall in the rate of the rouble on the currency market was particularly rapid after the 2 April price reform. In trading on 9 June 1991, a dollar cost as much as 49.6 roubles (*Izvestiya*, 11 July 1991, p. 1).

Falling standard of living

While a small portion of the population has been able to profit from the liberalization of the economy and the increasing shortages, most people's standard of living grew even worse in 1991. This may be seen in the decreased production and imports (and thus less consumption) of basic consumer goods. Judging from the data published on production and imports expressed in physical units, we are talking about a reduction of about 10-15 per cent. After the price rises on 2 April, the standard of living of a major part of the population deteriorated further. We can see this in the reduction in sales of a number of foodstuffs such as meat and sausages. In May 1991 cooperative and state retail-trade turnover in fixed prices was officially 23 per cent lower than in May 1990 ('Soobshchenie Goskomstata', 1991b). Since Goskomstat is underestimating the real growth of retail prices (by about 5-6 per cent) the actual decrease in state and cooperative (in the old meaning) retail-trade turnover would have been nearly 30 per cent in May 1991.

Evidence of the fall in the standard of living can be found in the unprecedented fall in house building. Medical care has sharply deteriorated. Appropriations to medical care are increasing more slowly than costs. Take, for example, the situation in Moscow: the city's healthcare budget in 1991 was supposed to be 2.4 billion roubles in order to supply all non-paid medical services. Instead, only 1.2 billion was allocated (Repin, 1991).

So far the growth of unemployment has been limited. Officially, it is not large: two million people at the beginning of 1991, or less than 2 per cent of overall employment. In fact, unemployment is higher than this, since a type of unemployment has turned up in the form of sending employees on long unpaid leaves. In the very near future unemployment will doubtless grow dramatically because of the shortage of raw materials, reduced capital construction, conversions, production cut-backs and bankruptcies.[19]

The deteriorating standard of living and the breakdown of the health-care system is already undermining the health of the population. In 1990, mortality grew noticeably (by 0.4 per thousand persons). A huge increase in the number of suicides speaks of the sorry state of affairs. In 1990, between seven and nine people took their own life every week in Moscow, but at the beginning of 1991, this figure was 19-21 people: that is, 2.5 times the 1990 level.[20] The situation in Leningrad is similar (Yunisov, 1991, p. 8). There is a similarity with the Great Depression of 1929–32, when suicides in the United States went from 14 per 100,000 population in 1929 to 17.4 in 1932 (*Statistical Abstracts*, 1934, p. 80).

Dire prospects for the future

If current tendencies persist, a model for development of the Soviet Union in the near future could be based on the experience of countries with war economies. The Soviet economy has much in common with these coun-tries in its share of military spending as a part of the national product, in the level of sacrifice of its population, in the economic system (command economy), and in the level of isolation from the outside world.

Agriculture is seriously weakened in terms of labour and material resources. Agricultural workers have decreasing incentives to increase production because of the deteriorating price relationships between the output of industry and construction and the output of agriculture.[21] We can realistically expect a decrease by 20 per cent in the area under grain crops and a decrease in yield by 30 per cent (in a period of unfavourable climactic conditions).[22] This should lead to a reduction in grain produc-tion by 44 per cent compared to 1990: that is, down to 92 million tons or 300 kilos per capita for the year. It was at this level of per capita grain production (or only slightly higher) that the Russian famines of 1921, 1932 and 1946 broke out. Perhaps there might not be enough grain on the world market just when it is needed to compensate this huge drop in production. Even at a slightly higher level of grain production, sections of the population might experience serious food shortages in the near future.

The unfavourable price relationships, the depreciation of the rouble, the breakdown of the consumer market, the growing proportions of barter trade and the simultaneous breakdown of command methods makes it necessary for *kolkhozy* and *sovkhozy* to cut sharply the proportion of their output available for outside distribution. These cuts had already become significant by 1990 when extraordinary measures had to be taken to keep state grain procurements from being disrupted. Despite this and despite the record harvest, procurement levels were much lower than in 1989. On 16 July 1991, after threshing the harvest from 25 m. hectares, *kolkhozy* and *sovkhozy* surrendered only 3.7 m. tons to state procurements (*Pravda*, 18 July 1991, p. 1), while on 16 July 1990, when they had harvested from 20 m. hectares, they handed over 7.5 million tons, and, in 1989, 12.5 m. tons.[23] This sharp drop in grain procurements could bring the population to the brink of a famine in the cities of a number of regions (since some regional authorities will first send the procured grain to meet the needs of the inhabitants of the cities in their own regions), in Central Asia and in Transcaucasia. Such a deterioration of food supply will aggravate relations between the cities and the countryside, between population groups, between certain republics and between the republics and Moscow, and between the government and the population. Strikes would become more common, further diminishing production in industry, construction and transport, causing further devaluation of the rouble and further discouraging deliveries of agricultural output. Strike activity will inflict most severe damage to the mining sector, electrical energy and transport: these sectors have a relatively high concentration of labour and are more economically vulnerable because of fixed prices on their output.

The decrease in the production of raw materials and fuels, and disruptions in electricity supply and transport, will put the economy in further disarray. The reduction and often the temporary suspension of the production of electricity and heating (due to lack of fuel, strikes, accidents) in addition to the lack of food, will cause the city population to suffer from cold homes, electrical black-outs and from the disarray of municipal services and public transportation. The population of the cities will begin to flee to the countryside and to other countries.

As always in this type of situation, the spheres of culture, science and healthcare are very vulnerable. We can expect mass closure of the schools, vocational schools and scientific institutions, undermining the already modest cultural level of the country's population. The healthcare system will be short of many medicines, instruments and dressings. Patients will receive poorer quality food and experience colder hospitals. Deepening food shortages and insufficient heating will bring easy prey for epidemics; the hospitals and clinics will not be able to prevent them. The result of this will be a growing mortality rate. Meanwhile, because of economic troubles and social instability, fertility rates will fall: some regions have already plummeted to a third or fourth of their usual level.

Industry is in shambles and incapable of providing even minimal goods to the agricultural sector. Without petrol, lubricants, electricity and spare parts, it is impossible to do any agricultural work. As a result, the production and consumption of food will decrease even more and the crisis will deepen. Productive capital investments will be minimal because of the shortage of labour, materials and financial resources. This will further reduce productive potential and competitiveness on the world market. Scientific and technical progress will freeze. The country will be hurled back several decades in its economic and social development. Is there anything that can save the Soviet Union from the impending catastrophe? Perhaps there is, but that is another subject.

References

Aleksashenko, Sergei (1991) 'Ne gubite, muzhiki, ne gubite', *Nezavisimaya gazeta*, 6 April, p. 2.

Commission of the European Communities (1990) 'Stabilization, Liberalization and Devolution: Assessment of the Economic Situation and Reform Process in the Soviet Union', *European Economy*, No. 45, (December).

Demenin, O. (1990) 'Pochem zoloto', *Vostochnyi ekpress*, No. 1, p. 8.

Directorate of Intelligence (1990) *Handbook of Economic Statistics*, Washington DC.

'Ekonomika SSSR v 1 kvartale 1991 goda. Soobshchenie Goskomstata SSSR' (1991) *Ekonomika i zhizn'*, No. 17, pp. 16–18.

Gaidar, E. (1991) 'V nachale novoi fazy', *Kommunist*, 68, No. 2, pp. 8-19, (January).

Gosudarstvennyi byudzhet SSSR (1990), Moscow: Finansy i Statistika.

IMF, IBRD, OECD and EBRD (1990) *The Economy of the USSR. Summary and Recommendations*, Washington DC: 19 December.

IMF, IBRD, OECD and EBRD (1991) *A Study of the Soviet Economy*, Vol 3, Paris: (February).

Khanin, G. I. (1990) 'Krizis uglublyaetsya', *EKO*, No. 1, pp. 73-87.

Khanin, G. I. (1991a) *Dinamika ekonomicheskogo razvitiya SSSR*, Novosibirsk: Nauka.

Khanin, G. I. (1991b) 'Ekonomicheskii rost v SSSR v 80 gody', *EKO*, No. 5, pp. 25–34.

Legler, V. (1990) 'Zolotoe delo', *EKO*, No. 4, pp. 151–70.

Molodezh SSSR. Statisticheskii spravochnik (1990), Moscow.

Narodnoe khozyaistvo SSSR v 1988 godu (1989), Moscow.

Narodnoe khozyaistvo SSSR v 1989 godu (1990), Moscow.

Otdel sotsial'no-ekonomicheskoi politiki TsK KPSS (1991) 'O neudovletvoritel'nom obespechenii narodnogo khozyaistva syr'evymi resursami v 1991 g', *Izvestiya TsK KPSS*, No. 4 pp. 72-5.

Repin, I. (1991) 'Vse rukhnut po planu,' *Argumenty i fakty*, No. 9, p. 3.

Sel'skoe khozyaistvo SSSR (1988), Moscow.

'Soobshchenie Goskomstata SSSR. Ekonomika SSSR v 1990 godu' (1991a), *Ekonomika i zhizn'*, No. 5, p. 9–13.

'Soobshchenie Goskomstata SSSR' (1991b), 14 June 1991 (unpublished materials of the Stockholm Institute of Soviet and East European Economics, 30 pp.).

Statistical Abstracts of the United States (1934), Washington, DC.

Statistical Abstracts of the United States (1960), Washington, DC.

Yunisov, V. (1991) 'Konchitsya li nasha zima?' *Ogonek*, No. 13, pp. 6–8, 18.

Zoteev, G. N. (1991) *Spad sovetskoi ekonomiki v 1990-1991 godakh i krakh naivnykh reform Gorbacheva*, (unpublished manuscript) Moscow, (February).

Notes

1 Translated from Russian by Marion Cutting. I wish to express my thanks to

colleagues Albina Tretyakova, Anders Åslund and Igor Birman for fruitful discussions on the problems surrounding this paper.

2 These reasons are surveyed in Khanin (1991b).

3 These data do not aspire to be exact. They need to be made more precise using more detailed data on production volume in the third and fourth quarters.

4 The CIA has estimated Soviet gold reserves in 1989 at 2,416 tons, and the annual production at 330 tons (Directorate of Intelligence, 1990, p. 6).

5 The total number employed in goldmining (according to *Glavalmazzoloto*, the Central Board for Almaz gold mining) is 100-120 thousand people (*Pravda*, 5 February 1991, p. 4). The total number employed in the prospector artels subordinated to *Glavalmazzoloto* (which clearly are not included in the first figure of those employed by them) is more than 50 thousand persons (*Izvestiya*, 17 December 1990, p. 3). The ratio of labour productivity in state v. prospector mining is 1:2 (Legler, 1990, p. 156). The yield by prospectors in one of the gold fields of the Chukotka region was 1.4 kilos (Demenin, 1990, p. 8).

6 After this paper was submitted, the USSR Gosbank's balance for 1 January 1991 was announced, in which the gold reserves of Gosbank were given at 374.5 tons (*Izvestiya*, 16 July 1991, p. 2), thus confirming my figures.

7 At a seminar at the USSR Academy of Science's Institute of the World Economy and International Relations (IMEMO) in the mid-1980s.

8 One alternative would be to reduce employees' pay and give additional subsidies to enterprises experiencing financial difficulties, but this method is fraught with problems.

9 Tikhonov himself puts it at 135 m. tons, but he includes in it the losses of the irrational feeding of grain directly to livestock, thus bypassing the concentrated feed industry.

10 In May 1991 the national income decreased by 15 per cent compared to the corresponding period of 1990, according to Goskomstat data ('Soobshchenie Goskomstata', 1991b). Taking hidden price decreases into account, the increase was by 20 per cent.

11 The fall of the national income in 1990 by 5 per cent, a calculation based initially on the totals of the first half of 1990, was defined more precisely to 9-10 per cent based on the totals of the second half of 1990.

12 A special problem is how to cancel such a huge deficit. This concerns the union budget as well, although its deficit is much higher than the size, claimed for USSR Gosbank, of its payment. A still more difficult problem is how to reduce the deficit of the local and republic-level budgets. Most probably it will be at the expense of credits of the republics' central banks and their local offices.

13 Cited in a speech by V. S. Pavlov at the plenum of the conference of USSR trade unions.

14 Calculated as follows: we know that in the first quarter of 1991, the volume of capital investment of state enterprises and organizations was 39.6 billion roubles (using 'estimate' costs in prices on 1 January 1991). This figure had decreased according to official data, in the same prices, by 16 per cent compared to the first quarter of 1990, and thus was 47.1 billion roubles (39.6 : 0.84) in the first quarter of 1990 (in 1 January 1991 prices). This same volume in 1984 'estimate' prices was 32.7 billion roubles. This gives a price index for investment goods of 144 per cent (47.1 : 32.7).

15 The newspaper *Kommersant* (No. 17, 1991, p. 6) gives figures on the rise of retail prices after 2 April of 2.7 times. However, these data are contradicted by data in the same issue of *Kommersant* (p. 7) on the rise in the cost of a

consumer basket after 2 April. For the most well-off section of the population it is estimated at 1.47 times, for the middle section 2.5 times, and for the poorest 1.88 times what it formerly cost. Even without knowing the exact figures on the distribution of the population into income groups, it is evident that the first estimate is too high; the general price rise is close enough to the amount I named. Clearly, the methods used by *Kommersant* for computing the general price index are faulty.

16 This is much larger than the deficit calculated by Aleksashenko (1991) which amounted to 200 billion roubles. The reason for the divergence of these estimates is because in his calculations, Aleksashenko did not reflect the course of the fulfilment of the state budget and he specified the RSFSR's share in the budgets of the union republics imprecisely.

17 Because of limited space, I shall not perform the corresponding calculations.

18 Moreover, the domestic debt of the USSR, if we can believe V. S. Pavlov, even decreased from 550 billion roubles at the end of 1990 to 540 billion roubles at the end of the first quarter of 1991 *(Izvestiya*, 23 April 1991). At whose expense was the deficit for the first quarter covered? Apparently, at the expense of the balance of the union budget accounts that have been set aside since 1990 when the domestic debt rose by 150 billion roubles with a budget deficit equal to 60-80 billion roubles. In 1990, the union government, in a far-sighted manner,'took a loan' from Gosbank, counting on a deficit not only in 1990 but in 1991 as well.

19 See Susanne Oxenstierna's Chapter 3 in this volume.

20 It is possible that this rise is partly due to a seasonal variation in suicides.

21 Agricultural procurement prices for January-March 1991 (and this level was maintained up to the end of the first quarter of 1991) had risen by 61 per cent of the 1990 level for the same months. Meanwhile in January-May 1991, wholesale prices in industry had increased by 96 per cent and in construction, by 80 per cent from their levels for the same period in 1990, according to Goskomstat data (these understate the actual price level, since they do not take hidden price rises into account) ('Soobshchenie Goskomstata', 1991b). Retail prices for this period more than doubled.

22 In 1975, the grain yield was 70 per cent of the 1970 level (*Sel'skoe khozyaistvo SSSR*, 1988, p. 126).

23 Speech by N. I. Ryzhkov at a mutual session of the Presidential Council and the Council of the Federation (*Izvestiya*, 22 July 1990, p. 1). See also G. Evstif'ev, 'Mnogo khleba – eshche bol'she problem', *Izvestiya*, 25 July 1990, p. 1.

2

Public Attitudes to the Transition

Vladimir Kosmarskii

Economic consciousness during the period of transition

The main features of economic consciousness today are people´s attitudes towards the market, new forms of property and types of economic activity. At any rate they are formed under the impact of the following factors:

    (a) changes in the economic situation connected with the demolition of once stable and habitual stereotypes, such as the wages-tariff system, working place guarantees and steady state prices;

    (b) changes of social structure in respect of the appearance of new socioeconomic groups such as members of cooperatives, employers; alterations in the social status of traditional social groups such as workers, engineers and students;

    (c) the destruction of social values inculcated by the administrative system, with main features such as etatism and egalitarianism, and the mastering of opposing new values.

Micro- and macro-levels can be singled out in social consciousness. The first is linked with individual and small group motivation, and estimations of the concrete economic situation. The second level is connected with the basic social values of society corresponding to the existing social institution of production and distribution, and to the stereotypes of people´s mentality.

In a situation where the old socioeconomic system is being demolished and new forms of socioeconomic relations have not yet come into being, the main types of socioeconomic consciousness are determined by the correlation of pragmatic aims and motives on the micro-level on the one hand, and ideological stereotypes and ethical norms on the other.

We can therefore advance the following hypothesis:

1   In the Soviet Union we have an evolution of new views and a new mentality at the macro-level, in the discarding of old, incorrect slogans lauding the centrally-planned economy over a market economy, state property over private property. This evolution can be durable if it is accompanied by changes on the micro-level, in the motivation of people´s behaviour.

2   Four types of mass economic consciousness can be discerned today. Two of them are consistent and in conformity with micro- and macro-levels: (a) the conservative type of economic consciousness, which is a characteristic feature of the mentality of supporters of the 'command-administrative' system; (b) the radical type of economic consciousness, which prevails among those who are oriented to market values. Two other types of economic consciousness are not consistent. (c) The characteristic feature of a 'liberal' attitude is its support of new economic mechanisms, and the transition to a market economy on the macro-level. At the same time, however, everyday life appraisals are made under the impact of the usual ideas of egalitarianism and universal state social guarantees. (d) The main feature of a 'moderate-radical' economic consciousness is measured support of market-oriented ideas on a micro-level. This type of mentality is widespread among supporters of economic liberalization. Representatives of this group are sometimes sceptical about market-oriented reforms on the macro-level, and they are overly cautious about problems such as hired labour and private property.

3   The economic consciousness of the greater part of the population can be described as inconsistent, which appears to be a typical feature of a transition period from one type of socioeconomic system to another.

In my opinion, representatives of the third or the 'liberal' type of economic consciousness are the most numerous. At the same time, this type is the most unstable: under the impact of economic change it can disintegrate. Then either the 'moderate-radical' type can be strengthened, which would mean that market-oriented ideas would begin to take possession of people´s minds both on micro- and macro-levels, or the 'conserva-tive' type, connoting a return to the old, habitual norms of economic life.

Survey methods and data

Most interviews were conducted by the All-Union Centre for Public Opinion and Market Research (VCIOM) at standardized, 'face to face' interviews, at the homes of the respondents.

In all union republics, interviews were conducted in the local languages.

The respondents were selected through a multiple sampling process, including the following phases:

Table 2.1 Distribution of answers to the question 'How would you estimate the current economic situation (a) in the USSR and
(b) in the republic you live in?' (per cent of those interviewed in each republic)

Republics	Replies							
	The situation is favourable		The situation is unfavourable		The situation is critical		I don´t know	
	(a)*	(b)*	(a)	(b)	(a)	(b)	(a)	(b)
USSR	2	4	37	48	56	41	5	7
Russia	1	2	36	40	59	53	4	5
Ukraine	1	1	35	53	57	40	7	6
Belorussia	0	0	41	46	56	48	3	6
Estonia	0	1	24	52	74	43	2	4
Kazakhstan	3	5	31	56	60	27	6	12
Uzbekistan	5	15	47	53	39	23	9	9

* (a) represents an appraisal of the economic situation in the USSR; (b)
an appraisal estimate of the economic situation in the republic in which
the respondents live.

(a) identification of the regions and types of communities, as well as
the number of respondents therein;
(b) identification of the existing households within the selected regions;
(c) identification of the respondents in the chosen settlements through
the random selection from files of local address bureaux.

Respondents were assured of the absolute confidentiality of their
answers both verbally and in writing. All of them, of course, were free to
refuse to be interviewed.

This paper is based on data from a large number of surveys done by
VCIOM from December 1988 to March 1991.*

People´s general estimation of the economic situation

The results of the survey held in December 1990 showed that more than
half of the respondents (56 per cent) considered the economic situation
in the Soviet Union to be critical, and another third (37 per cent) regarded
it as unpromising. The economic position of the country as a whole was
estimated as being more dangerous than the situation within specific
republics whose inhabitants were questioned (see table 2.1).

The most similar and pessimistic assessments of the economic situation
in the Soviet Union as well as in the respondents' native republics are given

Table 2.2 Distribution of answers to the question 'How would the economy of the Soviet Union develop in forthcoming months?' (per cent of those interviewed)

Replies	Time of poll	
	January 1991	February 1991
Considerable improvement in the economic situation	4	3
Insignificant improvement in the economic situation	16	13
Slight deterioration in the economic situation	29	27
Significant deterioration in the economic situation	37	43
I do not know	14	14

by the citizens of Russia; the most optimistic by those living in Uzbekistan. Many reasons could be adduced to explain a situation in which the economic position of the Soviet Union is rated as 'critical' and the economic position of the respondents' native republics as 'unpromising'. First, the perception that the situation in the Soviet Union is more dangerous than in its republics is reinforced by the apparent collapse of the Union, the disintegration of inter-republican economic relations and the conflicts between the republics. Second, secessionist ideas and negative attitudes towards the central government may have an impact on comparisons between the economic position of the country and its regions. Third, reactions depend on how the situation is described by central and republican mass media.

Still, the objective regional differences in the evolution of mass consciousness and the peculiarities of the local economic situation strongly influence people's reactions. For instance, in Estonia and Kazakhstan, the differences between the appraisals of the economic position of the Soviet Union and their own republic are the most marked. There the assessment of the economic situation is positively influenced by people´s respect for their local government´s policy.

The prospects for economic performance are rated by people as very unfavourable. The year 1990 was far more difficult than 1989 (see table 2.2). But people´s expectations about the future of the Soviet economy are very pessimistic. More than half (54 per cent) of those interviewed in December 1990 thought that an economic catastrophe was in the offing in 1991; 49 per cent thought that mass unemployment would occur; 42 per cent feared hunger; 51 per cent were apprehensive about irregularities in the water and electricity supply. More than 40 per cent of those interviewed predicted a rise in the number of strikes; 70 per cent foresaw a surge in emigration. Although these figures are estimates, they are indicative of the high degree of social tension in Soviet society.

'Marketization' of the Soviet economy: people's attitudes

To all appearances, curiosity – the original reaction of people at the mere mention of the notion of the 'market' – and expectations of a speedy resolution of current socioeconomic problems have been replaced by a deep, rational interest. About four-fifths of those questioned in December 1990 confirmed that they were interested in discussions about the market as reported in the newspapers, as well as on radio and television. The number of those indifferent to market problems was seven times smaller (13 per cent). Another 7 per cent could not assess their attitude to market discussions.

The reasons for such a situation are quite obvious. On the one hand, many think that 'marketization' of the economy is the only way out of the entire current economic crisis. In any case, every fourth person (25 per cent) who participated in the December 1990 survey confirmed that the reasons for the current troubles were contained in the very essence of socialism, and that the only solution was the creation of a different society, based on a free market economy. On the other hand, the difficulty of taking the first steps towards the free market evoked people's intransigence on these issues. Almost half the respondents (45 per cent) assumed that management blunders committed during the perestroika period were the real reason for the crisis.

It is very significant that the five-year period since the beginning of economic reform was felt to be quite sufficient to improve the economic situation in the country. However, only every tenth citizen of the Soviet Union declared that the errors of economic policy before perestroika were directly to blame for the current crisis situation.

At the same time a 'free market' is still a very vague concept for most Soviet citizens. Their notions about the type of society which may come into being if the marketization of the Soviet economy can be successfully brought about are as follows (in per cent of those interviewed).

'Market economy would produce...'
– renovated socialism	10
– capitalism	18
– a society combining the best features of both capitalism and socialism	20
– a society combining the worst features of both capitalism and socialism	12
No answer	40

Table 2.3 Existence of good anti-crisis programme, December 1990 (per cent of those interviewed)

I consider that the government of	Has a well-thought-out anti-crisis programme	Does not have a well-thought-out anti-crisis programme	Do not know
Russia	28	32	40
Ukraine	14	55	31
Belorussia	23	48	29
Estonia	23	37	40
Kazakhstan	25	30	45
Uzbekistan	27	32	41

It can be seen that the number of those who cannot divine the future of society at the end of the marketization process is about two-fifths of the respondents. At the same time, many people anticipate a sort of economic chimera combining the worst features of capitalism and socialism. Although the ideological stereotypes of negative attitudes towards capitalism are becoming more and more feeble, they still dominate the mass consciousness.

Considerable numbers of Soviet citizens think that, although the market-type transformation of the Soviet economy is absolutely essential, this development must be gradual (two of five respondents felt that it must be so). The proportion of radicals voting for a rapid transformation of the economy on market terms is half as large (about 20 per cent). Another 16 per cent of the respondents thought that the 'marketization of the Soviet economy was unnecessary, and the only thing that needed to be done now was to perfect the methods of planning and centralized management'.

As mentioned above, the generally positive yet restrained attitudes towards a market economic development are partly caused by errors committed by the 'architects' of perestroika. Lively discussions about the market are based on the opinion that the government do not have any well-thought-out anti-crisis programme at all (see table 2.3).

Judging by the results of the polls, people consider that the parliamentary debates on economic problems are a constructive search for an effective solution, but that they are mainly a struggle for power among different political groups. In December 1990, 55 per cent of the respondents regarded the on-going economic discussions in the Supreme Soviet of the USSR as a mere struggle for power; 20 per cent thought that these discussions were an inevitable clash of different scientific approaches to the problem of economic reconstruction; and 25 per cent did not express any view.

The proposition of restoring economic order by strengthening the power of the president of the USSR is assessed quite sceptically. Only 22 per cent of the respondents felt that concession of larger economic rights

Table 2.4 Preparedness to undertake sacrifices, August 1990
(per cent of those interviewed)

	Are ready to help their government even at their own expense	Demand that the state 'pay the debts'
Estonia	27	32
Georgia	18	45
Ukraine	8	54
Russia	6	56
Tadzhikistan	6	63

to the president would improve the economic situation; 43 per cent of them disagreed with such a notion; and 35 per cent did not answer the question.

It may be assumed that public consciousness and public opinion in the USSR are at the same crossroads as economic and political life in the country. This situation is rather dangerous, because the instability in practically every sphere of public life heightens the probability of accidental, possibly fatal developments. The following example illustrates this.

Today the slogan 'Towards the market at the expense of the state, not the citizens' is very popular in the Soviet Union. It is the overt intention of the 'architects' of reform. But what do the citizens themselves think about it? I shall try to answer this question on the basis of the results of the all-Union survey undertaken in August 1990.

More than half the respondents (54 per cent) thought that 'up to now our state has too often solved its own problems at the expense of the citizens, and today we all have the right to demand the improvement of our life in a short period, and not to consent to the policy of "belt-tightening" any more'.

Another quarter (24 per cent) believed that 'our state today is in a very tough situation, and cannot give us more than it already gives. That is why everybody has to rely on himself.' Every tenth (9 per cent) respondent gave the following answer: 'Our state is in such a dangerous position, that we have to help it even at our own expense, and we have to tighten the belts now.' (Some 13 per cent of the respondents did not have a clear stand.) More than half the respondents qualified the state as a debtor which is not insolvent.

The regional features of people-state linkage merit comment. I think that the more legitimate the state power is in one or the other union republic, the higher is the proportion of those among the republic's population who are going to support this power, even at the expense of personal goals. On the other hand, if local authorities are associated with totalitarian central power, the level of personal claims is much higher (see table 2.4).

Table 2.5 Popular attitudes to destatization, December 1990
(per cent of those interviewed)

Models of destatization	Positive attitude	Negative attitude	Indefinite attitude
Free transfer of state property to work collectives	64	16	20
Sale of state property to work collectives	45	29	26
Sale of state property to individual private owners	32	47	21
– sale of small workshops and stores	68	21	11
– sale of large enterprises	21	56	23
– sale of plots of land	88	6	6
Sale of state property to foreigners	17	64	19

Of course, we must remember that the objective capability of citizens to adopt a belt-tightening policy depends on the prosperity of different regions. Nevertheless, my conclusion seems plausible.

Popular attitudes towards privatization

One of the central problems of the transition period is the destatization of the Soviet economy. This can be effected by the transfer of state property to individual or collective owners. Until the summer of 1991, popular views on the process of privatization were not taken into account, although they are decisive for the success of privatization. Attitudes to different modes of destatization are illustrated by the above data (see table 2.5).

The most attractive method of privatization is the free transfer to work

Table 2.6 Public attitudes to purchasing shares

Republics	Attitudes to share purchasing (per cent of those interviewed)			People's motivation in share purchasing (per cent of those interviewed wishing to buy shares)			
	Want to purchase	Do not want to purchase	No answer	To gain extra profits	To retain in savings	To parti- cipate in mana- gement	Could not deter- mine the purpose
USSR	25	40	35	57	17	10	16
Russia	21	42	37	60	11	10	19
Ukraine	24	45	31	57	13	17	13
Belorussia	19	52	29	59	11	2	28
Estonia	40	36	24	59	24	9	8
Kazakhstan	30	27	43	59	12	9	20
Uzbekistan	22	42	36	48	30	10	12

Republics	Reasons for people´s refusal to buy shares (per cent of those interviewed who refused to buy shares)					
	Do not know what shares are	Do not have enough money to buy shares	Doubt shares would bring extra profit	Fear of losing money in buying shares	Not interes- ted in share buying	Could not determine the cause of refusal
USSR	22	37	11	12	11	7
Russia	17	39	8	12	12	12
Ukraine	18	36	10	14	10	12
Belorussia	17	34	15	12	14	8
Estonia	10	38	12	24	7	9
Kazakhstan	22	35	14	12	8	9
Uzbekistan	39	29	11	5	11	5

collectives. In general, collectivistic methods are favoured. Presumably attitudes towards property transfer remain ideological. The sales of state property are less popular than free transfer, but preferred work collectives of state enterprises are the buyers. There are sharp differences in people´s attitudes towards privatization: 37 per cent of those interviewed in December 1990 thought that state property and land must not be sold to private persons; 39 per cent of the respondents expressed the contrary opinion, while 28 per cent did not state their attitude. Views of the privatization of state property are decisive for the kind of privatization that can be implemented. Those in favour of privatization support all possible methods while the antagonists of privatization are opponents of all kinds of destatization.

The model of the destatization of state property that seems likely to enjoy the people´s confidence is rather simple: it is the free transfer of large state enterprises to their work collectives, i.e. their communization, while small enterprises and land should be sold to individual owners. One of the most discussed methods of privatization is the issuing of shares to the public. Popular attitudes on this issue may be illustrated with data from the December 1990 survey (see table 2.6).

Unemployment: what people think about it

One of the most powerful, ideological stereotypes is the basically dogmatic idea of full employment as an intrinsic part of the socialist economic system. It implies that the worker has an absolute guarantee of employment, and the coexistence of socialism and unemployment is seen as an anomaly. Gradually, most Soviet experts have come to concede that some unemployment is inevitable as market relations influence labour. Even so, many experts assume that unemployment is caused by errors in management or planning.

Public opinion polls conducted by VCIOM between 1988 and 1991 showed a considerable change in the public´s attitudes towards unemployment. During this period public opinion became much more tolerant of unemployment. This is illustrated in the distribution of answers to the question 'What judgement about unemployment do you agree with?' (See table 2.7).

At the same time I wish to stress the following:

1 People will tolerate some unemployment, but only if it is quite minimal. The number of radicals who think that unemployment is one of the most powerful negative incentives with which to achieve economic efficiency is diminishing.
2 Even today, when the situation on the labour market is changing dramatically, public opinion about unemployment is largely uninformed, since there is little unemployment in most regions.

Nevertheless, times have changed. At the beginning of 1990, every second citizen of our country (49 per cent) remarked that 'unemployment does exist in the USSR'; about a third of those questioned (34 per cent) expressed a contrary opinion; and another 17 per cent did not answer the question. Thus a large proportion of Soviet citizens no longer deny on purely ideological grounds that unemployment exists.

The unemployed: potential models of behaviour

Table 2.7   Attitudes to unemployment
(per cent of those interviewed)

Replies		Polls	
	December 1988	November 1989	December 1990
'Unemployment in our country is inadmissible'	58	45	39
'Unemployment is quite a tolerable thing'	17	6	20
'Some extent of unemployment is even useful'	–	22	18
'Unemployment is a necessity if we want the economy to be effective'	13	11	9
No answer	12	16	14

The regulation of the labour market would be ineffective if the state bodies enforcing it did not know the probable models of behaviour of the people in the labour market, especially in a situation of mounting unemployment.

From 1989 to 1991 the situation changed drastically:

1 Concern grew among all categories of employees because of the increasing likelihood of job losses. The proportion of those who did not know what to do if they became unemployed grew 1.3 to 2.8 times during this period.
2 The demands of most of the employed have become much more rigid. The proportion of those who would prefer to remain unemployed, while waiting to get a job equivalent to what they had lost, grew for different categories of employees from 1.4 to 1.8 times.
3 Work in cooperatives or the private sector has become increasingly attractive. The proportion of those intent on opening their own businesses, or looking for work in cooperatives, increased 1.2 to 2.8 times.
4 The probability of social protest actions because of complications on the labour market has also increased.

We can conclude. The mentality of people is conditioned by the growing demands with regard to their potential workplace and increasing anxiety prompting unpredictable behaviour in the event of job losses. Therefore the emergence of large-scale unemployment could trigger severe social reactions.

Yet, although the labour market is becoming increasingly unstable, a permanent job is not the main criterion for the choice of a job. In January 1991 only one of 25 respondents (4 per cent) answered the question 'What workplace would you prefer, irrespective of the job you are doing now?' with a workplace secured against dismissals; many more respondents (30 per cent) preferred a well-paid job.

This does not mean that the subjective value of the guarantee of employment as such is declining: more than half (55 per cent) of those participating in a survey conducted in January 1991 said that the state must ensure work for every employee that would be compatible with his education and profession. The proportion of those who declared that the state must ensure any kind of work for the unemployed was 32 per cent of the respondents. When speaking of additional training for the unemployed, even stricter claims on the state were made by people. Some 90 per cent of those questioned in the January 1991 survey said the state must provide the unemployed with additional training. Only 4 per cent of the respondents expressed a contrary opinion.

To all appearances, the redistribution of property rights in the Soviet economy will lead to a change in the public opinion on the paternalistic role of the state in labour affairs. The severity of claims made on the state by the people is diminishing as the connection between the state and the sector of the economy in which a respondent is working becomes looser.

Hence the proportion of respondents assigning the state the role of a total or partial guarantor of employment shifts from 2.25:1 for those working in the state sector to 1.57:1 for workers in leaseholds to 1.06:1 for people working in cooperatives. The same tendency is typical for the views on the role of the state in providing additional training for the unemployed. The ratio of those entrusting the state with complete responsibility for the additional training of the unemployed to those holding a contrary opinion is 28:1 in the cooperative sector and only 4.5:1 in the state sector.

Inflation and stabilization policies in public opinion

The main short-term problem of economic reform in the Soviet Union is monetary stabilization. The entire economic situation of the economy, but particularly labour incentives, depend on the successful stabilization of the economy. We can judge the changing view of money in the public consciousness by the answers to the question 'Do you personally agree that today everything depends on money?' asked in March 1991. Half the respondents declared that they agreed with it absolutely; another 28 per cent were prone to think so, and 19 per cent did not agree with this statement. Some 7 per cent of the respondents found it difficult to answer the question.

Today, there is a universal sense of the inflationary decline of the purchasing power of the rouble. Only 3 per cent of respondents questioned in March 1991 considered that they could buy more goods for the same amount of money as in the preceding year. Every tenth (11 per cent) respondent felt that the amount he could purchase was the same, and four out of five persons (79 per cent) remarked that the purchasing power was

Table 2.8 Distribution of answers to the question 'What probable ways of rouble stabilization do you personally support?' (per cent of those interviewed)

Replies	
Confiscatory monetary reform	31
Public sale of small enterprises, plots of land	29
Public sale of flats	24
Public sale of stocks	21
The increase of interest rates for saving-bank deposits	17
Different systems of consumption rationing	14
Forced loans, public sale of state bonds	5
Foreign loans	5
Public sale of gold and hard currency	4
Auction sale of imported consumer goods	4
Conducting lotteries	3
No answer	19

much less than a year earlier. (7 per cent did not answer.) The state of affairs is quite obvious, and the decline of real incomes takes place simultaneously with a substantial growth of nominal incomes.

People are very pessimistic about the possibility of suspending the fall of the purchasing power of money. Every second person (50 per cent) questioned in March 1991 and answering the question 'Will money depreciate in future?' said that 'the rouble will be totally devalued very soon'. About 8 per cent thought the 'situation would stabilize in a year or so'; another 15 per cent expected to see an improvement in the near future. The question itself was quite specialized, so it is understandable that 27 per cent of the respondents could not answer it.

People's hopes about currency stabilization prompt the question about the mechanism of such improvement. The poll conducted in Moscow in November 1990 permits us to analyse people´s attitudes towards different modes of stabilizing the purchasing power of the rouble (see table 2.8).

Confiscatory monetary reform is still the most popular. Still, the number of supporters of market-oriented mechanisms of currency stabilization, based on sales of new real property items (such as flats, land and shares) is growing. Classical monetarist ways of stabilization, such as internal and external loans and gold-currency interventions, do not enjoy much support. Presumably, people would be more likely to support stabilization measures based on the restructuring of expenditures, reducing investment expenses as well. As already stressed, the popularity of confiscatory monetary reform was very high at the end of 1990. Even after the March 1991 exchange of banknotes of 50 and 100 rouble denominations, the situation has not changed drastically.

Notes

* The following are details of the most important surveys used as information sources:

1 A representative nationwide study of unemployment problems was made in December 1988. It included 2,000 interviews in cities and towns in Russia, the Ukraine, Belorussia, Estonia, Georgia, Armenia, Kazakhstan and Uzbekistan.

2 A representative nationwide study of economic reform problems was undertaken in December 1989. It included 1,148 interviews in cities and towns in Russia, the Ukraine, Belorussia, Latvia, Moldavia, Georgia and Uzbekistan.

3 A representative nationwide study of property problems made in January 1990 included 1,073 interviews in cities, towns and rural communities in Russia, the Ukraine, Latvia, Armenia and Kazakhstan.

4 A representative nationwide study, carried out in August 1990, included 2,500 interviews in cities, towns and rural communities of Russia, the Ukraine, Estonia, Georgia, Tajikstan and Uzbekistan.

5 A representative all-Russia study, carried out in October 1990, included 2,000 interviews in cities, towns and rural communities of the Russian Federation. It had a focus group of 500 Muscovites.

6 A representative nationwide study of economic reform problems, carried out in December 1990, included 3,399 interviews with city and rural dwellers in Russia, the Ukraine, Estonia, Kazakhstan and Uzbekistan.

7 In three telephonic polls, held in January, February and March 1991, some 2,000 persons from cities, towns and rural regions in Russia, the Ukraine, Estonia and Kazakhstan were questioned in each survey.

8 A representative nationwide study, conducted in March 1991, included 3,006 interviews in cities, towns and rural regions in Russia, the Ukraine, Belorussia, Estonia, Armenia, Kazakhstan and Uzbekistan.

3

Trends in Employment and Unemployment

Susanne Oxenstierna

Introduction

The economic reform process which began in 1987, and the crisis situation which has eventually overtaken the Soviet economy, have produced noticeable changes in the Soviet labour market. Previously, only employment in the state and collective farm sector was counted as productive employment; the rise in employment was guaranteed by the extensive growth of jobs in the state sector; the risk of being laid off was minimal; wages were centrally fixed and stable; and labour relations were kept under strict control. Today, people are displaced from their jobs in the socialized sector and they have been given the opportunity for self-employment and work in cooperatives. Even work in private subsidiary agriculture is counted as productive employment. However, besides these changes in official attitudes and actual developments, from which both individuals and the economy as a whole may profit, there are negative consequences of the transformation with which the policy-makers have immense difficulties in dealing. Nominal wage increases have been dramatic and strikes have become a common phenomenon. Moreover, the existence of unemployment has been officially recognized, and sharp rises in unemployment are envisaged as the process of transition continues. This has given rise to all sorts of unemployment estimates circulating in the Soviet press and official writings, creating a rather confusing picture of current and future unemployment figures in the Soviet economy.

The inconsistent evidence of unemployment which these contradictory figures provide is partly due to the fact that different authors imply different things when they talk about the numbers of unemployed and unemployment rates. Some refer to the people making up the gross flows out of the state sector as unemployed, some to the estimated stock of unemployed, some have in mind those people who will become eligible for unemployment benefits, and some appear to include a certain proportion

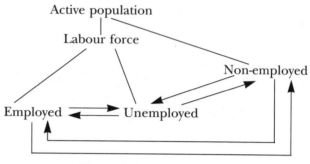

Figure 3.1

of the non-employed population in their estimates. The latter approach reflects a concern with the regional aspects of unemployment. Central Asia and Transcaucasia[1] have significantly larger shares of a non-employed active population than the USSR average, and some observers take this as evidence of quite a large group of long-term unemployed in these regions. Apart from varying definitions and regional aspects adding to the complexity of the issue, a basic problem is that available labour statistics are inadequate to describe and estimate unemployment properly.

This paper attempts to give a tentative picture of the development of Soviet employment, non-employment and unemployment in recent years. First these categories are defined and the kind of data necessary to provide a relevant picture of this development is discussed. Then the development of employment is described with data which is available, and the causes behind the changes are debated. The fourth section contains a discussion on unemployment and non-employment. The fifth section comments on some unemployment scenarios, and in the sixth section, the proposed policies for mitigating this problem are dealt with. Finally, there is a section of conclusions that can be drawn from the foregoing discussion.

A note on definitions and data

According to Western standards, the active population may be divided into two major groups. One consists of those who choose to participate in the labour market and these constitute the labour force. The other is comprised of those who do not participate in the labour market and these make up the non-employed. The labour force may in turn be divided into those who are employed and those who are unemployed (see figure 3.1). The current numbers in each category make up the total number (or 'stock') of those employed, non-employed and unemployed. Individuals can change their labour-market status. This means that there are gross flows of individuals moving from the state of being employed into the state of being unemployed and vice versa. Individuals also enter or re-enter the labour force from the state of non-employment and can fall either into the category of the employed or of the unemployed. Similarly, individuals can leave the labour force, i.e. move from employment or unemployment into non-employment. The net flows between the different states determine whether the stocks of employed, non-employed and unemployed change or not.

In most Western countries the number of persons in employment, non-employment and unemployment are detailed in regular labour-force surveys. In the Soviet Union there are no such statistics: the only data on the labour force collected from the supply side is that provided in the population censuses. This data makes it possible to derive labour-force participation rates, the numbers in the labour force at the point of time the census was conducted, and information on the non-employed population. Information on the number of employed is also found in the employment statistics collated from the employers, regularly reported by Goskomstat (State Committee on Statistics). The only regular data available on unemployment comes from the reports on 'unplanned mobility' (*tekuchest'*) – the numbers of individuals (or percentage of the work force) quitting their jobs on their own initiative (or having been sacked for disciplinary reasons). Together with conjectures about the average duration of unemployment spells between jobs, these figures have also been used to estimate the frictional unemployment rates for the USSR before the start of perestroika.

Employment

The two major changes in the Soviet employment pattern since the start of the period of transition are the decline in state-sector employment and the rise in legal private employment. As indicated in table 3.1, state-sector employment has declined by about one million people per year since 1988, or by a total of over 3 million people between 1985 and 1990. (Including employment in the *kolkhoz* sector, the decrease over five years was 4.4 million.) As a result, the number of employed in the state sector is now down to the 1980-level. Meanwhile, employment in cooperatives and other legal private activities (outside agriculture) has risen from zero in the mid-1980s to over 4 million at the beginning of the 1990s. The Soviet authorities have started publishing figures for total employment, including private subsidiary agriculture. Altogether, employment in the state, the collective farms, the cooperative and individual sectors, rose to 139.3 million people in 1989. Thereafter total employment dwindled to 138.4 million people in 1990 (*Ekonomika i zhizn'*, No. 5, 1991). Further decline occurred in the first quarter of 1991, when total employment fell to 134.8 million people (*Ekonomika i zhizn'*, No. 17, 1991). The greater part of this decrease took place in the state and collective farm sector where employment fell by about 3 million people (see table 3.1).

The development in the last few years represents a sharp break with the previous trend in employment. In the 1960s and 1970s, state-sector employment rose by around 10 million people in each five-year period. In the first half of the 1980s, the growth in employment slowed down, but

Table 3.1   Trends in Soviet employment, 1986–1991 (thousand)

	1986	1987	1988	1989	1990	Jan – Mar 1991
State sector	118503	118572	117236	115433	114600	112800
Annual change	705	69	-1336	-1803	-833	-1800
Kolkhoz sector	12560	12236	11700	11600	11500	10300
Annual change	-127	-324	-536	-100	-100	-1200
State & kolkhoz sector	131063	130808	128936	127033	126100	123100
Annual change	578	-255	-1872	-1903	-933	-3000
Consumer cooperatives	NA	NA	NA	NA	3500	3500
Cooperatives[1] (excl. part-time)	NA	NA	743	3143	4208	4200
Annual change	–	–	–	2400	1065	-8
Self-employed[1]	NA	427	NA	300	200	200
Private subsidiary Agriculture	NA	NA	NA	4000	4200	3700
Private farmers	NA	NA	NA	NA	100	100

Sources: *Trud v SSSR*, 1988, pp. 30–1, 76, 276; *Narkhoz 1988*, pp. 322, 329; *Narkhoz 1989*, pp. 48–9, 268; *Ekonomika i zhizn'*, No. 5, No. 17, and No. 20, 1991; *Pravda*, 28 January 1990.

Notes: 1. The reported numbers for those in self-employment and those employed in cooperatives vary between different sources. Here the numbers for cooperative employment in 1988 and 1989 are calculated from the figures on total cooperative employment and the number of holders of several jobs in *Narkhoz 1988* and *1989* and that for 1990 from the corresponding figures in *Ekonomika i zhizn'*, No. 20, 1991. The numbers of self-employed in 1987 is the number reported in *Trud v SSSR*, 1988. The remaining figures for these two items are from the plan fulfilment reports in *Pravda*, 28 January 1990, and *Ekonomika i zhizn'*, No. 5 and No. 17, 1991.

Table 3.2   Change in employment stocks, 1965–1989 (thousand)

	1965-70	1970-75	1975-80	1980-85	1985-89	1985-89 per cent
State and kolkhoz Sector, total	11342	10432	8509	4643	-3452	-2.6
State sector:[1]	13271	11974	10338	5300	-2365	-2.0
Productive Sector:[1]	7597	6682	5113	2521	-4441	-4.5
Industry	4146	2461	2837	1212	-1689	-4.4
Agriculture	-1214	-440	-700	-67	-2161	-8.7
State	715	1102	1129	590	-1074	-8.8
Kolkhoz	-1929	-1542	-1829	-657	-1087	-8.6
Construction	1751	1522	666	252	1692	14.7
Transportation	733	1230	1109	554	-2194	-20.2
Rail	12	128	157	23	-276	-10.5
Road	699	1068	923	513	-1886	-24.2
Water	22	34	29	18	-32	-7.1
Trade	1528	1320	837	337	-154	-1.5
Communication	323	198	106	37	-132	-7.9
Forestry	31	20	5	-2	-63	-13.8
Others	299	371	253	198	260	13.7
Non-productive Sector:[1]	3745	3750	3396	2122	989	3.2
Education	1202	889	1031	721	1137	11.5
Health	803	689	454	561	713	10.5
Housing	666	753	707	382	155	3.2
Science	374	791	589	175	-449	-9.9
State administration	302	231	240	156	-792	-33.2
Culture	268	232	234	96	198	14.3
Finance	88	131	130	30	10	1.5
Art	42	34	11	1	17	3.7

Sources: Oxenstierna (1990) p. 233; *Narkhoz 1989*, pp. 48-9; *Trud v SSSR*, 1988, p. 76.
Notes: 1. Includes sectors listed below this heading.

nevertheless the increment was about 5 million people (see table 3.2).

As shown in table 3.2, the productive sector[2] has lost employment in absolute terms. Agricultural employment decreased by over 2 million people (including *kolkhozy*) between 1985 and 1989. The transportation sector employed 2 million people, or 20 per cent fewer workers, in 1989 than in 1985. Employment has decreased in railway transportation by 10 per cent, in road transportation by 24 per cent. The only productive sectors which have experienced an increase in employment during the period are construction and the unspecified activities included in the productive sector (table 3.2).

Employment in the non-productive sector[3] increased by almost 1 million

Table 3.3   Number of employed in the state sector in the republics, 1980-1989

	Average annual employment (thousand)			Change in employment			
				1980-1985		1985-1989	
				thousand	per cent		
	1980	1985	1989				
USSR	112498	117798	115433	5300	4.7	-2365	-2.0
Slavic	89700	92591	90194	2891	3.2	-2397	-2.6
RSFSR	65612	67641	65634	2029	3.1	-2007	-3.0
Ukraine	20042	20679	20249	637	3.2	-430	-2.1
Belorussia	4046	4271	4311	225	5.6	40	0.9
Moldavia	1511	1619	1491	108	7.1	-128	-7.9
Baltic	3363	3512	3399	149	4.4	-113	-3.2
Estonia	700	718	675	18	2.6	-43	-6.0
Latvia	1202	1231	1171	29	2.4	-60	-4.9
Lithuania	1461	1563	1553	102	7.0	-10	-0.6
Transcaucasia	4972	5591	5523	619	12.4	-68	-1.2
Georgia	1978	2178	2161	200	10.1	-17	-0.8
Armenia	1192	1355	1304	163	13.7	-51	-3.8
Azerbaidzhan	1802	2058	2058	256	14.2	0	0.0
Central Asia	6909	7985	8325	1076	15.6	340	4.3
Uzbekistan	4169	4834	5061	665	16.0	227	4.7
Tadzhikistan	927	1101	1161	174	18.8	60	5.4
Turkmenistan	711	811	854	100	14.1	43	5.3
Kirgizia	1102	1239	1249	137	12.4	10	0.8
Kazakhstan	6043	6500	6501	457	7.6	1	0.0

Source : *Narkhoz1989*, p. 52.

people between 1985 and 1989. All sectors, except state and local admin-istration, and the sciences, showed gains in employment. The rise in employment in the two largest non-productive sectors, education and healthcare, was around 10 per cent. The state bureaucracy has declined by a third compared to 1985, and the number of people employed by scientific institutions by 10 per cent.

Disaggregation over the republics shows that in absolute terms the major part of the decrease has taken place in the RSFSR. However, in rela-tive terms the decline in employment in this republic is rather small. State employment declined by around 3 per cent between 1985 and 1989 (table 3.3). Yet it is a significant change compared to previous periods, for instance between 1980 and 1985, when employment rose by 3 per cent in the RSFSR. In the three Slavic republics together, employment declined by 2.4 million persons (2.6 per cent). Other republics have more signifi-cant decreases in relative terms, for instance, Moldavia (8 per cent), Estonia (6 per cent) and Latvia (5 per cent). The Transcaucasian republics

Table 3.4   Number of women employed in the state sector, 1980-1989 (thousand)

	1985	1986	1987	1988	1989	1980-85	1985-89
Number	60011	60171	60054	59273	58729		
Change		160	-117	-781	-544	2442	-1282

Source : *Narkhoz 1989*, p. 53.

have experienced a decline in employment of only 1 per cent. However, in the first half of the 1980s, employment grew by 12 per cent in this area. In the Central Asian republics, employment has increased by about 300 thousand persons (4.3 per cent), but the increase is only a third of the increase in the period between 1980 and 1985.

Further, it may be noted that parallel to the decline between 1985 and 1989, the number of women employed in the state sector has decreased by 1.3 million. This corresponds to 54 per cent of the total decline (table 3.4). Since women make up over 50 per cent of the state labour force, this decline in female employment cannot be taken as an indication that women are displaced to a greater extent than men.

Why does state-sector employment decline?

The decline in state-sector employment raises several questions. Has the contraction of employment come about because labour demand has declined in this sector? That is, have state employers become subject to hardening budget constraints and consequently dismissed workers? Is the decline primarily due to competition for labour from the private sector? Or is it due to factors related to labour supply? Part of the decline may be attributed to the regional mismatch between jobs and job-seekers. The demographic situation is such that growth in the active population takes place mainly in the southern republics where job opportunities are scarce and people are reluctant to migrate to new jobs. Furthermore, the effects of wage rises, price increases and changes in taxation rules may have had both a positive and a negative impact on labour supply. Labour supply may increase or decrease when real wages increase, depending on whether the substitution or income effect dominates. A problem with the Soviet environment is that it is difficult to determine whether real wages have increased or decreased, and what the impact of income taxes on the take-home wage is. Moreover, the shortages on consumer markets complicate matters, since money incomes do not entail command over goods and services. Labour supply may have declined because of supply-multiplier effects: that is, people choose to be non-employed (or reduce their work time) because shortages in consumer goods markets have intensified.

Since we do not have data on quits and lay-offs (which would tell us whether people have left their jobs on their own initiative, or whether they have in fact been laid off), nor detailed information on the development of non-employment and unemployment in recent years, it is unfortunately not possible to give clear-cut answers to these questions. We can only point at factors which have probably contributed to this development.

The wage reform launched in 1986 appears to have had some impact on the level of employment. This reform aimed at raising basic wages in the productive sector by 20 to 25 per cent and also at increasing wage differentiation. Enterprises were supposed to cover the resulting rise in labour costs by their own means, through the rationalization of production and labour shedding (see Oxenstierna, 1990, pp. 242–4; Chapman, 1988). The reform was estimated to raise the wage bill in industry alone by about 20 billion roubles (Maevskii, 1986, p. 9). According to the latest reports, 5.5 per cent (3.3 million) of the work force affected by the reform have been dismissed (*Statisticheskii press byulleten'*, No. 13, 1990, p. 38). Many of the displaced have been re-employed in the state sector, often at the same enterprise. The figures for 1988 revealed that about 3 per cent of the workers transferred to the new wage scales were actually laid off, of which about a third were retired on pension (Oxenstierna, 1990, p. 251). If we assume that lay-offs are still around 3 per cent, this implies that the wage reform would 'explain' about 1.8 million or over 50 per cent of the total decline in state-sector employment between 1985 and 1990.

Because of the drastic changes in many variables simultaneously, too much cannot be read into this kind of mechanical calculation. In fact, some Soviet employment specialists tend to attribute very small importance to the wage reform and other reform measures in explaining the decline in state-sector employment.[4] In any case, the effects on labour productivity have been much weaker than those observed when the reform was tried out on an experimental basis,[5] and the effects on the nominal average wage level have been much more dramatic than expected. In 1988, the average nominal wages in the state sector rose by 8.3 per cent, in 1989, by 9.4 per cent, and in 1990, by 12.5 per cent,[6] compared to about 2.5 per cent per year in the early 1980s.

This is largely due to the fact that the wage reform was implemented in an environment created by the 1987 Law on State Enterprises[7] which was introduced in 1988. Among other provisions, this law gave enterprises some freedom in setting their prices and adjusting their product mix towards more expensive products. Combined with the absence of competition in the product market, this opened the opportunity to raise wages by increasing prices instead of shedding labour.

In addition, the wage determination mechanism in the enterprise law which was chosen by most enterprises had the potential of raising wages without improving labour productivity. The law offered the enterprise a choice between two alternatives with respect to wage determination. According to the first, the major part of the wage budget was dependent on revenues alone and only a small part was profit-related. In principle, this model copied already existing practices. In the second alternative, the total wage budget was dependent on net-revenues (total revenues minus all costs except labour costs).[8] Most enterprises adopted the first alternative, which implies that wages would be disbursed regardless of how bad overall results were. This shows that budget constraints have continued to be particularly soft with regard to wages.

The slowing decline of state-sector employment in 1990 further supports the view that the trade-off between wages and the employment level is very weak. State wages rose by 12.5 per cent, while state-sector employment declined by 0.7 per cent.

The situation during the first quarter of 1991, when state-sector employment was reported to have fallen by 1.8 million persons, might be a result of a staggered effect. A new enterprise law (a law applicable to all types of enterprises) has been introduced, together with a new tax legislation.[9] Enterprises might have expected continuing soft budget constraints, and therefore postponed dismissals until it became clear that loss-making enterprises would have to cut down employment or close down. If constraints have in fact hardened, the wholesale price reform in January 1991 and the postponement of retail price rises until April would have put many enterprises in trouble and led to dismissals.

The general disintegration of the material-supply system is another factor which has distorted production, and perhaps this is the major cause of the decline in employment at the beginning of 1991. Lack of input means that output levels fall with resulting loss of revenue. If enterprises are operating under hard budget constraints, this should lead to labour shedding. Whether this is the story behind the decline in the first quarter of 1991 can only be discovered by empirical testing.

The private sector

The legalization of employment outside the state and *kolkhoz* sector is certainly one of the factors underlying the decline in state-sector employment. The development of this sector is in itself a central element in the transformation of the economy.

The legalization of private employment started with the Law on Individual Labour Activity of 19 November 1986, which permitted people who were not required to work in the state sector to engage in a variety of activities such as private taxis, car repairs, housing construction, etc. The number of people in these activities has not been very great (see table 3.1), but the psychological impact of legalizing self-employment certainly prepared the way for succeeding reforms (see Plokker, 1990).

Permitting cooperatives has had a more substantial impact on private opportunities. The Law on Cooperatives was adopted in May 1988, and employment in this sector rose dramatically (see tables 3.1 and 3.6). Growth slowed down slightly between 1989 and 1990, and during the first months of 1991 employment was reported to have fallen by a few thousand persons (table 3.1).

In 1988, cooperatives engaged in consumer goods production and consumer services grew rapidly. By January 1989, there were a total of 77,500 cooperatives, of which over 50 per cent were in the consumer goods production field (Tedstrom, 1989). Public opinion became rather critical of cooperatives, and since then the growth in the number of cooperatives

Table 3.5   The cooperative sector 1990 (end of year)

	Number of cooperatives (thousand)	Number of workers (thousand)	Wage fund (million roubles)	Sales turnover (million roubles)
All	245.4	6098.2	26836.0	67313.0
Selected branches:				
Construction	75.5	2548.2	13015.4	25961.5
Consumer goods production	41.8	1010.0	4069.7	11994.4
Consumer services	27.6	420.8	1291.1	2888.3
Producer goods distribution	8.9	380.1	1730.5	5941.4
Data processing, Information services	4.0	77.2	287.0	1736.0

Source : *Ekonomika i zhizn'*, No. 20, 1991.

has shifted towards activities which are not so visible to the public.

At the end of 1990, the cooperatives employed about 6.1 million persons of which 31 per cent were reported as several jobs holders (*sovmestiteli*), implying that they did not work full-time in the cooperatives. Many probably had a job in the state sector as their first job. This means that about 4.2 million persons can be regarded as employed full-time in the cooperatives (*Ekonomika i zhizn'*, No. 20, 1991). The total sales turnover was 67 billion roubles, and the net revenues were 44.2 billion, of which 74 per cent, or 32.5 billion roubles was left to the cooperatives to dispose of (ibid.). The wage fund of this sector rose by about 10 billion roubles compared to 26.8 billion roubles in 1989. This implies that those employed in cooperatives (about 4 per cent of total employment) received 20 per cent of the total increase of 53 billion roubles in the economy-total wage fund. The average wage paid in the cooperative sector was 417 roubles per month (ibid.). This was 1.5 times the average wage in the state sector.[10]

As is evident from table 3.5, construction cooperatives now account for almost 40 per cent of total sales turnover, over 40 per cent of cooperative employment and almost 50 per cent of the total wage budget of the cooperative sector. Wage fund per worker was over 5,000 roubles per year (426 roubles per month), and sales turnover 10,385 roubles per worker. Consumer goods production, consumer services and public catering account for 40 per cent of sales turnover, a fourth of employment, and 20 per cent of the total wage sum in the cooperative sector. The wage fund

Table 3.6 Development of employment in cooperatives in the USSR and its republics, 1989-1990

(1) Number of employed (thousand)
(2) Proportion of part-time workers (*sovmestiteli*) (per cent)
(3) Change in number of employed

	Jan 1989		Jan 1990			July 1990	
	(1)	(2)	(1)	(2)	(3)	(1)	(3)[1]
USSR	1395.9	46.8	4855.4	35.3	3459.5	5219.5	364.1
RSFSR	707.9	47.0	2688.4	34.1	1980.5	2958.8	270.4
Ukraine	249.0	50.2	779.4	39.2	530.4	784.2	4.8
Belorussia	43.6	53.8	123.9	44.6	80.3	137.1	13.2
Moldavia	38.5	61.0	83.0	36.7	44.5	111.4	28.4
Estonia	21.5	68.4	42.1	54.9	20.6	47.1	5
Latvia	28.7	67.6	134.8	48.1	106.1	158.6	23.8
Lithuania	25.4	61.2	81.4	50.1	56.0	77.9	-3.5
Georgia	32.4	40.2	135.9	31.7	103.5	127.8	-8.1
Armenia	56.4	25.9	138.1	40.3	81.7	171.3	33.2
Azerbaidzhan	15.8	32.3	62.8	32.3	47.0	63.7	0.9
Uzbekistan	71.6	35.7	250.5	28.1	178.9	243.2	-7.3
Tadzhikistan	12.5	36.0	40.7	22.1	28.2	44.2	3.5
Turkmenistan	4.8	18.7	30.5	24.3	25.7	33.5	3
Kirgizia	15.8	37.3	38.7	28.7	22.9	34.4	-4.3
Kazakhstan	72.7	35.7	225.2	25.3	152.5	226.3	1.1

Notes: [1] Change during first six months 1990.
Sources: Malle (1990), p. 210; *Narkhoz 1989*, p. 269; *Statisticheskii byulleten'*, No. 20, 1990, p. 44.

per worker was lower than in construction, 3,700 roubles per year (306 roubles per month), but sales turnover per worker was of the same magnitude, 10,220 roubles.

A majority of all cooperatives were formed in connection with a state enterprise. In 1990, this proportion was as high as 80 per cent (*Ekonomika i zhizn'*, No. 20, 1991). This meant that in many cases a part of an enterprise's activities had simply been taken over by a cooperative formed by workers employed at the enterprise. Large Soviet enterprises have always included a vast spectrum of activities. For instance, they have had their own construction department, their own recreation facilities, social services and so forth. This kind of auxiliary activity, as well as parts of the main production, are now reorganized into cooperatives. For the cooperatives, the link to a state enterprise is essential because they can lease equipment and buildings and do not have to accumulate capital. The under-development of production capacities in the economy and the shortages make relations with a well-established enterprise in the old hierarchy crucial for getting access to capital goods and material inputs.

The close link to the state sector, and the fact that cooperatives to a large extent provide services to state producers, is one element behind the increased amount of money in circulation. By the sale of services to state enterprises, passive money in the state-enterprise sector enters circulation through the purchases of cooperatives and the wages and salaries paid to their personnel. The growth in the cooperatives' wage funds has been greater than the average for the state sector. Thus, although minor in size, the cooperative sector has contributed to the wage-price spiral. The proportion of wages in total costs is much higher in the cooperative sector (40 per cent) than in the state sector.[11]

Throughout their existence, a large share of those employed in cooperatives has consisted of people holding several jobs, which in most cases imply they have a state-sector job as well as their work in the cooperative. The distribution of cooperatives in the republics reveals regional differences in this respect (table 3.6). The proportion of part-time workers is lowest in the Central Asian republics. This might be an indication of cooperative jobs to a larger extent representing new job opportunities in that region than elsewhere in the USSR (see Malle, 1990).

The large number of cooperatives that are established in direct connection to state enterprises suggests that new workplaces are not created to any large extent. In 1989–1990, only 12.5 per cent of the growth in cooperative employment represented a growth in workplaces. That means, of the total rise in employment of 3.5 million persons, only around 400,000 persons had new jobs (ibid.). The most important impediments to further development of the cooperative sector are probably the lack of equipment and inputs. Changes in tax laws have not been advantageous for the cooperatives, and both the physical impediments and the less favourable financial situation have contributed to the slow growth of the sector.

Unemployment

Some unemployment has always existed in the Soviet Union. Primarily, this has been in the form of frictional unemployment because of people changing jobs and being dismissed for disciplinary reasons. In Soviet parlance this phenomenon has been discussed under the heading 'unplanned turnover' (*tekuchest'*). In Western literature, estimated frictional unemployment rates for the USSR have been calculated from data on *tekuchest'* and the estimated average duration of unemployment between jobs. The unemployment rate arrived at for the 1980s with this methodology has been in the range of 1 to 3 per cent[12] depending on the average duration of unemployment spells. For instance, in 1985, if the average duration of unemployment was one month, the frictional unemployment rate was 0.9 per cent. If the average duration was two months or three months, the unemployment rate was 1.8 or 2.7 per cent respectively (Oxenstierna, 1990, p. 224). In the 1980s, reported job changes involved about 13 to 14 per cent of the state-sector labour force (some 15 million persons) and the resulting simulated unemployment rates correspond to between 1.2 to 3.5 million unemployed on a yearly basis.

In addition to frictional unemployment, the most important types of unemployment have probably been unemployment due to rural-urban migration, and unemployment of first-time job-seekers. Unemployment in connection with migration has not been documented, and there is little knowledge about first-time job-seekers. In the 1980s, every year 4 to 5 million persons in the age-groups between 15 to 24 years finished school or graduated from higher educational establishments. It appears that typically, the time taken to find employment has been longer (three to six months) for these categories than for job-changers. To what extent the school-leavers and graduates have been actively looking for jobs during this period is uncertain, but a very rough estimate indicates that first-time job-seekers would add about 1 to 2 per cent to the simulated unemployment rates for the mid-1980s (Oxenstierna, 1989, p. 865). This implies that it is reasonable to assume a 'natural' or lower-bound unemployment rate of 2–5 per cent (2.4–6 million)[13] for the Soviet economy even before the start of perestroika.

How many unemployed?

In the light of these figures, the claim made by Goskomtrud (the State Committee on Labour and Social Questions) that there were approximately 2 to 2.5 million unemployed in 1990 appears a bit low (*Ekonomika i zhizn'*, No. 15, 1990). The number of people changing jobs has not decreased. The frictional unemployment rate because of *tekuchest'* was in the range of 1.1 to 3.4 per cent[14] and there are several indications that difficulties had increased for first-time job-seekers finding jobs. The figures for 'the number of school-leavers neither working or studying' have gone up and there are reports of graduates from higher educational establishments having increasing problems finding jobs. According to the Population Census of 1989, 422,000 persons aged between 16 to 29 years did not work. The number of school-leavers neither working nor studying has risen from 23,600 in 1985 and 36,200 in 1987 to 90,600 in 1989 (Kirillov, 1990, p. 59). This represents 4 per cent of the total group of school-leavers (2,250,000) in 1989 (ibid., p. 58). Of those neither working nor studying in 1989, 32,800 were engaged in private subsidiary agriculture; yet even if these are subtracted from the total number, there were over twice as many non-employed school-leavers in 1989 (57,800) than in 1985.

In addition, some of the decline in state-sector employment is due to people having been laid off, who are searching for new jobs, and who should be regarded as unemployed. Further, there are reports of increasing numbers of migrants and of migrant-refugees. Goskomstat reports that there were around 600,000 refugees on Soviet territory in 1990 (*Ekonomika*

Table 3.7 Job-seekers turning to the employment services, 1990

	Number of job-seekers	Found jobs for	Not found jobs for
Number of persons (thousand)	4142.0	2684.9	1457.1
Per cent	100	64.6	35.4

Source : Ekonomika i zhizn', No. 19, 1991.

i zhizn', No. 5, 1991; Volokh, 1991, p. 50). These are people who had to leave their permanent place of residence because of natural catastrophes, ethnic conflicts and suspected food problems in some regions that have put people on the move. In particular, the refugees come from Azerbaidzhan and Armenia (in 1988–1989, 422,000 persons left these areas; in the first quarter of 1990, 100,000). There are also refugees from Uzbekistan and Kazakhstan (in 1989, 100,000 left these areas). Among the refugees are also armed forces personnel and their families (about 50,000 thousand) (Volokh, ibid.). (The numbers of unemployed as a result of demobilization is not reported.) The problems of the refugees are not only concerned with finding work; but this nevertheless is one of their difficulties, particularly in big cities like Moscow and St Petersburg where refugees are now considered as a special category among the unemployed.

Apart from these indications that unemployment has risen, there is the latent non-employment–unemployment problem in the labour-surplus regions of Central Asia and Transcaucasia. Estimates of unemployment are uncertain, however, since they are based on the relatively larger share of non-employed in this region compared to the USSR average. In 1989, 22 per cent of the working-age population in Central Asia and 28 per cent in Transcaucasia were non-employed, as compared to the USSR average of 16 per cent.[15] In absolute figures this is 6 million persons. Some estimates indicate that as many as 3 million would be active job-seekers who cannot find work (Semenov, 1990, p. 49).

The Goskomstat report on the economy in 1990 states that the number of non-employed and non-studying in the working-age population exceeded 8 million persons, and that of the temporarily non-working population, 2 million could be regarded as unemployed. Meanwhile, there were about 3 million vacancies in the state sector (*Ekonomika i zhizn'*, No. 5, 1991).

The 8-million figure appears to be an estimate of the proportion of non-employed among the estimated total 'labour resources'[16] which were reported at 164 million people in 1989. Of the total of about 25 million non-employed (those in private subsidiary agriculture and private farming had been included among the employed), 12 million people were reported to be in education. The remaining 13 million were in the armed forces, staying at home, or temporarily out of work (*Ekonomicheskoe i sotsial'noe razvitie*, 1990, p. 43). The armed forces appear to include around

4 to 4.5 million persons,[17] so the number potentially available for work was 8.5 to 9 million. Of these, about 4 million persons may be assumed to be women not in the labour force.[18] Thus there are 4.5 to 5 million persons who are potentially unemployed. At least between half and one million of these may be considered people who do not wish to work,[19] so the potential stock of unemployed appears to be approximately 3.5 to 4.5 million rather than 2 million. Unemployment due to job-changing in the state sector has probably not been included in Goskomstat's figure of 8 million, so 1.1 to 3.8 million frictionally unemployed should be added. The estimated unemployment rate is thus in the range of 3.2 to 5.8 per cent.[20]

However, since it is unknown how long people go unemployed, and 'the number of labour resources' which does not take account of people's labour-market behaviour is dubious, this estimate is still very tentative. It comes closer to the Shatalin group's estimate of unemployment at the beginning of 1990. The figure they proposed was 6 million, of which 1.5 million was attributed to frictional unemployment and 4.5 million were permanently unemployed (*Perekhod k rynku*, 1990, p. 111).

Who are they?

Early reports on job-losers revealed that pensioners, women and white-collar workers were over-represented among the displaced and that these categories had difficulties in finding new jobs. Displacements among white-collar workers were three times higher than among blue-collar workers (Zaslavskii, 1988, p. 30). Moreover, first-time job-seekers with specialized or higher education have reportedly encountered difficulties in finding jobs, at least in the urban centres where they have studied (ibid., p. 28).

Data on job seekers provided by the employment services reveals that over 4 million persons registered at the employment offices in 1990. Of these, 65 per cent found jobs with the assistance of the employment service, and 35 per cent (1.5 million) did not find employment.[21]

The number of persons using the employment offices represents only a fraction of those looking for jobs during some period in a year. It is impossible to tell to what extent they are representative for the whole group of job-seekers, but this is the only group of people looking for jobs about whom there is some detailed information. Over half of those turning to the employment offices were persons who had left their jobs of their own volition (*Ekonomika i zhizn'*, No. 19, 1991). The remainder were school-leavers (about 10 per cent), students who wished to work in their free time (almost 10 per cent), and unspecified categories (over 10 per cent). Only 4 per cent of those turning to the employment service were laid-off workers. Persons engaged in the private subsidiary economy made up 5 per cent of the applicants, pensioners around 3 per cent, and persons dismissed for disciplinary reasons 2.5 per cent (ibid.).

Not surprisingly, the category having most trouble in finding a new job were those who had been laid-off. Over 60 per cent of these were not found jobs. By contrast, among those who quitted on their own initiative, only 35 per cent could not find a new job. Other categories with problems were pensioners, persons who returned from medical treatment, persons looking for a second job, and persons who had been dismissed for infringements of labour discipline. Around 40 per cent of these did not find jobs through the employment service (ibid.).

Unemployment scenarios

In the context of the various reform programmes presented during the autumn of 1990, and the formulation of the new employment law, different unemployment scenarios were drawn up. In these, the primary cause for the rise in unemployment was felt to be the reduction of manpower due to privatization and structural change. The duration of unemployment was also expected to rise, which in turn increases the unemployment rate even if the number of unemployed people remained constant.

Goskomtrud came forward with two projections on the labour-market implications of the move towards a market economy. The Shatalin group presented their unemployment scenario in relation to the 500-days programme. Furthermore, the joint study by four international economic agencies of the Soviet economy presents two hypothetical scenarios for 1991 and 1992 (*A Study of the Soviet Economy*, 1991, Vol. 2, pp. 148–9).

The first scenario described by Goskomtrud involved a transition period of eight to ten years and the second a transition period of two years. In the first, more gradual, scenario it was projected that employment in the state sector would fall by 40 million over eight to ten years, and by 9.5 million in 1991. Only about a third of the contraction in 1991 was expected to occur on account of redundancies; 500,000 would become unemployed because of ownership changes and reduced manpower, 1.5 million due to loss-making enterprises closing down, and 1.5 million as a result of structural changes in industry. The remainder were supposed to leave the state sector of their own accord (ibid., p. 147). In this scenario, the total employment level in the economy stayed at its 1990 level. This implied that the gradual increase of the number of unemployed persons from about 2 million up to 4.5 million (3.25 per cent of the labour force) in 1994, would be in line with the projected increase in the labour force of about 700,000 persons per year (ibid.). In the second, more radical, scenario, the lay-offs in 1991 were projected at 6 million, because of more rapid structural change and faster privatization (ibid.). Goskomtrud did not explicitly state the unemployment consequences of this alternative.

Goskomtrud also made projections on the regional distribution of those unemployed who would require assistance, primarily in income support, in 1991. This forecast revealed that 46 per cent of such persons would be located in the Slavic republics, 30 per cent would be located in the Central Asian republics (almost 40 per cent if Kazakhstan is included), and about 12 per cent to the Transcaucasian republics (ibid., p. 212). Even if we assume that the number of unemployed in need of help is only 3 million persons, it is evident that in relation to the numbers of the population, the proportion of unemployed would be largest in the Southern republics.

The Shatalin group put the figure for the number of unemployed at 6 million at the beginning of 1990, of which 4.5 million would represent long-term unemployment and 1.5 per cent frictional unemployment *(Perekhod k rynku,* 1990, p. 111). According to this prognosis, the number of unemployed would reach 6.3 million by January 1991 (ibid.). The rise in unemployment during 1990 was due to a rise in frictional unemployed (plus 10,000) because of an increasing number of displaced workers and a slight increase in the duration of unemployment between jobs (from 1 to 1.5 months), and a rise in the number of long-term unemployed (plus 20,000). During 1991, the number of unemployed will rise to almost 12 million due to long-term unemployment rising to 6.1 million, and a rise in frictional unemployment stemming from an increase in the numbers of job-changers and job-losers (from 17 million in 1990 to 25 million in 1991), and the longer time interval in the duration of unemployment between jobs (from one month in 1990 to two months at the end of 1992).

The two hypothetical unemployment scenarios for 1991 and 1992 presented by the joint study are based on Goskomtrud's forecasts, but have less modest assumptions regarding the degree of overstaffing at Soviet enterprises and the average duration of unemployment spells (*A Study,* 1991, pp. 148–9). In both scenarios, enterprises are assumed to eliminate overmanning in two years, and the initial number of unemployed is fixed at 2.5 million at the end of 1990. In the first, gradual, scenario, it is assumed that initial overstaffing is 12.5 per cent, and that the average duration of unemployment will rise to 7.5 months in 1992. In this scenario the unemployment stock rises to 8.3 million at the end of 1991 (which corresponds to an unemployment rate of 6 per cent), and to 13 million (9.4 per cent) at the end of 1992 (ibid., p. 200). In the second scenario, overstaffing is assumed to be 25 per cent initially, and the average duration of unemployment rises to ten months. In this case, the stock of unemployed will rise to 17 million at the end of 1991 (about 12 per cent) and then settle at around 15 million, or about 10 per cent at the end of 1992. The first scenario implies a rise of the unemployment rate from 1.8 per cent (2.5 million) at the end of 1990, to 6 per cent (8.3 million) at the end of 1991, to 9.4 per cent (13.2 million) at the end of 1992 (ibid, p. 200). The second scenario implies a rise of unemployment to 9.3 per cent (13 million) in 1991, and 10.8 per cent (15 million) in 1992 (ibid.).

Since none of the economic programmes presented in 1990 took off, none of these scenarios will materialize, yet they point to possible developments even if the timing might not be right. The hypothetical scenarios of the joint study highlight the importance of taking into account the contribution of prolonged duration of unemployment spells to the unemployment rate.

The present crisis situation in the Soviet economy indicates that unemployment could get worse than these forecasts. Recently, Prime Minister Pavlov has depicted three new scenarios (*Ekonomika i zhizn'*, No. 18, 1991). In the first, no measures against the crisis are undertaken, in which case the national income is supposed to fall by 20 per cent. According to Pavlov, this would result in 18 million unemployed persons (12–13 per cent of the labour force) by the end of 1991. Pavlov does not explain how he arrives at this figure, but presumably he means that 18 million persons would get displaced during the year. The second alternative is a *laissez-faire* scenario, where state intervention should cease completely. Setting the market forces free, the Prime Minister assumes that the national income would drop by 30 per cent and unemployment would rise to 30 million persons (21 per cent of the labour force). Again, it might be assumed that Pavlov has the number of displaced in mind, and does not take into account that this shock treatment might lead to new opportunities and job creation. The third alternative, which is the government's alternative, envisages measures which would prevent the national income from falling more than 10 per cent. Pavlov does not give an estimate for the number of unem-ployed in this alternative, but says that unemployment would fall to manageable numbers, and people could find work in small scale enter-prises, the developing services sector, road construction, and, as a last resort, be given unemployment benefits. The two other estimates indicate that for each percentage point decrease in the national income, employ-ment declines by 0.7 per cent of the labour force. This would mean that the number of people losing their jobs in the last scenario will be around 9 million persons, or 6 per cent.

This projection is close to the first Goskomtrud scenario, which assumed that 9.5 million persons would leave the state sector in 1991 and that around 3 million of these would become unemployed. The reason that Pavlov might find this a more manageable number probably has to do with the government's labour policy, which is designed to take care of the displaced and the unemployed and whose financing would provide a cover-age for about this number of persons.

Labour market policies to ease transition

A sharp rise in unemployment will cause concern and possibly lead to increased social tension. Therefore, it is important that there is a policy to mitigate the unemployment problem. After a lengthy discussion, an all-union law on employment was finally adopted in January 1991.[22] This law provides definitions of 'employed', 'unemployed', and 'suitable work', gives general directions for labour-market policy and employment programmes, and lays down minimal levels of income support to the unemployed. The republics, however, are supposed to work out their own employment laws which may differ in accordance with regional conditions.

Until the adoption of this law, the rights of laid-off workers had been regulated by a decree adopted by the CPSU Central Committee, the Council of Ministers, and the VTsSPS[23] in December 1987.[24] In March 1988, this decree was followed up by the Goskomtrud and the VTsSPS by an order spelling out the conditions in more detail.[25]

The new employment law clearly states that employment is voluntary and that voluntary non-employment cannot be used for legal prosecution of a person. Citizens are regarded as employed if they work for pay according to an agreement; if they are self-employed; if they have been elected to a paid position; if they are in military service; or if they work abroad temporarily (Articles I: 1–2).

A citizen is considered to be unemployed if he is of working age and capable of working but for reasons beyond his control does not have a job and work income; if he is registered with the state employment service; if he is searching for a job; or if he is capable and available for work, but has not been offered a suitable job by the employment service. If the employment service cannot offer the unemployed person a suitable job he can be offered retraining (Article I:2). A suitable job is judged in terms of the professional training of the job-seeker, his age and work experience, as well as the geographical location of the job. A job is not suitable if the job-seeker would have to move to less favourable living conditions; if it is too far from his present residence; if the wage and other working conditions are worse than at his previous job; or if there are 'valid' reasons, in particular personal or family reasons, for him to refuse it (Article I:3).

The law's definition of unemployed means that a person quitting a job on his own initiative will not be counted as unemployed. The argument for this is that the status of unemployed means the right to income support and if voluntary job-changers would be made eligible for benefits, they could prolong their spells of search unemployment. The definition of a suitable job appears generous regarding possible changes in labour demand. There is already a problem finding suitable jobs for displaced professionals with specialized secondary or higher education, particularly in big urban centres. These people must either accept jobs below their professional status or move in order to be redeployed. In a longer perspective, the problem with people with the wrong professional profile will certainly increase and involve blue-collar workers as well.

Rules for income support to the unemployed are differentiated for different categories. Laid-off workers would get a severance payment from their former employer corresponding to their average wage for a maximum of three months. The laid-off worker must register with the employment service within ten days after being dismissed. If no suitable job has been found for the displaced worker during the three-month period, he is regarded as unemployed (Article IV:26). If the person worked for at least 12 weeks during the 12 months preceding the unemployment spell, he will have the right to receive unemployment benefits for at least 26 weeks in a 12-month period. During the period the unemployed receives benefits, he must actively search for work (Article IV:28).

Re-entrants (persons absent from the labour market for at least one year) will get unemployment benefits from the 11th day after registration at the employment service for at least 26 weeks during any 12 month period (ibid.). First-time job-seekers have the right to unemployment benefits for 13 weeks from the 11th day after registration (ibid.). Job-seekers who have fulfilled their required years of service for receiving old-age pension can get up to 52 weeks of unemployment benefits (Article IV:29).

The sizes of unemployment benefits to laid-off workers are to be based on the basic (*tariff*) wage at the previous job (Article IV:30). This means that bonuses and extra payments which may be a substantial part of earnings are not taken into account. The minimum size of the benefit should not be less than 50 per cent of the former basic wage or the minimum wage (Article IV:31). For those displaced from military service and those graduating from professional training or retraining, the minimum size of the benefit must not be less than the minimum wage (Article IV:32, 35). For first-time job-seekers and re-entrants after long spells of non-employment, the minimum level is 75 per cent of the minimum wage (Article IV:33–34).

Apart from income support, the unemployed should be offered re-training if necessary. If an enterprise hires a displaced worker and organizes training for him, the worker has the right to receive his former average wage during the training period (from the new employer), but the enterprise will be able to deduct the costs of the training from its taxable profit (Article IV:26). Persons for whom jobs are difficult to find should be offered re-training possibilities by the employment service. The training could be organized either in centres under the employment service's management or in existing establishments for vocational training. In this case, costs should be born by the special state fund for employment assistance (hereafter the employment fund) (Article III:24). A person undergoing re-training should get income support corresponding at least to the unemployment benefit.

Besides income support and re-training, the employment law gives the outlines for the organization of employment programmes, public relief works and how labour policy should be administered. The most important element for the effective administration of labour policies is the establishment of a network of public employment services.

The resources to be made available for labour policies are to be raised by a one per cent levy on the pay-roll. At least 10 per cent of this revenue should be transferred to a central all-union fund, and the rest should be retained in republican employment funds for republican needs. The central fund is needed for redistributional purposes, since the tax base and the estimated number of persons who will be in need of assistance are unevenly distributed over the country.

Conclusions

So far, the transformation of the Soviet economy has led to a certain 'de-statefication' of labour through a decline in state-sector employment and some 'privatization' through a rise in employment in the private sector, primarily in cooperatives. However, the legal private sector does not account for more than about 6 per cent of estimated total employment, even if subsidiary agriculture is included.[26]

The decline in state-sector employment is due to changes in both the demand and supply side of the labour market. The wage reform launched in 1986 has induced state employers to shed some labour. However, the trade-off between nominal wage increases and the employment level is still very weak, which indicates that state employers have been operating under soft budget constraints at least up to 1990. The 1987 enterprise law has contributed to the development of high wage rises without improvements in labour productivity by granting monopolistic enterprises more discretion over price formation and the enterprise remuneration funds, and by a wage determination mechanism which does not link wage payments directly to profit. In addition, the legalization of private employment has drained the state sector of labour, and the increased competition on the labour market has also pushed nominal wages upwards.

With the data available it is not possible to say that these measures are the primary causes for the decline of employment in the state sector. To a greater or smaller extent, decreased labour supply may have interplayed. The demographic situation, with large increases in the labour force in Central Asia and Transcaucasia, where job opportunities are scarce, might have affected the employment level. Jobless people in these regions have a low propensity to migrate, and the proportion of non-employed is considerably higher in these regions than the USSR average. Thus, employment might have fallen because of a supply constraint.

The changes in wages, prices and tax laws might also have decreased labour supply (at least to the legal economy). Intensified shortages in consumer-goods markets may have produced supply multiplier effects: that is, people choose not to work since wages and salaries do not guarantee command over goods and services. Moreover, the ethnic conflicts, demobilization, natural catastrophes and the economic crisis have induced people to move, which also means they have left their jobs. These developments may also be reflected in declining employment. In order to analyse the trends in employment better statistics are necessary. For instance, if a time series of quits and lay-offs did exist we could be more precise about the decline in employment and whether it is primarily due to factors affecting demand or supply.

Also, the study of the development in unemployment is impeded by the lack of relevant labour statistics. Since there is no data which can clearly distinguish the unemployed from the non-employed, all unemployment estimates are extremely tentative. From the data available, an estimate of the number of unemployed is 3.5 to 4.5 million at the end of 1990 may be obtained, to which unemployment due to job-changing should add between 1 and 4 million. This means that the unemployment rate would be in the range of 3 to 6 per cent. In order to get a more adequate picture of the situation regarding unemployment, it would be desirable if labour force surveys could be conducted at least in some regions of the country. To know how many are actually unemployed, how this number develops and who are unemployed, is important for the shaping of labour-market policies. Better data is also crucial for forecasting the unemployment consequences of any reform programme.

Several tentative scenarios of the consequences of further transition on unemployment have been presented. These indicate that unemployment may increase sharply, and that an unemployment rate of around 10 per cent is not implausible when the economy is undergoing privatization and structural change. Unemployment will rise more sharply if economic deterioration continues.

The job creation capacity of the economy during the transition period is difficult to foresee, not least because today it is hard to tell what kind of transition the economy will have to undergo. A further deepening of the economic crisis will affect employment negatively and have serious social consequences. With impediments such as the lack of equipment and inputs and breakdowns in the transportation or energy sector, the entrepreneurial spirit will not be adequate to create new opportunities and new jobs. Obviously, the most important condition for avoiding the drastic consequences of unemployment is to create decent prerequisites for economically meaningful activities.

Even if a way out of the present crisis situation is found, open unemployment will rise and it is important that there is a preparedness to mitigate this problem to avoid increased social tension and a backlash to the whole transition process. It is also vital that labour policies are designed in such a way that they do not impede the transformation of the economy. In particular, labour policies should not be geared to conserving jobs without future prospects, but instead to helping the reallocation of workers from the shrinking sectors of the economy to the expanding sectors. Some income support programmes must also be put in place to provide short term help to the unemployed in order to avoid destitution among those affected.

The all-union employment legislation passed in January 1991 copies many elements of labour policies in market economies and is a reasonable beginning for implementing relevant labour policies in different republics. The possibilities of realizing the ambitions of this legislation may be questioned during the transition period. For instance, generous provisions have been made about the kind of job an unemployed person can refuse while still being eligible for income support. The aim of providing relevant re-training will be difficult to realize because of ignorance about the kind of professional profiles which will be in demand in the future. The possibilities of financing any employment programmes, even only those on income support for the unemployed, may be questioned as well, in the light of the general financial situation and the possible number of unemployed.

References

Åslund, A., (1991) *The Soviet Economic Crisis: Causes and Dimensions*, Stockholm Institute of Soviet and East European Economics, Working Paper, No. 16.

A Study of the Soviet Economy, (1991), IMF, The World Bank, OECD, EBRD, Paris.

Ekonomicheskoe i sotsial'noe razvitie soyuznykh respublik (1990), Moscow: Goskomstat.

Chapman, J., (1988) 'Gorbachev's Wage Reform', *Soviet Economy*, 4, No. 4, pp. 338–65.

Chizhova, L. (ed.) (1990) *Strategiya zanyatosti*, Moscow: Ekonomika.

Clarke, D. (1988) 'Gorbachev's Proposed Restructuring of the Soviet Army', *Radio Liberty Research Bulletin*, RL 544/88.

Kirillov, I., (1990) 'O zanyatosti molodezhi, okonchivshei srednyuyu shkolu', *Vestnik statistiki*, 10, pp. 58–60.

Maevskii, V. and Maevskaya, L. (1986) 'Proizvoditel'nost' truda i fond zarabotnoi platy', *Voprosy ekonomiki*, No. 8, pp. 51–62.

Malle, S., (1990) 'Labour Redeployment and Cooperatives in the Soviet Union', *Recherches Economiques de Louvain*, 56, No. 2, pp. 191–220.

Narodnoe khozyaistvo za 70 let., (1987) Moscow: Finansy i statistika (abbreviated *Narkhoz 1986*).

Narodnoe khozyaistvo v 1988 g., (1989) Moscow: Finansy i statistika (abbreviated *Narkhoz 1988*).

Narodnoe khozyaistvo v 1989 g., (1990) Moscow: Finansy i statistika (abbreviated *Narkhoz 1989*).

'Osnovy zakonodatel'stva soyuza SSR i respublik o zanyatosti naseleniya', (1991) *Izvestiya*, 26 January.

Oxenstierna, S., (1989) *Perestroika and Unemployment.* Papers of the Sixth Annual Conference of the Italian Association for Comparative Economic Studies, Urbino, 12–14 October 1989, pp. 859–80.

Oxenstierna, S., (1990) *From Labour Shortage to Unemployment? The Soviet Labour Market in the 1980s*, Stockholm: Almqvist & Wiksell.

Perekhod k rynku, (1990) Moscow: Arkhangel'skoe.

Plokker, K., (1990) 'The Development of Individual and Cooperative Labour Activity in the Soviet Union', *Soviet Studies*, 42, No. 3, July, pp. 403–28.

Polnyi khozyaistvennyi raschet i samofinansirovanie, (1988), Moscow: Pravda.

Semenov, A. (1990) 'Rynok truda i stoimost' rabochei sily', *Sotsialisticheskii trud*, No. 6, pp. 44–50.

Shcherbakov, V., (1991) 'Rynok truda i zanyatost': sostoyanie, problemy, perspektivy', *Sotsialisticheskii trud*, No. l, pp. 6–16.

Sobell, V., (1988) 'Perestroika and the Warsaw Pact Military Burden', Radio Free Europe Research, *RAD Background Report/*103.

Tedstrom, J. (1989) 'The Soviet Cooperative Movement: An Update', Radio Liberty, *Report on the USSR*, 1, No. 41.

Trud v SSSR, (1988) Moscow: Finansy i statistika.

Volokh, V., (1991) 'Nuzhen zakon o bezhentsakh', *Sotsialisticheskii trud*, No. 4, pp. 50–2.

Zakon SSSR (1987) 'O gosudarstvennom predpriyatii (ob"edinienie)', 30 June 1987, *Ekonomicheskaya gazeta*, No. 28, July.

Zakon SSSR (1990a) 'O predpriyatiyakh v SSSR', *Ekonomika i zhizn'*, No. 25, June.

Zakon SSSR (1990b) 'O nalogakh s predpriyatii, ob"edinienii i organizatsii', *Ekonomika i zhizn'*, No. 30, July.

Zaslavskii, I., (1988) 'Obespechenie zanyatosti v usloviyakh perestroiki', *Rabochii klass: sovremennyi mir*, No. 5, pp. 27–37.

Notes

1 Central Asia includes the republics of Uzbekistan, Tadzhikistan, Turkmenistan and Kirgizia. Transcaucasia includes Georgia, Armenia and Azerbaidzhan.

2 Soviet economics distinguishes between the productive sector (also called the material sphere of production), which comprises industry, construction, transportation, agriculture, trade and communications, and the non-productive sector (or the non-material sphere of production), which consists of education, healthcare, housing and other public services, science, state and local

administration, finance and banking, and art and culture.

3   See previous note.

4   For instance, in a discussion in Stockholm on 14 June 1991 Professor I. Maslova, Institute of Economics, Moscow, stressed the importance of people changing their labour-market behaviour (e.g. women being less inclined to work). Professor A. Kotlyar, Central Labour Institute at the RSFSR Ministry of Labour, Moscow, pointed at regional disbalances, claiming that there is still a problem of labour shortage in many areas.

5   The wage reform was tried out in the Belorussian railways during 1985 and 1986. Labour productivity rose by 32 per cent compared to 1983, and around 13 per cent of the work force was displaced. Wages rose by over 22 per cent. In 1987 the reform was adopted in the whole railway sector and employment decreased by about 10 per cent (Oxenstierna, op. cit. pp. 243–4).

6   These are the percentage growth rates for *state sector* wages which may be deducted from *Narkhoz 1989* (p. 78) and *Ekonomika i zhizn'* No. 5 (1991, p. 9). Åslund (1991, pp. 8, 30) presents higher growth rates based on the total remuneration paid out to the population in the years in question. Of course, if the earnings of *kolkhozniki* (which rose more than average state wages in 1989 and 1990) and the wages in cooperatives are included, wage and salary rises are higher. Still, I am not fully convinced of a 14 per cent increase for 1989, because total employment did not decline this year, only state and *kolkhoz* sector employment did.

7   Zakon (1987).

8   Oxenstierna, op. cit., Ch. 10, contains a detailed presentation and analysis of these models.

9   Zakon (1990a); Zakon (1990b).

10   In the construction field the cooperative average wage was 463 roubles, and that in the state sector was 339 roubles (1.34:1). In agriculture the average cooperative wage was lower (230r.) than in state agriculture (270r.). In trade the cooperative wage was 574r. while that in the state sector was 227r. (2.5:1), in healthcare the corresponding relation was 398 and 184r. (2.16:1), in scientific work, 484 and 333r. (1.45:1), and in construction design, 495 and 392r. (1.26:1) *(Ekonomika i zhizn'*, No. 20, 1991). Because the proportion of part-time workers is greater in the cooperative sector than in the state sector, the actual average cooperative take-home wage for full-time workers is higher than these figures reveal. On the other hand, work intensity is probably much higher in the cooperative sector than in the state sector.

11   The average share of labour costs in total costs was 14 per cent in Soviet industry in the mid-1980s (see e.g. *Narkhoz 1986*, p. 159). According to *Ekonomika i zhizn'*, No. 20 (1991, p. 12), the labour share in total costs in material production in the state sector was twice as low as in the cooperative sector, i.e. 20 per cent.

12   These figures apply only to the state-sector labour force (that *is, kolkhozy* are not included).

13   This interval is too large to be satisfactory.

14   Calculation based on the *tekuchest'* figures in *Narkhoz 1989* (p. 69) and one to three months average duration of unemployment spells. If anything, duration of unemployment should have increased.

15   Calculated from data in *Vestnik statistiki*, No. 6, 1990, pp. 62–77 and *Statisticheskii press byulleten'*, No. 13, 1990, pp. 78–9.

16   The estimated labour resources is a figure reflecting the numbers which could possibly be mobilized into the labour force. Thus, it does not take account of people's actual labour-market behaviour.

17 Sobell (1988) reported military personnel per 1,000 population in the USSR at 16.1. Calculated on the basis of the total population in 1987, this implies that the Soviet armed forces consisted of 4.5 million persons. According to *Pravda*, 28 January 1990, the armed forces numbered 4 million in 1989. Gorbachev, in his speech to the UN General Assembly on 7 December 1988, announced an overall reduction of 500,000 men in the Soviet military establishment until 1990 (Clarke, 1988).

18 This is the estimate reported for 1989 in *Pravda*, 28 January 1990.

19 Various numbers for this group are given. See e.g. Shcherbakov (1991, pp. 14-15) and Chizhova (1990, p. 64).

20 Here the rate has been calculated as the total number of full-year equivalent unemployed, 4.6 million and 8.3 million respectively, divided by total employment in 1990, 138.4 million, plus the respective stock of unemployed. That is, 4.6/142 and 8.3/143.

21 Calculated from data in *Vestnik statistiki*, No. 6, 1990, pp. 62–77 and *Statisticheskii byulleten'*, No. 13, 1990, pp. 78–9.

22 'Osnovy' (1991).

23 All-Union Central Trade Union Council.

24 Joint decree on efficient employment, job placement for laid-off workers, and the rights of laid-off workers to compensation *(Polnyi khozyaisbvennyiraschet*, 1988, pp. 117–33).

25 See Oxenstierna (1990), pp. 244–6.

26 The number of employed in the cooperatives and in private subsidiary agriculture, together with those who were self-employed, made up 8 million persons in the first quarter of 1991. Total employment was reported at 134.8 million people, which means that employment in the private sector was 5.9 per cent of total employment (see table 3.1).

PART II
STABILIZATION AND FOREIGN TRADE

4
The Emergence and Stabilization of Extreme Inflationary Pressures in the Soviet Union

Ardo Hansson

I Introduction

From the mid-1980s, the growing macroeconomic instability in the Soviet Union has been linked to two main factors: the *flow* problem of a large government budget deficit and rapid credit growth, and the *stock* 'monetary overhang' of excess purchasing power at prevailing levels of controlled prices and interest rates. In this setting, the bulk of excess demand pressure has appeared as 'repressed inflation' and a shortage of goods, rather than as open price increases. In 1990, the official inflation rate of around 5 per cent was still at traditional single-digit levels, and even the highest alternative estimates would put it well in the lower double digits.[1]

From the start of 1991, and slightly earlier in some of the republics, policy clearly shifted towards an attempt to release some inflationary pressure through a combination of administrative price increases and direct partial compensation of incomes. The result was a rapid acceleration of inflation: official indices in the first quarter of 1991 showed a price level that was 22 per cent higher than in the same quarter of the preceding year.[2]

In most republics, a much larger jump manifested itself on 2 April 1991, when the Soviet government raised fixed retail prices or price ceilings for some goods, while freeing the prices of others. Official appraisals show that this increased average retail prices by 60 to 70 per cent, but independent estimates have even exceeded 100 per cent (*The Economist*, 6 April 1991).

Given that this was a recent administrative increase, its impact on the core rate of inflation is still unclear. While few would probably claim that sustained price rises already reach the 50 per cent per month threshold often used to define hyperinflation, most prognoses are for a further acceleration of price rises. While some foresee a price rise of around 150 per cent during 1991, warnings of a collapse into hyperinflation are becoming ever more common.[3] These are sounded by Soviet politicians of different persuasions, and by domestic and foreign economists familiar with the Soviet economy.

Yet, beyond general warnings, we are unaware of studies which have examined the potential for extreme inflation in the Soviet Union more closely. This paper takes a modest step in this direction by asking three main questions:

1 Is the Soviet Union, in mid-1991, experiencing an extreme inflationary shock?
2 Does the Soviet economy have the propagation mechanisms for trans-lating this into persistent hyperinflation?
3 What stabilization policies or other measures could reduce the risk of extreme inflation?

To find the answers, we shall examine the historical experiences of countries which have gone through extreme inflation, and compare their pre-hyperinflationary experience to the Soviet situation in mid-1991. Early- and mid-twentieth century Europe, Latin America and Israel in the 1980s, and Poland in 1989, are included in the discussion.

These experiences show the difficulty of predicting exactly if and when hyperinflation might occur. Some countries have faced huge terms of trade shocks without high inflation.[4] In the 1980s, both Mexico and Italy ran budget deficits in the range of 12–15 per cent of GDP, yet price rises never reached hyperinflationary levels.[5] Factors separating curable, chron-ically high and extreme inflation are nebulous and varying. Uncertainty is exacerbated by the inherent instability of extreme inflation. It is not uncommon to observe long periods in which inflationary pressures appear to be under control. Then, when an invisible threshold has been crossed or the rules of the game change, any further shock can suddenly 'set the house on fire in no time'.[6]

For these reasons, we shall not make prognoses about short-run Soviet inflation. Our goal is simply to determine whether the present Soviet Union offers fertile ground for extreme inflation to emerge and grow, and what might be done to reduce this potential. We shall do this in several stages. Section II describes the types of shocks which have hit other economies before hyperinflation, drawing comparisons with the present Soviet economy. Section III proceeds similarly for the propagation mech-anisms of inflation. Section IV then examines the additional factors pecu-liar to the Soviet case. Finally, Section V summarizes our findings and the implications for Soviet stabilization policy.

II Types of hyperinflationary shocks

The shocks that might initiate hyperinflation can be divided into those emanating from outside the country, and those arising from within. As many are interrelated, the list of primary determinants would be shorter than the one we present.

External shocks

There are four types of external inflationary shocks. The balance of payments impact of a *terms of trade deterioration* can be counteracted through a devaluation. This raises inflationary pressures, especially when the tradables sectors are under government ownership and represent a major source of state revenues. Such shocks have been cited by Dornbusch, et al. (1990) as having played a role in Bolivian hyperinflation. A 22 per cent drop in the terms of trade during 1985–6, mostly from falling agricultural prices, also hurt Argentinian stabilization during the Austral plan.[7]

An *economic blockade* that reduces the volume of foreign trade is inflationary through its disruptive supply-side effects. As key inputs become difficult to acquire, the productive efficiency of the economy deteriorates. The First World War blockade of Germany has been ascribed a role in the subsequent hyperinflation (Guttmann and Meehan, 1975).

A *de facto* economic blockade can also be imposed by a country on itself. As in the case of Brazil in the early 1980s, which imposed restrictions on raw materials imports, this usually has a balance of payments motivation (Modiano, 1988, p. 240). The effect on productive efficiency and inflation is the same as that of an externally imposed blockade.

Possibly the most common form of external shock is a 'debt crisis', or a sudden *reversal or curtailment of net financial flows*. Without resorting to a partial or full suspension of debt service, this can be met in two ways: the improvement of the current account balance via devaluation, or a switch to greater domestic financing, including through money creation. Either response raises inflationary pressures.

The best-known example of such a shock is the case of German reparations after the First World War. An attempt to increase the German trade surplus through depreciation and relaxed credit led to inflation.[8] In the early 1980s, the debt shock was linked to a rise in world interest rates that made many countries either insolvent or illiquid. Argentina responded with an inflationary devaluation. Morales (1988, p. 310) also describes how devaluation induced by the 1982 reversal of external financing flows helped trigger Bolivian hyperinflation.

Finally, the extreme financing needs of a *war* are a classic source of inflationary pressure. More often than not the effects are felt after rather than during the conflict, when a combination of direct controls and appeals to patriotism can keep inflationary pressures bottled up. Once the war is over, the controls are eased, the patriotism disappears and the pressures erupt. Examples include Germany and Austria after the First World War and Israel and Argentina in the 1980s.

Internal shocks

There are at least six forms of internally generated inflationary shocks. Of these, the most common and almost universal precursor of hyperinflation has been a serious *fiscal imbalance*, especially when it is not debt financed.[9]

Second, the *exchange rate policy* adopted by a country can be inflationary in two ways: via its direct impact on tradables prices and through its indirect impact on the budget. Dornbusch and Fischer (1986, p. 6) stress the effect of exchange-rate collapse in the German case. The mechanisms of budgetary effect are more complex. Overvaluation can reduce tariff revenues by lowering the home-currency price of imports. Undervaluation raises the domestic-currency cost of servicing foreign debt. The net effect will depend on the relative size of tariff revenues and the stock of debt.

Third, inflation can arise from domestic *supply shocks,* or exogenous declines in the potential output of the economy at a given price level. These worsen the menu of available macroeconomic outcomes. An example is the drought preceding Brazil's hyperinflation.

Fourth, *real wage growth* in excess of the rise in labour productivity is also stagflationary. In Israel, a 16 per cent increase in real wages over three years preceded the hyperinflation of the mid-1980s.[10]

Fifth, a realignment of domestic *relative prices* can be inflationary. In a fully flexible economy, relative and absolute wages or prices would not be linked. However, when wages or prices are downwardly rigid, an attempt to keep average prices constant would face the hardest hit sectors with unemployment and a fall in output. The alternative of adjusting relative prices through some overall inflation rate can thus be viewed as being less painful.[11]

Finally, revolution or other forms of *political transition* could be fertile ground for hyperinflation. When the government is in a weakened state and the population is socially and politically divided, claims on the social pie grow unimpeded. Lacking legitimacy or the means to enforce a temporary reduction in overall claims, and facing growing tax evasion by an unsupportive public, the government must revert to the inflationary mechanism. As Dornbusch et al. (1990) note, '"Politically impossible" is the key phrase accompanying the progressive slide into hyperinflation.'[12]

Machinea and Fanelli (1988, p. 112) cite the interaction of political and economic instability as a key source of disequilibrium in the run-up to Argentinian hyperinflation. Those negatively affected by the stabilization – e.g. some trade unions – exerted pressure to obtain government subsidization of private-sector adjustment costs. In Brazil, economic policy was immobilized in the run-up to the 1985 elections. This continued after the election, when the death of the elected president led to a government lacking the legitimacy required to push through major changes. Finally Morales (1988, p. 309) describes the paralysis induced by intense political turmoil as a factor in Bolivian hyperinflation. Recognition of the impending crisis was delayed, although its symptoms were already present.

Comparison with the Soviet Union of mid-1991

In mid-1991, the Soviet economy is characterized by the simultaneous existence of nearly all of the noted shocks. The one possible exception concerns the terms of trade. From January 1991, most trade with the former CMEA region (which has accounted for about one-half of total Soviet trade) went over to freely negotiated prices. The price of oil, the major Soviet export to the region, jumped relative to the price of the manufactures imported by the Soviet Union, producing a clear improvement in the terms of trade.[13]

The terms of trade for the remainder of Soviet trade will also closely follow the price of oil. As the present world price is close to the average level during the period 1986 to 1990, there are no immediate terms of trade shock of any size.[14] The inflationary pressure coming from the repressed effect of the 1986 decline in world oil prices is discussed below.

Developments in trade volumes represent a serious negative shock. Having demanded a sudden end to the former financing arrangements for CMEA trade, and having rejected barter and other interim arrangements, the USSR has imposed what amounts to a severe economic blockade against itself. This arises from the absence of a workable finance mechanism combined with the paralysing effect of accumulated arrears in trade-credit payments. The latter have stayed in the range of $5–6 billion from the end of 1989. Guarantees by unknown Soviet commercial banks have little value, while the Vneshekonombank guarantees requested by trading partners have been increasingly hard to secure. The fear of the budgetary impact of massive bad loans has also made trading partners reluctant to provide guarantees themselves. Yet without these mechanisms it is difficult to see much trade occurring. The quantitative effect has been a 45 and 18 per cent fall in imports and exports respectively during the first quarter of 1991.[15]

In early 1991, the Soviet Union faced a severe external financing problem. Following an import spurt in 1987–9, during which purchases from the West grew by no less than 47 per cent, the Soviet hard-currency debt rose to around $60 billion at the end of 1989 (Åslund, 1991, pp. 19-20). In 1990, official foreign reserves dropped by $10 billion to $5.1 billion (*The Financial Times*, 31 January 1991). The combination of $11 billion of maturing debt, payment of trade credit arrears and a continuing trade deficit leaves a financing requirement of at least $15 billion in 1991.[16] While some progress has recently been made in repayment, the combination of an accelerating slump in oil production, lower international oil prices, and bottlenecks in the economy mean that the underlying determinants of 'ability to pay' do not appear to be improving. With commercial banks reluctant to lend, the key Soviet options are to seek official assistance or to squeeze imports, neither of which is particularly attractive.

Finally, the present financial instability can be better understood if one views the Soviet Union as a post- (cold?) war economy. As in wartime, the combination of controls, coercion and an outwardly unchallenged official ideology helped curb inflationary pressures. As in a post-war economy, their simultaneous erosion in the USSR has in turn released the pent-up pressures.

With reference to internal inflationary shocks, the problem of the Soviet budget deficit is well-known. Because of a complex mixture of policy mistakes (such as the anti-alcohol campaign and excessive wage liberalization) and unexpected revenue losses (the lower international oil price) and expenditures (Chernobyl, the Armenian earthquake), the official deficit rose from 1985 to a peak of 11 per cent of GNP in 1989.[17] The official 1990 figures are somewhat lower.[18]

In 1991, the problem appears to be even worse. Deficit estimates for the first quarter range from 26.9 billion roubles by Goskomstat to 34 billion by Prime Minister Pavlov.[19] All exceed the planned deficit of 26.7 billion roubles for the whole of 1991. The high figures must come largely from the subsidies to sustain retail prices after wholesale price rises, and a drop in republican transfers to the central government.[20]

The 'anti-crisis programme' and subsequent announcements give mixed signals about the direction of the budget. A moratorium on new investment based on central government finance is a positive sign (*The Economist*, 27 April 1991). However, a presidential decree in March, which lowered enterprise tax rates from 45 to 35 per cent, and the promise in the '9+1 agreement' to abolish a 5 per cent sales tax, are reasons for concern. Further sources of uncertainty are whether reductions in producer subsidies will be fully made-up by higher wage subsidies, and whether the military and bureaucracy will face serious budget cuts.

As the Soviet Union has numerous exchange rates, it is not easy to describe developments in this sphere. Following the April retail price rises, the chairman of Gosbank said that exporters were no longer competitive and needed to be compensated, presumably by a further rouble devaluation (*The Financial Times*, 2 April 1991). While the tourist rate was raised from 5.74 to 27.6 roubles/dollar, increases in other rates have not followed. However, the increasing role of the highly depreciated auction rate is clearly inflationary.

That the Soviet Union is experiencing a negative supply shock is shown by the accelerating output decline in a period of demand expansion. Official figures for 1990 already indicated a 4 per cent decline in national product (*The Financial Times*, 6 February 1991). In the first quarter of 1991, this was between 8 and 12 per cent, depending upon the measure used.[21] The predicted decline for the whole of 1991 ranges from 11.6 per cent by Gosplan to 20 per cent by other economists.[22]

The supply shock has two noteworthy causes. The first is the secular decline in energy (especially oil) production. Crude oil output fell from 12.5 million barrels a day (b/d) in 1987-8 to 11.4 million b/d in 1990. In the first quarter of 1991, production was down 9 per cent relative to the same quarter of the preceding year and some projections are for the decline to accelerate.[23] At the same time, electricity-generation capacity has suffered from environmental protest, while extensive miners' strikes have cut coal production for 1991.

A second supply shock comes from the flourishing of barter trade between enterprises. The extraordinary efforts needed to undertake such commerce reduce the productive efficiency and potential output of the economy.

Real wage trends have exacerbated inflationary pressures, and are particularly emphasized by Åslund (1991). Official estimates put annual Soviet real wage growth in the five years from 1986 to 1990 at 0.9, 2.4, 7.7, 7.3 and 5.0 per cent respectively, or at a cumulative rise of 25 per cent in five years (World Bank, 1990, p. 49). The acceleration in 1988 has been attributed to the law on state enterprises, which gave enterprise managers increased freedom in wage setting (Åslund, 1991, p. 7).

As the Soviet economy integrates more closely with the rest of the world, it will adopt a relative price structure very different from the current one.[24] While administrative adjustments need not lead closer to the new config- uration, the recent attempts have combined general and relative price adjustments. For instance, the 60.2 per cent measured rise in the Estonian cost of living between the fourth quarters of 1989 and 1990 is broken up into 100, 22.3 and 19.5 per cent rises in the price of food, industrial goods and services, respectively.[25]

Finally, that the Soviet Union is in a deep political transition with a rela- tively weak government does not need to be emphasized. The decline of some regions, sectors and classes have increased political pressures at all levels of government. However, governments, oppositions and legislatures have all shown an unwillingness to resist these pressures. For example, the populist Congress of Peoples Deputies has raised many social expenditures, which may be even more out of control than wages (Åslund, 1991, p. 9).

III Propagation mechanisms

To produce hyperinflation, the described shocks must interact with insti- tutional and other mechanisms that can turn a single price rise into gallop- ing inflation. These propagation mechanisms are characterized by their relatively slow workings: the requisite adaptions in the economy are only gradually introduced.[26] They can be grouped into monetary, fiscal and indexation-related mechanisms.

Monetary propagation

Central bank emission of money is an important way of financing a govern- ment fiscal deficit, especially when financial markets are weak. The govern- ment benefits either from the 'inflation tax' arising from the erosion of its real liabilities under open inflation, or from forcing the public to accu- mulate low-return savings in a setting of repressed inflation. The base for the inflation tax is roughly proportional to the real money holdings of the public.[27] These in turn depend on the availability of other stores of value such as durable goods, equities and real estate, domestic interest-bearing assets and foreign assets. The more easily these alternatives are acquired, the lower is the cost of switching out of domestic money and the more the switching will occur.

As the acquisition of durable goods is rarely legally constrained, the ability to switch out of money is limited by the extent of real private prop- erty, domestic financial liberalization and/or the 'dollarization' of the economy. The latter includes legality of, and access to, foreign exchange transactions and foreign bank accounts. All these compel the government to offer creditors more favourable terms for borrowed funds.

A second propagation mechanism is a passive monetary policy, especially under fiscal deficits. This can easily begin and sustain a spiral of inflation, depreciation and further monetary accommodation. Such a stance is more likely under a weak government fearful of unemployment. For instance, on the eve of the German hyperinflation, Reichsbank governor Havenstein declared it his 'sacred duty' to provide credit, claiming that without this the economy could not function (Guttmann and Meehan, 1975, p. 33).

A passive monetary stance also arises when authorities place almost sole emphasis on attaining external balance, without adjusting the overall level of absorption. In this situation, a nominal devaluation will quickly bring a proportional change in prices, the accommodation of which feeds back into the spiral.

Fiscal propagation

The main fiscal propagation mechanism is the so-called Tanzi effect. Not only can a budget deficit lead to inflation but an exogenous inflationary impulse can generate a fiscal deficit, the money finance of which then feeds an inflationary spiral. This arises when there are long lags between the assessment and collection of taxes. Following an unexpected price rise, real revenues contract automatically and are further reduced by citizens deferring payment to the last moment, increasing the fiscal deficit.[28]

The Tanzi effect is counteracted by 'fiscal drag' from the nominal specification of progressive tax rates and the reduction by inflation of the real value of government liabilities.[29] The net effect on the budget deficit is uncertain, but there is likely to be a threshold beyond which the Tanzi effect dominates and inflation becomes unstable in the absence of concerted action.

Indexation of contracts

The most visible propagation mechanism for high inflation is the indexation of prices, wages and interest rates. This almost always evolves in response to a previous bout of high inflation, as in Argentina and Israel.[30] Full indexation, which can include contracts specified in foreign currency terms to be translated at the prevailing exchange rate at the time of payment, occurs only in extreme cases.[31] Most often, the formal rules are for wages to increase less than proportionally to the rise in prices. However, as some workers will still reach settlements in excess of the mandated indexation rate, a partial rate would be adopted even if the desired end result was an equiproportionate growth in wage and price levels.

Similarly, financial contracts evolve indexed interest rates, or shrink to shorter maturities. If these developments become extensive, it is no longer possible to lower the real value of government interest-bearing debt, strengthening the likelihood of the Tanzi effect.

At modest rates of inflation, indexation can be based on long lags, which helps to stabilize the propagation of shocks. As inflation grows, economic agents try to raise the velocity of money by shortening intervals between salary payments and/or price adjustments. As the resulting fall in money demand further raises inflationary pressure, the shortening process can become unstable and act to accelerate inflation.

If the economy faces a pure demand shock, full wage indexation is not a barrier to concerted stabilization. In three other cases, it can make inflation intractable:

1 *When demand pressure is not eliminated.* Its full, mechanical accommodation sustains an inflationary spiral which might have been checked by partial indexation.
2 *Under a negative supply shock.* As this lowers the real wage at which full employment will be reached, real wage rigidity will bring unemployment. Attempts to raise employment via demand expansion will only raise inflation.
3 *Under extensive relative price adjustment.* As economic restructuring is induced, part of the capital stock becomes obsolete. Until this is transformed or replaced, and labour is reallocated, the marginal product of labour falls below its previous value. This has the same effect as a negative supply shock and is equally explosive if demand is not cut.

Propagation mechanisms in the Soviet Union

If the Soviet economy is unambiguously experiencing an inflationary shock, the evidence of a strong propagation mechanism for turning this into extreme inflation is more mixed. At the same time, the mechanisms required are becoming more evident.

Access to domestic non-money financial assets is not great. As privatization has scarcely begun, equities and real-estate are difficult to acquire. While fledgeling commercial banks offer interest rates above the token levels of the traditional banks, these are still below any reasonable measure of expected inflation. As the new banks deal almost solely with firms, they provide few new opportunities for households. Their danger of insolvency further reduces the attractiveness of their deposit rates.

Outside the large cities and the Baltic states, growing dollarization has still not reached the levels we might encounter in Latin America. While bans on foreign-currency trading have been little enforced, the available volumes of currency do not yet permit its wide circulation. It is uncertain whether the new Soviet law restricting foreign bank accounts and the use of hard currency, effective since 1 April 1991, will stem dollarization.

A very evident propagation mechanism is the passivity of monetary policy. As the banking system under central planning was by definition passive, the continuation of this *modus operandi* is not surprising.[32] Furthermore, the noted inability of an unpopular government to resist the pressures to expand money is at play. However, if recent reform plans which include the establishment of an independent central bank come to fruition and are implemented in spirit, this would be an important step.

Wage compensation has so far been *ad hoc* rather than according to an indexation rule. To compensate for the April retail price increases, the government paid a lump sum of 60 roubles in advance, while savings accounts were increased by 40 per cent but frozen for three years.[33] While the intention was to raise average monthly wages 50 per cent by April, some estimate the net effect to have been an equiproportionate rise in incomes and prices.[34]

The stated target rate of indexation has varied but has always been high. Originally, the Pavlov government promised full compensation for increases in the prices of food and basic products (*The Financial Times*, 13 February 1991). Later on, the discussions were of partial indexation: a rate of 85 per cent for wages and benefits was heard most often.

However, except for students and pensioners, the stated rate is almost irrelevant in the current situation. Under chronic excess demand, the danger is not that wages will lag behind prices (the only case when index-ation matters), but that salary growth will outpace inflation. Managers not reporting to a real owner face a soft-budget constraint and have many reasons to grant high wage settlements to ensure labour peace.[35] In this case, a ceiling to wage increases is more crucial than a floor.

Furthermore, an announced rate of indexation need not be politically feasible. When the government lacks support, sustained real wage cuts are unlikely to be accepted. As individual republican governments would lose political support while seeing the benefits dissipated over the whole union, they have even less interest in curtailing wage demands. If austerity brings unrest, an unpopular government will grant additional wage increases in an attempt to buy off the public, eroding partial indexation. The offer to double the wages of coal miners over two years is a good example (*The Financial Times*, 9 April 1991).

Three processes have not progressed much. There is little evidence of financial assets with floating interest rates (possibly because of the poor quality of price indices). Wage payments do not appear to be becoming more frequent. Finally, there are few contracts which are specified in hard currency, to be paid in roubles at the exchange rate on the payment date.[36]

IV Specific Soviet factors

Besides possessing the features of hyperinflating market economies, the Soviet Union has some characteristics which introduce other important differences. These will affect the initiation, propagation and control of inflation. Almost all of them increase rather than reduce the prospects of extreme inflation. In discussing these, we again divide them into mone-tary, fiscal and indexation aspects.

Monetary factors

So far, the most characteristic feature of the Soviet financial imbalance has been the existence of *repressed inflation*. While also seen in some other cases (e.g. Brazil), the degree of price control and the cumulative pressures in the USSR are incomparable to most peacetime market economies. Poland in the late 1980s is the most comparable example of repressed hyperinflation.

Dornbusch et al. (1990, p. 4) note that, starting in a situation of repressed inflation, extensive price liberalization can quickly lead to extreme inflation. Controls suppress the warning signals, giving a false impression of stability which ends when controls are removed without correcting the sources of pressure. Fear of this outcome led the German and Allied authorities to opt for a confiscatory monetary reform in the much more extreme repressed inflation of post-Second World War western Germany.[37]

A central part of the Soviet loss of financial control has been the explosion of inter-enterprise credits, which alone went up from about 3 billion roubles in 1987 to 16 billion roubles in 1988 (*The Economist*, 20 October 1990). As some *de jure* non-financial firms have thus begun to act like banks, their possible illiquidity could spread to other firms and precipitate a financial crisis. The combination of poor information and a collapsing economy makes bad loans extremely likely. When these surface, the government may need to restructure the debtor firms to avoid a crisis. The probable budgetary cost of any financial clean-up must be included in estimating future government outlays.

An analogous potential for a government rescue exists in the banking system, which has been termed a 'financial Wild West'.[38] Both traditional banks and the more than 2,000 scarcely regulated commercial banks potentially carry many bad loans which, if properly accounted for, would show that many of these institutions are insolvent. The cost of future loan write-offs by the government must also be included in prognoses of the budget deficit.[39]

The Soviet Union also lacks experience of indirect macroeconomic control and does not possess many financial and regulatory institutions that are required in a market economy environment. This increases the possibilities of policy mistakes which could set off an inflationary spiral.[40]

Fiscal factors

In addition to the budgetary impact of any financial bail-out, two fiscal properties that characterize the USSR deserve mention. The first is that the Soviet Union faces pressure not only from present deficits, but also from the cumulative effect of previous imbalances in the form of the monetary overhang. Their cumulative effect can be measured by the increase in the government's interest bill which would arise from issuing bonds that the public would voluntarily exchange for enough liquid assets to reduce inflationary pressure to near zero.

Second, as McKinnon (1990) and Åslund (1991) have argued, economic decentralization can have a negative impact on government revenues. Under traditional state ownership, most or all enterprise profits automatically accrue to the government. As firms become autonomous or private, government revenues can be maintained only if a well-functioning system of enterprise taxation is in place. As new tax legislation has been slow in coming and enforcement has been difficult, the tax base has been eroded and the fiscal deficit increased.

Indexation of contracts

Possibly the most important differences exist in the area of indexation. As this will be according to official price indices, it is important to recognize that the imperfect inclusion of unofficial prices introduces a crucial bias into Soviet price statistics. As shortages grew and the black market expanded, official indices understated the true rate of inflation.[41] If the USSR now undertakes serious price liberalization, these statistics will not capture the diminution of the black market and will thus overstate the rate of inflation.

In such a case, the *de facto* rate of indexation will exceed the stated amount. If, as is likely, it is not possible to adjust price indices to capture accurately the true average transaction prices, an apparently partial wage indexation scheme could in fact become one of more than full indexation, producing an extremely unstable situation.

Other factors

Two further factors are operative in the Soviet Union. One which could lead to high inflation is the certainly low elasticities of export supply and import demand, at least in the unreformed economy. Not only are state firms with soft budget constraints less likely to respond to the price signals resulting from devaluation, but extensive licensing and quantitative restrictions in the foreign sector will preclude the desired responses.[42] Attempts to improve the balance of payments through devaluation alone could well bring about enormous price rises.

A favourable factor is the large inventory stocks which have been accumulated under repressed inflation. Given a policy of credible stabilization with positive real interest rates, the additional supply of goods from their release would have a short-run anti-inflationary effect.

Comparison with the Polish hyperinflation of 1989

Several past experiences would form especially interesting case-studies from the Soviet perspective. The Austrian hyperinflation of the 1920s (with successor states to a collapsed empire becoming increasingly autarkic) and the Yugoslavian experience of the 1980s (with a loose federal state and 'socialist' economy) are two examples.[43]

For reasons of brevity, we examine a third case which is comparable and recent – the Polish hyperinflation of 1989.[44] As in the USSR today, three developments in the mid-1980s were a prelude to hyperinflation. First, wage setting was decentralized and liberalized, producing a wage explosion. As enterprise managers confronting labour shortages faced weak financial discipline, they had little reason to resist wage rises. In spite of a technically sound adjustment programme in early 1988, real wages rose further 'because of a profound lack of popular support for the government'.[45]

Second, to reverse the losses in competitiveness from wage increases, there was an attempt to devalue the exchange rate faster than the rate of inflation. Neither this nor a subsequent import squeeze were able to improve the balance of payments. Finally, the economy moved to budgetary and financial imbalance.

In this setting, the final collapse was brought on in 1989 by three key factors identified by Lipton and Sachs (1990):

1 the March 1989 legalization of the parallel foreign currency market, which supported the flight from currency;
2 the adoption, at the request of Solidarity, of a formal 80 per cent wage indexation rule in April, following the round-table talks;[46]
3 the August freeing of most retail food prices, and a sharp reduction of food subsidies by the outgoing Communist government.

By September, hyperinflation was well under way.

A comparable crisis besets the Soviet Union, since the combination of rising wages and low-wage discipline, a balance-of-payments crisis and a budget deficit are well evident. Dollarization is rising and wage indexation is being put in place. If the parallels can be drawn, then a simple price liberalization could be one event that could take the economy over the threshold of extreme inflation.

V Conclusions and implications for stabilization

Given the severity of the inflationary shock, and the steady establishment of the mechanisms for its propagation, it can be argued that steps to slow galloping inflation in the USSR are more urgent than minor adjustments or measures which gradually put in place the macroeconomic stabilization instruments of a market economy. This entails a comprehensive, consistent strategy which includes short-term emergency measures.

A fully elaborated plan would include measures to reverse all controllable shocks and dampen all propagation mechanisms. However, the core of any package likely to succeed would contain the following five measures:

1 A correction of the public-sector deficit, which has been a part of all successful stabilizations.[47] This would include a strengthening of revenues via both emergency short-run measures (higher public-sector and utilities prices, shorter tax-collection lags, greater tax indexation and enforcement, etc.) and longer-run reforms (a wider tax base, new taxes). On the expenditure side, there would be a similar combination of immediate measures (drastic subsidy cuts, investment moratoria) and longer-term steps (restructuring the government). These cuts would be implemented by officials uncompromisingly dedicated to budget balance.[48]

2   Moving decisively from a passive to an active monetary policy via formal central-bank independence. Whether this new body would have the underlying political support to achieve real autonomy is less certain, but heading it by officials with an overtly anti-inflationary outlook would build credibility.[49]
3   A wage pact, including the disallowance or dampening of indexation, and ceilings on wage settlements. A reduced real wage at the start of the programme would also make it more credible that inflation will not be used to reduce wages in the future.
4   Foreign assistance in the form of a stand-by agreement for the balance of payments and budgetary support. This was particularly important in the Israeli stabilization, where access to a line of credit raised confidence, even when it was never used.[50]
5   A political pact to achieve some social consensus, both across social groups and across regions which choose to remain in the union. A further round of austerity would only be tolerated if citizens support the government, as in the Polish stabilization of 1990.

The specifics of the Soviet case mean that a successful stabilization will appear harsher than those used in other countries. A programme to reduce current fiscal imbalances still leaves the cumulative impact of past imbalances in the form of the monetary overhang. It also does not account for three future possibilities:

1   The likelihood of extraordinary expenditures in bailing out financially distressed enterprises and banks;
2   The need for serious relative price adjustments and the inflationary pressure this creates;
3   The tendency for privatization and decentralization to reduce the flow revenues from enterprises.

Similarly, if indexation rules are used, they must take into account the bias in official price indices which will overstate the true post-liberalization inflation rate. Nominal rates of indexation must be reduced below target levels to achieve stability.

The Soviet economy is distinguished from the other examples we have studied by its large size and closedness. This could influence the source of ultimately explosive shocks and the mix of policies used in stabilization. Domestic price liberalization could constitute a much more severe shock than a sudden devaluation.

As extreme inflation can erupt suddenly, the worst mistake would be to become complacent, taking any apparent calm as an indication that things are under control. The longer stabilization is deferred, the more the propagation mechanisms of inflation become established. This raises the vulnerability of the economy to future shocks, and makes it more immune to subsequent stabilization efforts.

References

Åslund, A. (1991) 'The Soviet economic crisis: Causes and dimensions', Stockholm Institute of Soviet and East European Economics, Working Paper No. 16, January.

Bruno, M., G. Di Tella, R. Dornbusch and S. Fischer, (eds) (1988) *Inflation Stabilization: The Experience of Israel, Argentina, Brazil, Bolivia and Mexico*, Cambridge, MA: MIT Press.

Canavese, A. and G. Di Tella (1988) 'Inflation stabilization or hyperinflation avoidance? The case of the Austral Plan in Argentina, 1985-87', in M. Bruno, et al. (eds), pp. 153–90.

Cukierman, A. (1988) 'The end of high Israeli inflation: An experiment in heterodox stabilization', in M. Bruno, et al. (eds), pp. 48-94.

Dornbusch, R. and S. Fischer (1986) 'Stopping hyperinflations past and present', *Weltwirtschaftliches Archiv* 122, No. 1, pp. 1-46.

Dornbusch, R., F. Sturzenegger and H. Wolf (1990) 'Extreme inflation: Dynamics and stabilization', *Brookings Papers on Economic Activity*, No. 2, pp. 1-84.

Fischer, S. (1981) 'Relative shocks, relative price variability, and inflation', *Brookings Papers on Economic Activity*, No. 2, pp. 381-431.

Guttmann, W. and P. Meehan (1975) *The Great Inflation: Germany 1919-23*, Westmead, England: Saxon House.

Hansson, A. (1990) 'The 1948 West German economic reforms: A model for Eastern Europe?', University of British Columbia, Department of Economics, Discussion Paper No. 5/1990, March.

Hansson, A. (1991) 'The importance of being earnest: Early stages of the West German *Wirtschaftswunder*', UNU/WIDER working paper, Helsinki, May.

Lipton, D. and J. Sachs (1990) 'Creating a market economy in Eastern Europe: The case of Poland', *Brookings Papers on Economic Activity*, No. 1, pp. 75-147.

Machinea, J. L. and J. M. Fanelli (1988) 'Stopping hyperinflation; The case of the Austral Plan in Argentina, 1985-87', in M. Bruno, et al. (eds), pp. 111-52.

McKinnon, R. (1990) 'Stabilising the ruble', *Communist Economies*, 2, no. 2, pp. 131–42.

Modiano, E. (1988) 'The cruzado first attempt: The Brazilian stabilization program of February 1986', in M. Bruno, et al. (eds), pp. 215-58.

Morales, J.-A. (1988) 'Inflation stabilization in Bolivia', in M. Bruno, et al. (eds), pp. 307-46.

Sachs, J. and D. Lipton (1990) 'Poland's economic reform', *Foreign Affairs*, 69, No. 3, Summer, pp. 47-66.

Sargent, T. (1982) 'The ends of four big inflations', in R. Hall, (ed.) *Inflation: Causes and Effects* Chigago: University of Chicago Press, pp. 19-72.

Tanzi, V. (1977) 'Inflation, lags in collection and the real value of tax revenue', *IMF Staff Papers* 25, pp. 154-67.

World Bank (1990) *The Economy of the USSR*, Washington, DC: The World Bank.

Notes

1 See World Bank (1990, p. 49) and Åslund (1991, p. 5).

2 *The Financial Times*, 20 April 1991. In Estonia, the concomitant annual increase in consumer prices was already 100 per cent.

3 For more modest forecasts, see *The Economist*, 13 April 1991. Predictions of extreme inflation are reported in *The Financial Times*, 26 January, 30 March, and 14 April 1991.

4 Saudi Arabia, for instance, had a 3 per cent rate of deflation in 1986, when the price of petroleum fell sharply.

5 IMF, *International Financial Statistics Yearbook*, 1990.

6 Dornbusch, et. al. (1990, p. 5). For instance, in Argentina in 1981, there was no reason to believe that there would be hyperinflation (Canavese and Di Tella, 1988, p. 170). Bolivia had not had chronic inflation, nor were many of the required propagation mechanisms initially in place (Morales, 1988, p. 308). In both cases, inflation occurred very suddenly.

7 Machinea and Fanelli (1988, p. 145). The inflationary impact of terms of trade shocks on most industrial countries subsequent to the oil price rises of the 1970s is perhaps the most well-known example.

8 For more, see Guttmann and Meehan (1975).

9 For examples, see Machinea and Fanelli (1988, p. 111) for Argentina; Morales (1988, p. 312) for Bolivia; Bruno et. al.(1988, p. 288) for Brazil; and Cukierman (1988, p. 49) for Israel. The German hyperinflation has also been linked to deficit spending. For a description of the theoretical link between deficits and high inflation, see Dornbusch and Fischer (1986).

10 Cukierman (1988, p. 49). See also the discussion of the Polish experience below.

11 For more on the theoretical and empirical links between relative price shifts and inflation, see Fischer (1981).

12 Dornbusch, et. al. (1990, p. 50), who also list some historical cases when this held true. The political economy of hyperinflation and budgetary stabilization is relatively unexplored and deserves much more study.

13 While prices of individual goods in barter deals can be misleading (as relative prices are all that matter), the jump in the price paid by Poland for Soviet oil, from one-sixth the world level to near the world level (personal communication, Polish Ministry of Foreign Economic Relations) is indicative.

14 The simple arithmetic average of annual world oil prices for 1986-90, as reported in IMF *International Financial Statistics*, is $17 per barrel. This is almost identical in real terms to the $19.73 per barrel price of North Sea Brent on 21 May 1991 (*The Economist*, 25 May 1991).

15 *The Economist*, 20 and 27 April 1991. The latter includes a one-fifth shortfall in promised oil deliveries to Eastern Europe, which were already below traditional volumes.

16 *The Financial Times*, 31 January 1991 and *The Economist*, 16 March 1991.

17 See World Bank (1990, p. 10), which also provides earlier figures. For more analysis, see Åslund (1991).

18 *The Financial Times*, 27 April 1991. See also *The Financial Times*, 4 April 1991.

19 *The Financial Times*, 20 and 27 April 1991.

20 See *The Financial Times*, 30 March 1991.

21 See *The Economist*, 13 and 27 April 1991, and *The Financial Times*, 20 April 1991.

22 *The Financial Times*, 11 March 1991 and *The Economist*, 6 and 13 April 1991.

23 *The Financial Times*, 20 April 1991. This has been attributed to a poorly maintained infrastructure, outdated technology, lack of funding for new investments, etc. (*The Economist*, 13 April 1991).

24 For discussion of the differences between Soviet and Western relative prices, see *The Economist*, 2 February 1991.

25 Personal communication, Estonian Ministry of Economy.

26 Dornbusch et. al. (1990) cite this sluggishness as one of the main puzzles of hyperinflation.

27 More precisely, this 'tax' is collected from any government liabilities bearing below-market interest rates.

28 The higher the inflation rate and/or its acceleration, the lower will be real revenues.

29 For further discussion of the Tanzi effect and other channels, see Tanzi (1977) and Dornbusch, et. al. (1990).

30 Dornbusch and Fischer (1986, p. 12) cite the introduction of monthly wage indexation as a key step in the acceleration of Austrian inflation in the 1920s.

31 During hyperinflation, the exchange rate may be the single best indicator of the current price level.

32 The claim by the chairman of Gosbank, that money printing had to be expanded because the previous confiscation of large notes had not left enough cash to pay compensation to wage-earners and pensioners, is one example that monetary policy is viewed as simply accommodating payment decisions made elsewhere. See *The Financial Times*, 2 April 1991.

33 The actual compensation is much less, since at the 7 per cent interest rate offered, inflation will erode much of the real principal.

34 *The Financial Times*, 26 March, and *The Economist*, 6 April 1991.

35 For instance, dockers in Lithuania ended a two-day strike after managers doubled their pay (*The Financial Times*, 24 April 1991).

36 One mechanism we have not been able to explore is the Tanzi effect. Determining its role if any requires a close examination of both Soviet and republican tax laws, and the indexation and payment delays which they include.

37 For more, see Hansson (1990).

38 See *The Wall Street Journal Europe*, 6 June 1991.

39 In 1990, the Soviet government wrote off 93 billion roubles of bad loans to the agricultural sector alone (*The Wall Street Journal, Europe*, 6 June 1991). This has been seen in previous hyperinflations. In Argentina, interest-rate rises were induced by the insolvency of some domestic banks. As bank supervision was weak and the government provided full deposit insurance, the growth of debt arrears brought financial fragility to a climax in 1981 (Machinea and Fanelli, 1988, p. 118).

40 Morales (1988, p. 310) traces some pre-hyperinflation mistakes in Bolivia to an isolation from discussions in international academic and official circles.

41 For evidence of hidden inflation, see Åslund (1991).

42 For example, in discussions with the author, Estonian authorities have suggested that volumes of foreign currency exchanged by tourists declined following the introduction of the tourist rate. Given the visa-induced inelasticity of travel and the shortage-induced lack of ways to spend, this is not surprising.

43 It would also be useful to study policies adopted in those cases in which shocks were large but hyperinflation was successfully avoided. These might include France and Italy after the Second World War, and Mexico in the mid-1980s. Even these are not alike and we cannot draw general conclusions.

44 For this, we refer to the descriptions of Lipton and Sachs (1990) and Sachs and Lipton (1990).

45 Lipton and Sachs (1990, p. 109). The measured real wage rose by 14 per cent in that year, while prices rose by 60 per cent.

46 As this came on top of increases already granted, measured real wages rose by 45 per cent from August 1988 to August 1989.

47 Dornbusch and Fischer (1986, p. 6).

48 That technically sound policies must be combined with a clear will to implement them in the face of many pressures is shown in the experience of Western Germany after the currency reform of 1948. For a description, see Hansson (1991).

49 Sargent (1982) stresses the common role of a legally independent central bank in quickly ending hyperinflations. See Dornbusch and Fischer (1986, pp. 7-8) for the mechanics of its implementation in Germany.

50 See Dornbusch et. al. (1990, pp. 56-7). For the role of foreign assistance in the Austrian and Polish stabilizations of the 1920s, see Dornbusch and Fischer (1986).

5

The Role of the External Sector during the Transition[1]

Pekka Sutela

With the possible exception of a few cranks, the need for economic modernization is universally accepted in the USSR.[2] It is also widely accepted that there is no known example of successful inward-oriented economic modernization. Consequently, it is difficult to find serious advocates of economic autarky in current Soviet economic debates. Given the ideological background, history and current state of the Soviet economy, this is a matter of some importance.

The necessity of opening up the Soviet economy has long been recognized by specialists inside the USSR, and yet this has not been unanimously accepted by Soviet economists. A leading Russian nationalist economist (Lemeshev, 1991) thus attacked the 'colonialist policies' of Western countries allegedly intent upon exploiting the natural resources, environment and cheap labour of the USSR, and 'especially of Russia'. It may be pointed out that this critic, a leading expert on natural resource economics, is no proponent of economic self-containment. He readily accepts mutually advantageous trade and even some unspecified joint ventures. But he strongly disapproves of the current plans for 'open sectors' and 'special zones'. They would, in his view, surely jeopardize the organic unity of Russia. Basically, they remind him of little else but the notorious Eastern war goals of Nazi Germany. And, literally, he would rather have Russia stick to its *kvas* – for which some hundreds of recipes are to be found in *Rus'* – instead of buying licences for Pepsi (Lemeshev, 1991, p. 168).

This, to many of us, was the way all Russians were supposed to think. In fact, traditionally Russian as such views may sound, their current political significance is peripheral. Much to the surprise of many observers, when the Supreme Soviet had the first hearing of the new law on foreign investment on 29 May 1991, even the conservative *Soyuz* group supported it. Certainly, the official Soviet policy towards actual opening has been rather less than consistent (for comments, see, for instance, Spandaryan and Shmelev, 1990). Prominent spokesmen and decision-makers of the current regime are still capable of highly xenophobic pronouncements. In practical policies, the credit-worthiness crisis of 1991 brought about recentralization and increased the regimentation of foreign trade and payments. Nevertheless, though I share the opinion of those who think that an illiberal and authoritarian backlash in Soviet popular opinion and politics is almost inevitable, a return to ideologically glorified autarky seems impossible. The basic choice in favour of a market economy has been made, as also has that in support of opening up the economy. Furthermore, this opening is no longer merely seen as a question of decentralizing foreign trade rights or of allowing joint ventures. Rather, the governmental emphasis is now on capital imports.

Foreign investment is in fact increasingly seen as a crucial – sometimes even as the sole – magic cure for many of the major ills of the Soviet economy. A sceptical spectator surely cannot help wondering whether we may not be witnessing another of the seemingly endlessly recurring Soviet fads and campaigns, all feverishly adopted but also easily forgotten once the wondrous expected effects fail to materialize. There is an obvious possibility that should the current drive towards opening the economy fail for one reason or another, a nationalistic revival will follow.[3] Only time will tell, but outsiders should remember that these are issues on which our attitudes and actions will also contribute to the final result. This paper, therefore, proceeds from the premise that the current policy of opening up the Soviet economy is 'serious and for a long time'.

Official spokesmen still have to insist that they are not planning to 'sell Russia', but there is clearly a new emphasis in their statements. The current crisis programme of Prime Minister Pavlov calls for both export promotion and the import of capital 'on the basis of a programme agreed upon between the republics and under social control' ('O polozhenii', 1991, p. 2). Pavlov expects foreign investment to help increase domestic competition and provide access to modern technologies. According to him, the country needs to invest some 500 billion roubles in fixed capital. That could be financed domestically, Pavlov asserts, but only at the expense of 'the standard of living, people's health, the environment' ('Investitsii', 1991). A better way out of the crisis is to take advantage of foreign public and private investment.

Earlier, competition, advanced technologies and managerial know-how were supposed to be the fruit of trade and joint ventures. As these remedies for the ills of the Soviet economy have failed in their assumed modernizing mission, the wager is now on direct investment. Foreign capital 'is not only money, but also modern equipment, technology, the style of management in a market environment', Pavlov emphasizes ('Investitsii', 1991). Wholly foreign-owned subsidiaries, concessions and the guaranteed repatriation of earnings, as well as other advantages, now seem to be in the offing. The USSR has in the summer of 1991 finally ratified the investment-protection agreements negotiated and signed together with several countries some two years earlier.

In another move, in mid-May 1991 the President of the Russian Federation authorized the founding of two new 'Zones of Free Enterprise', one in Leningrad and the other in Vyborg ('Zony', 1991). The actual contents of these decisions, made by El'tsin using his recently-acquired extraordinary powers, remain unclear even if at least the Leningrad zone allegedly already exists.

Arkadii Volskii, an aspiring spokesman for Soviet managers, shares Pavlov's new-found enthusiasm for direct foreign investment (Volskii, 1991, pp. 55–6). Both men have recognized that the USSR has been unable rationally to utilize the Western credits that used to be so freely available. Direct investment with foreign control has better potential for productivity than credit could ever have, Volskii, in particular, argues. He admits that capital is globally scarce[4] and the USSR a late starter in the game of attracting capital. Still Volskii believes that the Soviet market will be able to compete for investment if the relevant political and legal conditions and institutions are established. Foreign companies must have the right to set up wholly-owned subsidiaries, 'at least in the critically important, high-technology branches'. Soviet national interests will be safeguarded by picking those industries which are most in need of modernization and those regions where social conditions are especially acute. These industries and regions will then be given the best conditions for attracting foreign capital.

Such views are a breakthrough and their importance should in no way be belittled. However, this innovation still comes with a string attached. The process of direct investment, both Pavlov and Volskii argue, has to be programmed and guided by the state so that national interests will not be endangered. Both see the inflow of capital as a pivotal remedy; both also want to control and plan it. Neither really asks whether the capital will be available, especially for those industries and regions where the existing capital stock is most antiquated and the social conditions most acute. But then, Western businessmen have told Volskii that objective conditions for attracting investment in the USSR do exist (Volskii, 1991, p. 56). Perhaps they were not told that – to parody the above-mentioned foreign investment criteria of Volskii – they might be asked to invest in the textile industries of Nagorno-Karabakh.

Soviet interest in the allegedly state-directed modernization of dynamic Asian economies has manifestly grown. The views of Pavlov and Volskii may also reflect this learning process. As a whole, this is a wide, complicated and poorly understood topic.[5] The interpretations of the Asian experience differ, not least in the countries themselves. The Asian experience figures prominently in current Hungarian policy debates, and it will certainly also do so in the USSR (see, for instance, the translation of Katz, 1991, in *Ekonomika i Zhizn'*). The dynamic Asian economies are generally cited as examples of state-guided modernization, to be followed by the European economies in transition. And really, the least that their experience shows is that the fundamentals of market economy can be adapted to widely different historical and cultural environments. This is certainly something that those who are overly worried about the peculiarities of the Russian mind should remember. Without trying to address here the complex issues raised by this proposition, it may yet be pointed out that surely the dynamic Asian economies have never had the decades-long history of central planning. As the liberals in Eastern and Central Europe argue against policies that may help to lengthen the life of existing state-centred structures, that may well make an enormous difference.

Such are the prevailing official views on the opening up of the Soviet economy. The spectrum of less-official views is as wide as ever. The nationalist view has already been noted above. Reformist Soviet economists keep pushing for their favourite proposals. Viktor Belkin still sees salvation in the introduction of a parallel currency ('Otstupat' ', 1991) while Nikolai Shmelev continues pressing for credit-financed consumer goods imports (Shmelev, 1991). Grigorii Yavlinskii and associates insist that Soviet integration into the world economy is an objective development that needs to be accelerated just now (Yavlinskii et al., 1991; 'Soglasie', 1991). However, there is an important difference between the means and ways of integration as seen by the current Soviet government on one hand and Yavlinskii and associates on the other. While the former counts upon foreign direct investment ('Programma', 1991), the latter assigns the key role to Western assistance and credits.[6]

This paper was written when both Soviet legislation on foreign investment and the Grand Bargain/G7 processes were ongoing concerns. This paper, therefore, bypasses the topical problems of international and Soviet politics. Instead of trying to shoot a rabbit that is running fast in the cloud of secretive policy formulation, this paper will address some questions of a more essential character. A natural starting-point is the issue of convertibility.[7]

Convertibility: the definitions

Convertibility means different things to different people. Therefore we have to start by defining some terms.

The main characteristic of money is its *liquidity*. Anything that is generally accepted as a means of payment should be defined as money. Money can therefore by definition be easily exchanged into commodities and assets with no restrictions other than availability and price. Barring hyper-inflationary and other anomalies, the liquidity of money drastically reduces transaction costs compared with a barter economy. This is the social productivity of money, one of the mainsprings of economic modernization and welfare in economic history.

The liquidity of money is sometimes also called *domestic commodity convertibility*. It is obviously a prerequisite for any other convertibility.

In a classical planned economy, money is not liquid or convertible into commodities within the state sector as allocation is based on plans and distribution certificates. The liquidity of money in the non-state sector exists in principle, but it is actually restricted in many well-known ways. For reasons that have been thoroughly analysed in the literature, modified planned economies easily slide into severe monetary disequilibria which further restrict the liquidity of money. Uncertainty, barter, and attempts at regional as well as branch- and plant-level autarky duly follow. As transaction costs consequently soar, there will be fewer transactions, less coordination of economic activities and therefore a smaller volume of production. Nothing is as practical as good theory: the recent Soviet débâcle is a classic illustration of such first principles of monetary economics.

If socialist money is thus only liquid in an extremely incomplete sense, there is no reason why it would be *externally convertible*. A currency can be regarded as fully convertible when any holder is free to convert it at a market exchange rate – fixed or flexible – into one of the major international reserve currencies. Thus, a currency can in principle be convertible even if there are restrictions on international trade or capital flows. Usually, however, convertibility is needed for the purpose of establishing the external liquidity of domestic money so that convertibility and the abolishing (or at least the reducing) of restrictions on trade and capital flows go together. Convertibility and external liberalization are natural bedfellows.

On the other hand, if socialist money cannot buy domestically available goods, there is no reason why it should be able to buy foreign goods (or capital) through external convertibility into the major international reserve currencies. In fact, such convertibility would be a clear anomaly under traditional socialism and arguably would undermine the sacred goals of central planning.

Internal convertibility of a currency means that residents of the country concerned are free to maintain domestic holdings of certain assets denominated in foreign currencies. Thus they may convert domestic currency internally into foreign-currency assets. The term of domestic convertibility is also used.

Furthermore, there are many forms of partial convertibility. *Current-account convertibility* means that domestic currency can be freely converted for current-account transaction purposes (that is, to put it bluntly, for trade). *Capital-account convertibility* also allows for conversion for capital-flow purposes. Sometimes a further distinction may be made between convertibility for residents and non-residents.

In practice most countries have for most of the time maintained some sort of partial convertibility. Existing restrictions on trade and capital flows have often further limited the value of adopted convertibility arrangements, though conceptually – if the above terminology is followed – they should be seen as a separate issue from convertibility proper.

The argument for convertibility is rather self-evident in the light of the definitions offered above. Fundamentally, convertibility means widening the scope of liquidity of domestic money. It is therefore a means for larger choice sets, competition, specialization and consequently efficiency. Opposition to convertibility can therefore primarily only arise from an unwillingness to widen the choice sets of economic agents or from an inability to maintain relevant exchange rates. The first-mentioned objection should no longer be relevant after the demise of central planning, but the latter problem still remains.

Convertibility: the Soviet intentions

According to preliminary press reports the Soviet government also seems to be aiming at something less than full convertibility. Gerashchenko, the state bank governor, gives three examples of the limitations it is planning to retain even after 1 January 1992, when partial convertibility has been declared to be introduced (see 'Vnutrennaya', 1991). Capital-account convertibility for investment abroad is not to be introduced for Soviet enterprises. The Soviet currency market is to be open to residents both for selling and buying, but for non-residents the sale of roubles will only be allowed for the sums they have earned on Soviet territory. Finally, Soviet enterprises will be obliged to sell all their currency earnings.

This is what Gerashchenko calls 'internal convertibility'. He expects it will mean a sharp devaluation of the rouble and therefore also major changes in relative domestic prices. State intervention in the currency market, Gerashchenko explains, will be the method for maintaining the profitability of import-dependent enterprises. There will, he adds, be a further liberalization of prices as well as demonopolization and new domestic competition. The details of the programme still remain unclear.

The effects of current-account convertibility

In general, in addition to being a natural extension of the liquidity of money, convertibility reduces the costs involved in the administrative allocation of foreign exchange. Also, we should not forget that convertibility is a powerful symbol of openness, economic freedom and the return to Europe. The real question, however, is the robustness and credibility of such a symbol.

Internal convertibility makes domestic holdings of foreign currencies available to financial intermediaries and thus eases the foreign-exchange constraint faced by the country. Obviously, the rationale for internal convertibility will depend on the degree of dollarization of the economy concerned. As a whole and distinct from the main streets of some cities, the Soviet economy still seems to have undergone relatively little dollarization. Under these circumstances, internal convertibility of the rouble might in practice turn into a vehicle of further dollarization without bringing the benefits that domestic convertibility has had in a country like Poland.

Current-account convertibility, together with trade liberalization, is – as is well understood by Pavlov and others – a source of competitive discipline. It offers obvious short-term benefits for the supply side of the country, both for the availability of consumer goods and of industrial inputs. Over a longer period, current account convertibility with trade liberalization will create a more competitive environment and contribute to better choices by providing new information and incentives. Domestic prices will automatically be rationalized as they can no longer drastically differ from those prevailing in the world market. This would be a major step towards efficiency.

Finally, import competition should promote innovation and quality improvement. At the same time current account convertibility and trade liberalization, at any rate, also pose short-term risks for domestic employment and the level of income. Because of the peculiarities of the closed, centrally managed economy, such effects are hard to measure. A new kind of macroeconomic instability may also arise.

Nevertheless, we should not expect import competition to be a panacea. In economies with sufficiently concentrated production structures and a relatively small foreign-trade share, domestic monopolies may well be able to find ways of protecting their markets, even to the extent that the nominal opening up of the economy may prove further to monopolize the economy. A belief in infant-industry arguments and in the necessity of economies of scale for international competitiveness may well combine with political corporatism in a way that will show surprising robustness, even in the face of declared market contestability.

The effects of current-account convertibility are crucially dependent upon the level of the exchange rate originally adopted. Assuming that domestic producers are generally not value subtractors, a sufficiently depreciated exchange rate will make domestic production profitable even after the introduction of convertibility. That will give domestic producers time for adjustment. Yet such periods of adjustment are also periods during which price distortions and associated inefficiencies remain.

In the Polish case, some observers argue that the rate of exchange originally chosen was so depreciated that it actually contributed to a net resource outflow and therefore unnecessarily deepened the recession in the economy (Gabrisch, 1991; Kolodko, 1991). This argument may perhaps be disputed, but it highlights that there is no need to be too dogmatic about an exchange rate once it has been selected. Given the inevitably existing distortions and great uncertainty about the supply responses and future competitiveness of domestic industries, no simple rule for choosing the initial exchange rate to be introduced with current account convertibility can ever produce an equilibrium rate other than by chance.

There may well be economically rational informational and second-best arguments for government intervention in the emerging markets of an economy in transition, when imperfections of various kinds will be numerous.[8] Independently of economically rational arguments, there will certainly be much political pressure for interventionism. The outcome may at worst prove to be a market economy of the Latin American type and not of the European (Kolodko, 1991). One way an economist has for approaching such perils is to ask for the best ways of adopting and maintaining credible policy commitments. Unfortunately, as will be seen below, this approach delivers few ready answers. It is often simply a matter of conjecture which fundamental policy line will be the most credible one in a given policy environment.

If the alternatives are either maintenance of non-price trade restrictions or the kind of collapse of domestic production that has been seen in the eastern *Länder* of Germany after the overnight introduction of the currency union, the distortions generated by a depreciated exchange rate seem well worth living with (see also 'The Soviet Economic Crisis', 1991). As the determining of a 'correct' exchange rate is anyway impossible in practice, it would seem preferable to make a mistake on the depreciated side rather than on the appreciated.

In general, the difficulty of choosing the 'correct' initial exchange rate may be a good argument for adopting an infrequently adjustable peg instead of an, in principle, completely fixed exchange-rate regime. Given the uncertainties of an economy in transition, the latter can hardly be a credible commitment over a longer period of time.

The effects of capital-account convertibility

There are various reasons why the economies in transition from socialism to capitalism will in general not be able to generate large domestic savings. This is a crucial difference between them and typical dynamic Asian economies.[9] The restructuring necessary for attaining competitiveness, higher living standards and a better environment will therefore require capital and other productive resources from abroad. As official assistance will be limited, foreign private capital and expertise will be crucial. Capital-account convertibility helps to attract foreign capital, managerial resources and technology by allowing for the repatriation of income.

Needless to say, capital-account convertibility is not a sufficient condition for foreign direct investments. Their availability depends on the economic, legal and political environment as a whole that is encountered in the country in question.

If introduced both ways, capital-account convertibility also opens the doors for capital flight and possibly great volatility in exchange rates, currency reserves and interest rates. This is an important reason why most countries have first made their currencies convertible on current account and only later – sometimes much later – on capital account. Furthermore, long-term capital movements are usually liberalized long before short-term capital movements.

The standard order of introducing foreign convertibility thus runs from current-account convertibility to long-term to short-term capital movements. This mode of thinking, however, currently has less weight than it used to have. Developments in market technologies have made restrictions on foreign-capital transfers very difficult to enforce. Restrictions on capital account can often be circumvented through the current account. This has been the major reason for liberalizing capital-account transactions in countries like Finland.

Still, the accepted wisdom that convertibility should first be introduced on current account and only later on capital account has much to recommend itself even now (for a different view, see Schrettl, 1991). Developments in financial instruments and market technologies have made short-term capital movements highly volatile and often speculative. Furthermore, their mere volume can easily flood the inevitably thin domestic markets of a small country.

Also, there is no reason why liberalizing capital movements beyond those necessary for attracting foreign productive investment should have any priority in transition. It is perfectly possible to encourage an inflow of long-term capital while limiting the possibilities for capital flight and volatile, short-term capital flows.

To attract foreign productive investment, rules guaranteeing non-residents the right to repatriate their assets as well as any investment and employment earnings need to be enacted. These changes should be implemented together with an investment code that allows non-residents to own, manage and exercise control over domestic enterprises. As has already been mentioned, the Soviet law on foreign investment under discussion in parliament during the summer of 1991 may fulfil such formal conditions. Still, the road to a favourable overall investment environment remains a long and winding one.

Exchange rate regimes

It is generally acknowledged that it is impossible for a country simultaneously to enjoy a stable exchange rate, unrestricted capital mobility and control over interest rates or other instruments of monetary policy. But it also seems impossible to forecast or even to explain *ex post* the observed variation in flexible exchange rates. Such uncertainty is a major real cost to economies and helps to explain why most financial authorities currently have a strong preference for fixed exchange rates. The exchange rate is not just one price among others. Rational economic decision-making needs some stability in the economy. The nominal anchor that seems best suited for maintaining the crucial credibility of economic policy is the rate of exchange, pegged to a suitable basket of currencies.

Stabilizing exchange rates and thus interest rates under modern conditions sets stringent requirements not only upon the policy institutions and instruments available, but especially upon the credibility of policy commitments. Such credibility is extremely difficult to attain and maintain.

There are also other strong arguments for an exchange-rate peg in the transition economies. The institutional and structural transformation that these countries undergo will be so profound that there can really be no reliable domestic framework for a monetary policy, which may therefore at best be guided by an exchange-rate target (Bofinger, 1990).

In the process of the opening-up of the economy, as domestic prices adjust towards international prices huge relative price changes will occur. Exchange-rate instability would make it even more difficult to arrive at any kind of predictability and thus equilibrium.

Nevertheless, an absolute commitment to an exchange rate once it has been adopted would be a folly (Fischer, 1990). As already emphasized, there is really no way of choosing the 'correct' initial rate of exchange. Any attempt at rigidly maintaining the rate ultimately opted for would not be credible. The need for stability and an economic-policy anchor would probably best be reconciled with the necessity for flexibility by adopting the policy of an infrequently adjustable peg.

It may be that an élite club of European market economies has decided that civilized nations do not devalue, come what may. However, this cannot be a policy prescription for economies in transition.

Current-account restrictions?

Countries in transition must weigh the benefits of removing all current-account restrictions against the advantages of exchange-rate stability and greater monetary independence. Perhaps the cause of economic opening in the end will be well-served by continuing to maintain some current-account restrictions in the first phases of transition: the alternative would be recurrent external-payment imbalances, high volatility and uncertainty and hence the vulnerability of the whole reform commitment. The international financial community cannot – and certainly does not – expect the economies in transition immediately to introduce full convertibility, even on current account.

The conditions for convertibility

Accordingly, convertibility is a means and not a goal in itself. In particular, convertibility should not be introduced to destabilize the economy or the domestic currency even further, as intended in various proposals for a parallel (convertible) currency for the USSR (see Nuti, 1990, pp. 174–5).

To make sense, convertibility has to be preceded or accompanied by other economic changes. In the light of past experience, the most important among them would seem to be:

1 trade and capital movement liberalization;
2 an appropriate exchange rate;
3 sound macroeconomic policies; and
4 incentives for economic agents to respond to market prices, which should be free of major distortions.

Each of these requirements or conditions for convertibility is a topic for separate discussion.[10] Therefore, without going into the four conditions in any detail, it should be clear at the outset that they include major institutional reforms – the creation of functional policy institutions and instruments for stabilization, together with privatization, liberalization and demonopolization.

The pace at which the economy can be opened-up will thus depend on whether there is strong political support for a comprehensive and rapid reform in general. Opening-up the economy is not something independent of the inner workings of the domestic economy.

The arguments for gradual opening

The arguments for opening-up the economy as part of a gradual transition to a market economy have not died down, as any reader of the publications of the Vienna-based WIIW institute will know (see, for example, Levcik, 1991). As the statistically measured economic crisis of some of the economies in transition deepens, perhaps a strengthening of the voice for 'moderation' in transition policies is to be expected.

The basic argument for gradual opening up is as follows:

> Questions over questions can be asked which show that to make price liberalization and convertibility work, many other conditions have to be fulfilled and the listing of only a few of the issues proves that these conditions cannot be satisfied overnight (Levcik, 1991, p. 47).

In particular, this approach argues that liberalization (including convertibility) does not make sense without the fourth condition listed above being fulfilled. That entails privatization, which has to be a lengthy process, as 'extravagant schemes like distributing national property to citizens free of charge in the form of coupons ... give[s] no automatic rise to entrepreneurship in the Schumpeterian sense' (Levcik, 1991, p. 49). In general, the gradualist approach argues that the four conditions must totally or at least in the main *precede* the introduction of convertibility, and thus the opening up of the economy as a whole.

Arguments for rapid transition

The strange thing about the arguments for a gradual transition is that, to the best of my knowledge, nobody has ever seriously believed that everything could change in the economy simultaneously, much less 'overnight' (see, for instance, Lipton and Sachs, 1990). The emphasis has always been on the necessary pace of policy change, not on some assumed speed of societal reaction and adjustment. The idea of an overnight 'big bang' is a straw man.

The real argument for rapid transition has thus always been about the credibility and political robustness of transition. The credibility of reform policies requires clear symbols. Furthermore, if there is fundamental political change and a popular willingness to bear the inevitable, and some of the not-so-inevitable, burdens of transition, these have to be utilized to the highest degree possible. Proposals for shock therapies really do relate to the necessary pace of policy change, not to the possible pace of social adjustment.

There are also important technical economic arguments for simultaneity. As most economists may have heard, economic issues are interconnected. Some of the general arguments flowing from that somewhat self-evident fact have been referred to above. Quite as obviously, all decisions simply cannot be taken at the same time. Some of them have to precede others. Naturally, some processes will take longer to produce results than others. This has to be taken into account in policy design. It is simply not enough to say that reform measures should be adopted as fast and as simultaneously as the political process and social response will ever allow. Everything cannot be done at once. Talk about phasing-in policy measures is therefore not just an attempt to postpone and water down the inevitable, as has sometimes been asserted. Surely, bureaucratic and other resistance exists and endless debates about sequencing are one of its possible tools. But the fact remains that some degree of sequencing must always exist. That much is inevitable. But it is also clear that debating sequencing comes fast upon diminishing returns.

It may well be argued (see Portes, 1991) that the transition to openness, or to current-account convertibility for residents more specifically, should take place early during the transition just because there are so many requirements for a meaningful convertibility. A commitment to early convertibility, backed by international institutions and generally perceived as a key element of the whole transition programme, will raise the political cost of reneging. Thus it is a commitment that may well enhance policymakers' credibility. That may itself help to push the alleged preconditions of convertibility through, not really as preconditions, but as elements of a coherent package.

The peculiarities of the USSR

It would be pertinent to consider several peculiarities of the USSR while discussing the opening up of its economy. First, as with large economies in general, the share of foreign trade in Russian/Soviet aggregate production has always been rather small. Second, the economy still has a fairly reliable basis for export revenue. Third, the country is not only large, but also geographically, culturally and economically heterogenous, so there is little reason to expect all parts of the country to become involved in the international division of labour at the same speed and to the same degree. Fourth, the industrial structure of the country is highly monopolized. Fifth, the degree of dollarization of the economy remains low. Sixth, the domestic distortions and inflexibilities of the economy are exceptionally deep-rooted. Seventh, the domestic support and credibility of the central government is weak. Eighth, the existing institutional infrastructure for markets remains embryonic.

What are the consequences of these peculiarities of the USSR as far as the opening of the Soviet economy goes? To offer some preliminary and tentative answers, let us proceed from the general to the particular.

On the gradual v. rapid transition issue, it can be generally concluded that the current state of the Soviet economy makes rapid, comprehensive, radical and, quite possibly, dirty change inevitable, if any success is to be expected ('The Soviet Economic Crisis', 1991; Schrettl, 1991). But there is also a structural feature of Soviet society that makes any attempts at gradual transition illusory. The present government has an exceptionally low legitimacy and popular support. That may change in the future, but any foreseeable Soviet government will be the executive of a weak state, torn between the conflicting interests of its constituent parts. Whether gradual transition is in general feasible or not, at least such grand social engineering, to be effective at all, would require a strong state and an extremely competent administration (Bicanic and Skreb, 1991). That will simply not be available in the USSR.

Clearly, the prospect of opening-up the economy is interesting only if there is a government that can first adopt a comprehensive and credible transition programme and second can believe that the population is willing and able to bear the sacrifices involved. If the first is not possible, opening-up would only imply a continued dollarization and possibly some marginal colonialization of the economy in the form of incoming speculative short-term investment. In this case, we should not expect notable amounts of long-term foreign investment. In the second instance, without popular support it would probably be better for the government to limit itself to the traditional kind of attempts at marginal change in the economic system. Such *sovershenstvovanie* should not now be understood as the building of developed socialism but rather as damage limitation and the establishment of administrative and other institutions suitable for market infrastructure. Those would thus stand ready for the more or less distant future when the population will have learned that the costs of adhering to the old order are indeed much higher than those of change.

One of the problems of the USSR is that, unlike Hungary and Poland, earlier Soviet modifications of the planned system have been so cosmetic that they have left very few institutions of social and economic infrastructure that could be suitable for a market environment now or in the near future.

The first economic task of a potentially reformist government, indeed of any reasonable government, will be to restore the macroeconomic equilibrium.[11] The stock disequilibrium problem – monetary overhangs – would soon be taken care of by price increases, possibly by some privatization, and by increasing uncertainty about future income flows so that voluntary savings will increase. The flow equilibrium problem is a question of budget balance and money supply. These can in principle be tackled by conventional measures, though in the Soviet context the need to create new fiscal federalism, a working taxation system, a framework of financial markets and monetary-policy instruments will tend to lengthen the period of stabilization. At the same time the whole programme of transition implied in the four conditions will need to be addressed.

The measures for opening-up the Soviet economy would not include anything out of the ordinary.[12] As the amount of domestic holdings of foreign currencies is rather low, internal convertibility of the rouble, as defined at the beginning of this paper, would not be an economically important issue. The adoption of current-account convertibility would be of primary importance. This implies a uniform rate of exchange on a level that can reasonably be expected to be approximately consistent with current-account equilibrium. Obviously, foreign balance-of-payments support will be needed.

The inflow of long-term capital is dependent on political stability domestic equilibrium as well as on the adoption of an investment code of the kind referred to above. Convertibility other than for current account is not a priority.

Because of the peculiarities of the USSR enumerated above, the Soviet case offers exceptionally good arguments for initially restricting even current-account convertibility and trade liberalization. There is no way of knowing whether large sections of Soviet industry are value subtractors or not, but McKinnonian arguments should probably be taken seriously in the Soviet case (McKinnon, 1991).

At least two kinds of transitional restrictions might be acceptable for the international financial community. The government may want to control the total amount of foreign exchange available for imports. At the same time it is essential that available foreign exchange should have the same price for every prospective importer. There are no sound economic arguments for currency self-sufficiency of enterprises, industries or regions.[13] There are many ways of reconciling these requirements: compulsory currency remittances and auctions, both ostensibly now advocated by Soviet authorities, is one of them.

Second, because of the exceptionally deep-rooted imbalances and inflexibilities in the Soviet economy, there may be a case for temporary import tariffs (Portes, 1991). Their use, however, is obviously a dangerous path and would need to be closely controlled by international authorities.

The Polish stabilization programme has been criticized for applying market economy macroeconomic policies to a country with non-market structures (see, for instance, Kolodko, 1991). Whether such criticisms are valid or not in the instance of Poland, they would certainly have to be considered in the Soviet case.

In the USSR, under no circumstances can import competition play a role similar to that in Poland. The size, heterogeneity and state of communications in the country make it impossible. Import competition, therefore, cannot be a substitute for domestic demonopolization. Furthermore, neither most Soviet consumers nor virtually any Soviet producers have the knowledge and experience of choosing or competing with foreign products. Cushioning the regime switch with import tariffs therefore seems exceptionally defensible.

References

Bicanic, Ivo, and Skreb, Marko (1991) 'A Paradox of the Transition to a Market Economy: Will the Role of the State Increase?', mimeo.

Bofinger, Peter (1990) 'The roles of monetary policy in the process of economic reform in Eastern Europe', *CEPR Discussion Paper* No. 457.

Bondarev, Yuri et al. (1991) 'Slovo k narodu', *Sovetskaya Rossiya*, 23 July 1991.

Borensztein, Eduardo, and Montiel, Peter J. (1991) 'Savings, Investment, and Growth in Eastern Europe', *International Monetary Fund, Research Department*, June, unpublished mimeo.

Fischer, Stanley (1990) 'Comment', *Brookings Papers on Economic Activity*, No. 1, pp.

134–5.

Gabrisch, Hubert (1991) 'Restoring the Growth Potential of Formerly Centrally Planned Economies', *Intereconomics*, 26, No. 2, pp. 88–94.

'Investitsii, kontsessii, svobodnye ekonomicheskie zony', (1991), *Izvestiya*, 30 May, pp. 1–2.

Katz, S. Stanley (1991) 'East Europe Should Learn from Asia', *The Financial Times*, 24 April, p. 15; translated in *Ekonomika i Zhizn'*, No. 21, p. 17.

Kolodko, Grzegorz W. (1991) 'Inflation stabilization in Poland: a year after', *Institute of Finance, Warsaw, Working Papers*, No. 17 (an abbreviated version in Russian in *Voprosy ekonomiki*, No. 5, pp. 119–34).

Lemeshev, Mikhail (1991) 'Razorenie', *Moskva*, No. 3, pp. 156–69.

Levcik, Friedrich (1991) 'The Place of Convertibility in the Transformation Process', *WIIW–Mitgliederinformation* 91/4, pp. 44–58, forthcoming in Williamson, John, (ed.) *The Economic Opening of Eastern Europe*, Washington, DC.

Lipton, David, and Sachs, Jeffrey (1990) 'Creating a Market Economy in Eastern Europe: The Case of Poland', *Brookings Papers on Economic Activity*, No. 1, pp. 75–133.

McKinnon, Ronald (1991) *The Order of Economic Liberalisation*, Baltimore, Johns Hopkins University Press (forthcoming).

Nuti, Domenico Mario (1990) 'Stabilisation and Reform Sequencing in the Soviet Economy', *Recherches Economiques de Louvain*, 56, No. 2, pp. 169–80.

'O polozhenii v strane i putyakh vyvoda ekonomiki iz krizisa' (1991). Doklad chlena TsK KPSS premier-ministra SSSR V. S. Pavlova', (1991) *Pravda*, 26 April, pp. 1–2.

'Otstupat' nekuda, pozadi – propast'', (1991) *Sobesednik*, No. 17, p. 7.

Portes, Richard (1991) 'The Transition to Convertibility for Eastern Europe and the USSR', *CEPR Discussion Paper* No. 500, January.

'Programma sovmestnykh deistvii Kabineta Ministrov SSSR i pravitelstv suverennykh respublik po vyvodu ekonomiki strany iz krizisa v usloviyakh perekhoda k rynku', *Izvestiya*, 10 July 1991, p. 2.

Schrettl, Wolfram (1991) 'Structural Conditions for a Stable Monetary Regime and Efficient Allocation of Investment: Soviet Country Study', in Hans Blommestein and Michael Marrese, (eds) *Transformation of Planned Economies: Property Rights Reform and Macroeconomic Stability*, OECD, Paris, pp. 109–125.

Shmelev, Nikolai (1991) 'V chem ya vizhu shans na spasenie' , *Izvestiya*, 29 March, p. 3.

'Soglasie na shans' (1991) *Delovoi mir*, 2, 3 and 4 July.

Spandaryan, Viktor and Shmelev, Nikolai (1990) 'Otkrytaya ekonomika na slovakh i na dele', *Kommunist*, No. 12, pp. 31–40.

Stiglitz, Joseph E. (1991) 'The Invisible Hand and Modern Welfare Economics', *National Bureau of Economic Research Working Paper* No. 3641, March.

The Soviet Economic Crisis: Steps to Avert Collapse (1991), Executive Report 19, February, IIASA, Laxenburg, Austria.

'Vnutrennaya konvertiruemost' rublya – prokhozhdenie proidennogo drugimi?' (1991) *Izvestiya*, 18 May, p. 2.

Volskii, Arkadii (1991) 'Rynok i ekonomicheskaya stabilizatsiya', *Kommunist*, No. 6, pp. 46–57.

Yavlinskii, Grigorii, Zadornov, Mikhail, and Mikhailov, Aleksei (1991) "... plyus "Bolshaya Semerka"', *Izvestiya*, 20 May, p. 3.

'Yellow light for Eastern Europe: Beware four economic development myths', (1990) *The Heritage Foundation Backgrounder*, 13 November.

'Zony svobodnogo predprimatelstvo' (1991) *Izvestiya*, 24 May, p. 2.

Notes

1 The opinions expressed in this paper are those of the author and do not reflect the views of the Bank of Finland.

2 In this paper, 'the USSR' and 'Soviet' refer to the present-day USSR or those parts of it that ultimately decide to sign a future union treaty, whatever the composition, name or constitutional character of the future 'USSR' may prove to be.

3 One sign of such an attempted revival is the July 1991 declaration of prominent Russian nationalists in *Sovetskaya Rossiya* (see Bondarev et al., 1991). Still, such sentiments continued to be politically on the losing side at the time of writing.

4 This is in fact a crucial matter which is not given appropriate attention in Soviet discussions. Because of the huge investment needs of Eastern Europe, Germany and the Gulf, as well as the lifting of sanctions on investing in South Africa, interest rates are generally expected to remain high during the next few years. In order to materialize, investments in the USSR should offer even better combinations of total yield and risk than those available elsewhere in the world economy. Only then would foreign investment in the USSR be commercially viable and also make a contribution to global growth and welfare. If such conditions do not exist in the USSR, international financial organizations as well as foreign governments would make themselves guilty of supporting wasteful practices if they encouraged private investment in that country.

The scepticism that the USSR will most probably not become a locomotive of the world economy within the foreseeable future seems well-founded. The chances of the USSR attracting foreign investment on a scale that would really matter for Soviet growth, competitiveness and technical progress during the next ten years seem slim indeed. Niches of profitable private investment will certainly exist, but the more foreign investment concentrates only on blue-chip opportunities, the higher will be the probability of a public and political backlash. There is no easy way out of this dilemma.

5 Work on the possible implications of the experience of dynamic Asian economies for European economies in transition is underway in various international organizations.

6 In an interview Yavlinsii has even seen this as the crucial difference between him and the Soviet government (see *The Financial Times*, 23 July 1991).

7 In addition to the literature cited, this paper has benefited greatly from various documents circulated by the IMF and OECD.

8 For an introductory discussion on constrained Pareto efficiency, see Stiglitz, 1991.

9 The argument that Eastern Europeans actually do have plenty of capital, but it is in the form of foreign exchange, precious stones, VCRs and art ('Yellow light for Eastern Europe', 1990), is hardly convincing. Anyway, most people would certainly not exchange their gadgets for shares of an utterly uncertain value. For a general discussion of these issues, see Borensztein and Montiel, 1991.

10 Below, they will be referred to as the four conditions.

11 Indeed, the costs of stabilization and partially restructuring should not be seen as the costs of transformation into a market economy. Assuming that governments accept some responsibility for the wellbeing of the population, such costs are essentially sunk costs that have to be carried whatever economic system is adopted.

12 It seems highly improbable that foreign assistance of the scale assumed in the plans of Yavlinskii and associates would be forthcoming. Neither is it clear at all that such transfers would be advisable.

13 It is somewhat surprising that Yavlinskii and associates demand, as a short-term measure, increasing the currency self-sufficiency of enterprises (see 'Soglasie', 1991).

6

Monetary, Financial and Foreign Exchange Policy: a Key to Stabilization and Economic Reform in the USSR

Boris Fedorov

The simple notion of a monetary, financial or foreign-exchange policy is as yet practically non-existent in the USSR. This is not at all surprising in view of the traditionally insignificant role of the rouble in the economic system. It stands to reason that this indicates the absence of a general economic policy in the conventional sense of the word. At least nobody in the Soviet government has ever tried to think about economic policy using something like the most rudimentary analytical scheme outlined in the Annex on page 111. This understanding just does not exist.

Until very recently, the understanding of money was based entirely on the nineteenth-century writings of Marx, with the result that the rouble was constantly losing its money functions. In all recent economic programmes monetary and financial issues have played a secondary role. Concrete actions or intentions of the authorities at all levels evince a distorted understanding of problems facing the country.

This paper tries to outline what, in my view, are the most important monetary, financial and foreign-exchange issues demanding urgent action as well as some of the more fundamental changes in the system. A general and fairly accurate description of the system and its deficiencies now exists in the form of a joint study prepared by four international economic agencies.[1]

I am aware that the best recommendations will be futile unless there is some kind of a consensus in the country and strong political will among its leaders. Both these prerequisites are currently lacking, but hopefully not for long.

The most pressing task is to define properly the functions of all levels of government. The absence of a clear-cut division of functions between the centre and the republics is one of the main reasons for the slowing down of the reform process. Confrontation and a war of laws have superseded the more important economic issues.

The way out is to agree upon a detailed division of labour by drawing up a list of concrete functions. Proposed divisions of functions must follow clear-cut principles of economic policy. For example, unwillingness to compromise cannot justify a decentralization of monetary, foreign-exchange or customs policy or that the central government is left without powers of taxation. All entities wishing to leave the union must start the relevant legal procedure in the meantime, abiding by existing laws.

A division of functions connotes readjusting legal collisions and giving clear-cut rights to all authorities. The centre must curtail its excessive authority and the republics should not infringe on what, judging by international experience, are the undisputable functions of the centre. One cannot be in the Union and at the same time participate in its elimination. The main underlying criterion is maintenance of the *common economic space* (market).

The exclusive functions of the centre must include a monetary, foreign-exchange and customs policy, export-import licensing, the federal budget and taxes, a common foreign policy, defence, a common energy system, main transportation systems, standards, and space programmes. Once such a division is agreed upon, the only prerequisite is the willingness of political leaders to change the system, not merely a façade.

Sound money and stabilization

The core element and anchor of any healthy market economy is sound money. Without efforts in this field we cannot hope to curb inflation or sustain decent standards of living. Without sound money Soviet citizens and enterprises have no incentive to work harder or to enhance the quality of their services and products, while emerging entrepreneurs and markets have no reliable bench-mark of value.

It is clear that in order to create sound money, immediate changes have to be implemented in the mechanism of money creation, banking, the budget, tax and foreign-exchange systems. But this cannot be provided without speedy action to achieve the macrobalance of the economy via relevant instruments in the same areas.

The idea of macroeconomic stabilization is not original but it is rather new in the Soviet environment. In effect, it was proposed and more or less developed for the first time only in the 500-days' plan of August 1990, and not without opposition from some members of the group. This plan could be briefly summed up as the energetic curbing of money creation and the mopping-up of excess liquidity to make price liberalization more socially acceptable.

Subsequently, the idea of macroeconomic stabilization was developed further by some economists guided by international experience but it did not really take off officially. For instance, all union government documents speak about preserving economic links and fighting inflation, but they never really tackle the key issues. Since outright price liberalization is still politically unacceptable, balancing the economy seems to be an unattainable target, and hence the union government´s projections about speedy economic recovery and the introduction of convertibility seem like wishful thinking.

The above-mentioned deficiencies are characteristic of the current government anti-crisis programme as well as other proposals. The former principally strives to preserve the old system although there are a lot of positive signs in the final version. The latter appear to be based – to put it crudely – on runaway inflation with the West paying the cheque.

It is my opinion that what is badly needed is real macroeconomic stabilization, essentially through domestic efforts, in order to ensure the creation of sound money, less painful adjustments, the credibility of the government and its ability to proceed with reforms. Stabilization is a basis for more profound reforms. Stabilization can be tantamount to the anti-crisis programme, but only if it is a part of or the first step of a comprehensive package of reform actions.

Because of the political situation in the USSR, the authorities have to do their utmost – more so than perhaps in any other East European country – to put the burden of stabilization on the state and to lessen adverse social consequences. This primarily means that state assets should be the cushion and will be used to pay the bill. At the same time, the strengthening of a social safety net must not compromise the idea of stabilization.

Contrary to the popular beliefs of Western economists, the Soviet stabilization of the future is not a simple repeat of the usual IMF recommendations. The IMF or any other international institution has never yet tackled anything akin to the Soviet economic system. That is why price liberalization cannot be immediate, and a restrictive policy is needed to a major degree in formulating any policy at all. Nevertheless, it would be a waste of time to try to invent anything entirely new.

From personal experience I know that in any discussion of reform, both by conservatives and reformers, prices represent the most debatable topic. The line of thinking usually centres around the question of how fast to liberalize. Not many people now believe in a calculation of prices.

The authorities, notwithstanding all their faults, took certain steps towards price liberalization. Price increases in April 1991 and the liberalization of a limited group of prices did not solve any problems (apart from bread, no other goods are in plentiful supply) but we must admit that the gap between implicit market prices and state fixed prices somewhat narrowed. On the other hand, the side effects of price reform in the form of a huge injection of cash, as well as the unabated pace of government-fuelled depreciation of the rouble, perhaps neutralize all the positive changes. Nevertheless, further action is relatively simple. Attention needs to be concentrated on the following priorities:

1 prices which generate the largest amount of subsidies (obviously agricultural);
2 prices of goods mostly linked to external competition and imports; and
3 prices of goods not suffering from excessive monopolization.

Once the priorities are clear, only the political will is needed to proceed with liberalization. If all the differences between the republics are settled through negotiations, the mess could be sorted out once and for all. It is vitally important not to allow different price regimes in what remains of the Soviet Union because that would entail fragmentation of the common economic space.

This process should have intermediate targets and for the next six months the target could be a 50 per cent cut in food subsidies; price liberalization must be harmonized with corporatization and budget priorities; as for corporatization, free prices should not be imposed on non-market entities. The government should also avoid big price rises leading to unhealthy cash compensation.

Only a limited list of prices should ultimately remain under control, but this means gradual changes, not an unrealistic pace of liberalization, which will be an important, but by far not the only, instrument of stabilization. In the initial stages, much more will depend upon budget constraints and restrictive monetary policy.

The problem of the budget deficit has been finally conceded but hardly understood in the USSR. The lack of proper statistics makes it difficult to evaluate the situation, but it is clear that it is coming to a climax:

– for all the incessant talk in 1988–90, nothing was done about the budget deficit; attempts to finance it through issues of bonds proved fruitless;
– in the first quarter of 1991 the deficit of the union budget reached 31.1 bn. roubles compared to official projections of 26.7 bn. for the whole year;[2]
– nobody really tried to limit the sky-rocketing expenditure at all levels of authority and because of the economic crisis, revenues are falling;
– republics are refusing to make contributions to the union budget and compensate for falling revenues by cutting transfers where they take place;
– for all the talk about the independence of the State Bank of the USSR and the so-called central banks of republics, they are still milked in order to finance budgets. In the spring of 1991, the union parliament decided that the State Bank should give the government another cheque of 5 billion roubles.

Since the budget is the main source of money creation, hence inflationary, the reduction of the budget deficit is still at the top of the agenda of any economic reform plan. The methods of these cuts and additional curbs also cannot be too original:

- the deficit can be financed only if government bonds are sold on the securities market;
- a freeze on new expenditure plans and on still undisbursed programmes which must undergo a thorough revision;
- a visible programme of budget cuts with an across-the-board 10 per cent cut of non-social items;
- a programme of phasing out food subsidies;
- unorthodox revenues and taxes (selling assets, taxing things like company cars etc.).

Simultaneously, a general reform of the financial system must begin, including the following legislative and institutional measures:

- a decree stipulating principles of the budget system;
- a set of policy measures to fight budget deficits;
- the creation of a small body responsible for national debt financing;
- an immediate agreement on a federal tax preferably both on institutional and personal incomes in the form of a fixed percentage.

The last point is very important because without tax powers the union government will always be at the mercy of republican authorities and hence will not constitute a real government.

The second vital side of macrostabilization is the imposition of proper curbs on money creation. This presupposes both quantitative (increased interest rates and higher reserve requirements for commercial banks, the penalization of credit expansion of banks, etc.) and institutional measures.

The second set of measures is really of paramount importance since it creates a basis for the first. Before implementing the restrictive monetary policy usually recommended by the IMF it is worth ascertaining if it is viable. It stands to reason that the first steps should be to determine at least the simplest monetary aggregates, to set up a proper banknote issue mechanism (sales of banknotes to commercial banks) and central bank refinancing facilities. Without knowing what is really happening it is useless to try to influence anything.

An interesting question of the role of cash in the Soviet Union is usually underestimated by Western economists. The proportion of banknotes in the overall money supply is abnormally high and nearly all wages are disbursed in cash. All other factors being equal, this creates a more inflation-prone system where consumer demand pressure on the retail market is always high even without taking into account the non-existent credibility of the government and the official banking system.

For this reason, in my opinion, the compulsory introduction of non-cash payments is one suitable method of combatting monetary overhang. Other methods include the sales of state-owned assets (including all forms of privatization), increases of deposit rates, the securitization of the national debt and the introduction of innovative assets such as precious metals into the market etc. Admittedly, perhaps the biggest coup of the union government till now has been the three-year freeze on the 40 per cent compensation of saving deposits. This measure has had the maximum stabilization effect and surprisingly did not lead to a major social commotion.

Other measures intended to reconstruct the monetary system should include steps to develop intercompany credit, money and capital markets, facilitating the flow of capital and interest rate formation, and to decrease the dependence of economic agents on state-provided financing.

The withdrawal of foreign exchange from the internal settlement system is also very important. The reasons for this are two-fold. Very simple arithmetic shows that the introduction of foreign money as a mode of payment (so-called dollarization) tends to depreciate the value of domestic currency (the rouble) faster than ordinary money creation. Monetary controls are complicated by the lack of statistics on the foreign-exchange component of the money supply. And lastly, discrimination against the national currency, which is ostensibly the only legal tender, creates social difficulties.

But none of these measures will work if the obvious question of the disintegration of the banking system is not solved. All the leaders of the republics which have opted to stay in the union must at long last admit that in a single country there can be only one central bank and one monetary policy. That means that any decisions to the contrary are detrimental to the public interest and must be repealed.

For my part, I would still recommend the creation of a united reserve system of the USSR, where the State Bank of the USSR would be transformed into something like a board of governors, and all the central banks of the republics would be integral parts of one system conducting one policy. All the basic parameters (the discount rate, reserve requirements, etc.) must be the same all over the USSR, also preventing all barriers to interrepublican money flows. Obviously a unified settlement system is also essential.

Stabilization presupposes some kind of control over wage formation. The peculiarity of the situation is that administrative controls are still rather stringent in the state sector, whereas in the new commercial sector they are virtually non-existent. That is why a general wage liberalization must be accompanied by the creation of a new system of controls, including a rational approach to indexation:

– an obligatory but rather loose across-the-board fixed limit to quarterly increases of wage funds of enterprises;
– special taxes to curb non-wage remuneration;
– avoidance of 200 per cent indexation as a source of inflation in itself;
– centrally agreed principles of indexation to avoid the import of inflation from other republics.

In the second half of 1991 it is impossible to make profound changes in the Soviet economy. But the process of transformation should really take off, and the short-term target is to define the direction of change properly as well as to undertake basic measures. If a certain degree of stabilization were achieved, further progress would be much easier.

Foreign-exchange policy and convertibility

The deficiencies of Soviet foreign-exchange policy are well-documented and do not require additional *proof.*[3] In the first half of 1991 the situation has grown more acute, mainly due to the confrontation with the republics and deteriorating fixed personal incomes. Practical actions are obviously of paramount importance today.

Convertibility is the other side of soundness of money and its introduction can no longer be delayed. Limited internal convertibility – free access of residents to hard currency via the exchange market – must evidently be achieved in a matter of two to three months with steps towards current-account convertibility following. The more gradual approach, of which I was a proponent earlier, now seems to be politically unacceptable.

The most important and pressing task is to dismantle the existing system of hard-currency allocation and planning, abandoning the practice of authorities at all levels actually buying and selling goods. This must be parallel with price liberalization so that enterprises can adjust to the necessity of buying supplies for roubles or buying hard currency at the market rates. Introducing a free market-exchange rate without liberalizing prices is evidently fraught with enormous dangers.

In view of the foreign-exchange shortages, unfavourable external markets and mounting indebtedness, Soviet authorities are confronted with the spectre of, if not actually experiencing, international bankruptcy. But opportunities for reducing state foreign-exchange expenditure are limited and the government has enormous obligations linked with food problems, supplies to light and chemical industry, the entire non-productive sector. The republics, moreover, are trying to take control over foreign-exchange revenues themselves.[3]

We cannot leave enterprises with all the export revenues because there are central debt obligations and the oil/gas industry earns most of the country´s hard currency. At the same time the government can no longer satisfy all demands and is in confrontation with other levels of authority. Ninety-five per cent of Soviet enterprises are isolated from the world market because they are oriented towards domestic consumption. One of the very grave dangers of the situation is to give in to the demands of the republican authorities and to divide export revenues between levels of government. This will only reproduce the old system on a smaller and less professional scale.

There is also the question of the undervaluation of the rouble, indicating an artificial shortage of hard-currency supply. The black market and the prevailing market rate of the Soviet rouble at the level of 40 roubles to 1 dollar is also an inflationary factor which the government brought about through its own efforts, and evidently does not take this effect into account in its current actions.

It is interesting to note the evolution of the official approach to convertibility. When the union government was more or less in command of the situation, the introduction of convertibility was a matter of the distant future. Economic collapse and the ever-increasing pressure from the republics to divide hard currency revenues made the cabinet of ministers come much closer to a realistic position. That is why the chairman of the State Bank of the USSR, V. Gerashchenko, presented a case for convertibility in May 1991 which can hardly be criticized.[4] Unfortunately, he is perhaps the only senior official with any understanding of the problem, and it is doubtful whether there will be a convertible rouble on 1 January 1992, since it should be introduced only in conjunction with the macrostabilization plan and relevant institutional changes.

The immediate measures in this particular sphere are to be based on an assumption that the union government should have enough hard currency to service debt and for some specific needs. Non-agreed default is highly detrimental to the introduction of convertibility. Obviously the existing rule that enterprises surrender 40 per cent of their export earnings to the union treasury at the official exchange rate is necessary (with a higher figure for between three and five main export items). At the same time the authorities should swiftly cease to act as sellers and buyers of goods and commodities.

For the time being there must be only *two exchange rates* : the official high one for the 40 per cent obligatory surrender of currency to the central government (fixed for a year at 2-3 roubles per dollar) and a free-market rate for all other operations. A target could be to phase out the official fixed rate in three to five years, or even sooner.

All other foreign-exchange revenues should be sold to authorized banks (there is already a short list of these banks) at market rates within one to three months after the implementation of a commercial deal. This will create equal opportunities for exporters and importers, especially those who work primarily for domestic consumption. All public authorities, enterprises and citizens buy foreign exchange from authorized banks at market rates for import, tourism or other purposes.

Special licences at the initial stage will have to be obtained for the export of capital and the import of certain types of goods. That means that a comprehensive centralized system of foreign-exchange controls must be built with gradual but steady liberalization as reform progresses. And this in turn means that the recent decision of the Soviet government (reiterated in the 1991 anti-crisis programme) to decentralize export-import licensing should be repealed.

The new foreign-exchange market should be based on a limited number of the most professional banks, which will act as agents for foreign-exchange control and compile the necessary statistics. Unlike auctions and current practice, the new exchange market should be open to all Soviet legal entities (including joint ventures, cooperatives and individuals) with only few regulations as to the aims of currency purchases.

All enterprises will have to have roubles to buy necessary supplies. Success in working for the domestic market must result in better access to hard currency. The liberalization of prices in areas dependent on imports should be an immediate priority. State trading agencies should be corporatized as soon as possible, severing links with the state. At the same time the foreign economic relations ministry should have clearer supervisory functions.

An important element in the reform of the Soviet foreign-exchange system is the protection of the rouble as the only legal tender in the country. All types of internal payments in any other currency than roubles should be explicitly prohibited, even if a hotel room will cost between 5,000 and 8,000 roubles a night. That means closing down all currency shops and restaurants, or rather, converting them into high price commercial establishments. This can be done overnight, after 20 or 30 days notice.

The other side of this problem is the gradual widening of money functions of the Soviet rouble *vis-à-vis* non-residents. There is already a practice of opening rouble accounts. (I actually signed the first licences for that in Russia.) The question is to give non-residents the powers to engage in commercial activities in the USSR in order to earn roubles. The danger is that because of distorted prices, non-residents will have too high a purchasing power, thus crowding out domestic economic agents. To maintain fair competition and a more or less realistic situation on the foreign-exchange market, the 'internationalization' of the rouble will have to be gradual, meaning in fact a phased lifting of exchange controls.

There is also the important question of external debt. Republican authorities in pursuit of sovereignty demand a division of the external debt, also implying by that a division of the exchange and gold reserves, of all exchange revenues. There is a clear-cut desire to divide and spend in the same way as the union government and there is nothing to prove that republican governments will be better at it.

Seriously speaking, the external central debt cannot be divided between the republics although the cabinet of ministers, out of its desire for a truce, now goes along with this idea. While reserves are easy to divide, it is difficult to imagine how the sovereign debt could be divided. What would our creditors say if tomorrow part of a Deutsche Bank loan were suddenly to be attributed, not to one of the major powers of the world, but partly to Turkmenia, partly to Moldavia, etc. In the first place, none of the republics is a sovereign state by international law, and, second, the inherent risk is too different. In a civilized world things are just not done like that.

The overall amount of the Soviet external debt should, in my opinion, be frozen in so far as it is possible with an international agreement to reschedule it, partly to ease the immediate debt-service burden. New centralized borrowing should be explicitly linked to the reform process. If the authorities want to achieve something through additional expenditure, it must be done via the rouble budget with the possibility of buying hard currency at the market.

Summing up

1 Monetary and financial policy measures are crucial to economic reform.
2 Notwithstanding the events from October 1990 to the spring of 1991, macroeconomic stabilization still remains a top priority.
3 Economic reform must be tackled first with stabilization and the simplest institutional measures, mainly in the domain of regulation.

4 Sorting out the major constitutional issues is an absolutely necessary prerequisite of successful economic reform.
5 Soviet economic reform can only be implemented by Soviets, although well-thought-out international assistance could facilitate progress.

Annex: the basic structure of economic policy of the USSR

1 Foreign exchange rate: generally floating but needs to be supported.
2 Interest rates: increase within certain limits to avoid further disruption of production.
3 Wages: straightforward control.
4 Prices: fast but gradual liberalization.
5 Balance-of-payments deficit: extraordinary measures to achieve surplus or at least to stop deterioration.
6 Budget deficit: cutting at all cost and proper financing.
7 Level of taxation: maintenance of the existing level.
8 Money supply: tight control over monetary expansion.

Changes in all the above mentioned structure are necessary to influence:

- output;
- employment;
- standard of living.

Parallel action should include:

- fight against internal barriers in the way of capital and goods flows;
- privatization;
- drastic changes in the functions of the state (stop commercial activities).

Notes

1 *A Study of the Soviet Economy*, IMF, IBRD, OECD and EBRD, Paris, February 1991, vol. 1, pp. 237–98, 359–420.
2 'Gosbank upolnomochen' zayavit' ', *Izvestiya*, 3 April 1991, p. 1.
3 Fedorov, Boris G. (1990) *Valyutnaya politika SSSR*, Finansy i Statistika, Moscow.
4 'Vnutrennaya konvertiruemost' rublya – prokhozhdenie proidennogo drugimi?', *Izvestiya*, 18 May 1991, p. 2.

PART III
POSSIBLE NEW FEDERAL STRUCTURES

7

The Economic Union of Republics: Federation, Confederation, Community

Sergei Aleksashenko

The Soviet Union is undergoing a difficult time of change which affects all aspects of social life. Admittedly, this change is not as rapid as in Eastern Europe, but if we compare today's picture with 1984 the difference will be obvious.

It is possible today to select three main streams of on-going changes: from a totalitarian society to a democratic one, from a command economy to a market one, and from a unitarian country to some undefined type of union. Any changes in society's life provokes a certain instability to the Soviet case. The higher the level of instability, the less likely is the success of general reforms. This means it is extremely important for the USSR to try to stabilize the situation, at least in one of the reforming structures, in order to facilitate the resolution of its other problems. To my mind, the sphere of the country's internal organization has to be mostly coherent for this resolution. First, a consensus in a small circle of political leaders is necessary, now that the democratization and marketization processes seem to be spontaneous and unwieldy. Second, such an agreement could be limited to a time period.

Unfortunately, it is just in this sphere that reforms have been the slowest and a lot of possibilities to reach an agreement have been lost. Today, the problem of the future organization of the USSR is a factor which any reform plan has to take cognizance of in its analysis.

The draft Union Treaty published in the Soviet press shows that no mutually acceptable solution to economic challenges has been found, and that most of the outstanding issues fall within the joint jurisdiction of the central and republican governments[1] without specifying ways of putting solutions into practice.

The purpose of this paper is to make a comparative study of the economic aspects of the various forms of the union of republics (federation, confederation or community) in terms of the prospects for ending the economic crisis. The form of the union as a unitary state is not under consideration, since this option of reconstitution appears unrealistic. The first part of this paper highlights the basic points of the on-going reform of the Soviet Union´s political structure. The second part explores the condition of the existence of three forms of economic union, and the merits and demerits inherent in each of them.

In analysing the economic aspects of the union of republics, the emphasis will be on those spheres which will play a major role in normalizing the financial situation in the country and in overcoming the crisis:

- the banking and financial system;
- the budgetary and taxation (fiscal) system; and
- the system of supporting undeveloped regions.

While being aware of the importance of the changes in the system of the command economy of the Soviet Union for successful market reforms, we nevertheless will not consider them at the moment, since it is fairly evident that each republic (region) will have to act on its own in this sphere. The proportion of political and legal matters relating to the dovetailing of the legislation of different republics is far greater than that of economic matters, so these aspects of a single economic zone are not included in this paper. In closing, we are going to draw conclusions about the anti-crisis potential of the various forms of the union and set out our personal views on future prospects.

Reform of the political structure of the USSR: basic points

Hardly anyone today can predict what the future political structure of the Soviet Union will be like. The traditional view was that the Soviet Union was a federative state with a heavily centralized power although its 15 republics had their own parliaments and governments. But even if we disregard recent events, this view cannot be considered as being entirely correct.

The existence inside the country of widely different civilizations, religious faiths and economic systems with different levels of development is typical of the Soviet Union and has had a major effect on the way all domestic problems are being handled.

The realization of the full extent of the gap between the Soviet Union and the developed nations in terms of living standards has led to an upsurge in nationalist feelings in all parts of the country. The simplest answer to the eternal Russian question of 'Who is to blame?' is now either 'aliens' – those who live outside a particular republic – or those of a non-indigenous ethnic group who live in a republic. Today it can be said that the answer is most common in the European part of the country, and the second in Central Asia as well as in the Transcaucasus. The former prompts efforts to break away from the

Soviet Union; the latter involves ethnic violence.

The disintegration of the country finds expression in what is called 'the parade of sovereignties', with all 15 union republics declaring their independence and claiming full political power. In the process, some of them flatly refuse to be part of the union in any way; others agree to be part of the union but cannot adopt a common stand on the issue of the functions of this union and the powers to be vested in it. (Statements by republican leaders reveal their determination to retain the old system, replacing Moscow´s control with local control, rather than to reshape the economic system.)

Virtually all constituent republics have proclaimed the establishment of their own monetary, financial, credit and customs system: that is to say, the political decisions on the abolition of the Soviet Union as a common economic zone have already been made. They have not yet been acted upon in view of the high costs involved and the lack of competent personnel, etc. (However, the Baltic republics, the Ukraine, Belorussia, Uzbekistan, and even some regions of Russia have, to a certain extent, set up their own customs systems.) Most of the practical steps being taken by the republics are intended to restrict the access to their consumer market and to reduce the 'export' of industrial goods mostly in short supply. This practice disrupts the economic links between producers, increases social tensions and exacerbates the general economic crisis. In turn, this boosts centrifugal feelings in many republics, while allowing the centre to blame the deteriorating economic situation on the republican leaders.

It appears that an understanding of the danger of such behaviour is occasionally evident in both the centre and the republics, if only intuitively. Accordingly, it is possible to forecast the following trends:

1 the continued existence of the union as a single economic space, with some republics likely to secede in the near future, preserving some economic contacts because of technological dependence;
2 the republics will have a greater say in running the economy, with most issues falling within their jurisdiction. There will be central economic management bodies where all republics will be represented (interrepublican bodies);
3 the dismantling of the rigid centralized command economy in favour of a market system, with a largely decentralized management in all sectors, and the possibility of greater centralization in the future.

Choice

Definitions

A *federation* will mean an economic system based on the demarcation of rights and responsibilities in decision-making, on a single monetary system with a central bank, on a fiscal system underpinned by the distribution of revenues and expenditures between the budgets of various levels. An important function of the centre will be the reallocation of resources for equitable distribution and for overcoming vertical and horizontal imbalances.

A *confederation* will mean an economic system based on the supremacy of its members, a single monetary system the stability of which is supported by common action by the central banks of the members of the confederation and a budgetary system based on the principle of forming the central budget predominantly through contributions from the budgets of the confederation's members.

A *community* will mean an economic system like the European Community of the early 1980s, with a national banking and monetary system, a mechanism of coordinating and supporting exchange rates, with a central budget and regional funds which are formed exclusively by the contributions of the Community's members. All three arrangements imply a single customs zone, with the absence of customs barriers (even though in the case of a community this is not so obvious), freedom of labour, commodity, capital and information flow and single or coordinated rules of competition.

The banking and monetary system

The country cannot overcome the economic crisis and switch to a market system without a tough monetary and fiscal policy, with the Central Bank playing a crucial role in its execution.

The prevailing conditions in the Soviet Union – a large territory and different conditions of management – make it desirable that, in the process of forming a federation, the system of the central bank should be similar to the federal reserve system of the US. Such a reorganization of the central bank will make it possible to allow for the specific features of various regions during the execution of macroeconomic policy and to ensure the implementation of the set targets.

Given this approach, it would be best to set up regional reserve banks, rather than republican banks (they may coincide), which would have direct contacts with commercial banks. This would make it possible roughly to balance the potential economic influence of reserve banks, putting them on an equal footing in decision-making.

The system of the federal central bank will make it possible, in the case of the implementation of the stabilization policy, to guarantee equal economic conditions throughout the country, to exercise effective control over the money supply, to make it much easier to control the process of lending to the government, to achieve rouble convertibility and to support its market exchange rate.

However, it is most unlikely that such a banking system will now be set up in the Soviet Union. The law on the USSR Gosbank passed by the USSR Supreme Soviet provides for a different banking structure, which can be characterized as semi-confederative – the establishment of a reserve system of the union as an association of central banks of the republics and a network of commercial banks. It is implied that, being part of the reserve system, the central banks of the constituent republics will delegate their money-creation and regulatory functions to it. The idea is that the union reserve system will be headed by a board of governors including the chairman of the board, four deputy chairmen (all to be appointed by the President of the Soviet Union) and ten members from among the governors of the republican central banks. All decisions will be taken by simple majority vote at board sessions.

This kind of a banking system is inherently unstable for the following reasons:

1 The size of member banks will vary. For example, the Gosbank of Russia will represent more than half the country´s economic potential, yet each republican bank will get only one vote. As a result, votes will not necessarily reflect the weight and economic impact of the various banks, creating a situation of potential conflict if a decision is taken against Russia´s views.[2]
2 In the case of an agreement between republics on the reform plan, the republican central banks have to delegate most of their monetary and credit functions to the union reserve. In fact, they will not act as real central banks, but will only retain some functions of secondary importance. The following of these should be mentioned:

  – the registration of commercial banks and the supervision of their activities on the territory of a given republic; and
  – the organization of a system of interbank insurance.

Moreover, even the execution of only these functions may generate certain problems in relations between republics. First, there is a danger that all commercial banks will operate on the territory of only one republic. Second, this may erect barriers to an interbank, interregional movement of financial resources. Third, this will create difficulties for enterprises operating in several republics, since local authorities will demand that money be placed in banks or their territory, while all financial budget dealings will be handled through a bank serving the central office of the enterprise concerned.

There are many similar problems, from which it may be concluded that to ensure the efficiency of the banking system – even in the form enshrined in the all-union legislation – the central banks in the republic will need carefully to coordinate all their activities and make appropriate regulations. Furthermore, there is a need to devise ways of barring banks from exercising their influence. Meanwhile, the reality of politics has gone much further: it is evident that because of their political ambitions, the republics today are not ready to sacrifice such a significant aspect of their sovereignty as the banking system.

The law on the Russian federation's Gosbank devolves to the Russian central bank all powers relating to the regulation and organization of money circulation on the territory of the republic. The programme of the Russian government seeks 'the organization of a parallel system of money circulation', as well as the enforcement of Russia´s own principles on the legislative regulation of the circulation of the rouble on the territory of the republic ('Programma ...', 1991). The Russian federation´s Gosbank began to draft directives on monetary and credit policy, and to lobby for these in the Russian federation´s parliament. In his pre-electoral programme, B. El´tsin supported the transfer of control over money issue to the republics. A Russian deputy prime minister proposes that specially marked roubles – in effect, Russia's own money – should be put into circulation on the territory of the republic (Malei, 1991). The law on the Gosbank of the Ukraine gave the central Ukrainian bank the right to issue its own money at any time. Simultaneously, the Ukraine is contemplating putting what is termed 'food money' (Fokin, 1991) into circulation in the near future, as an alternative to a blanket rationing system. Continuing to vie among themselves in building up a social defence system, the republics are not in a hurry to agree on matters of fiscal policy. It is hard to imagine how the idea floated by the governor of the Russian central bank will be put into practice: that the USSR Gosbank as the main plank of the banking system should be replaced with a coordinating council of republican central banks (Matyukhin, 1991). This arrangement may prove workable in a period of economic stability, but, given the current economic crisis, an obvious inflationary process, and the disastrous weakening and depreciation of the rouble, any decentralization of the banking system would lead to the erosion of control over money-creation and, consequently, the increased likelihood of the introduction of republican or interrepublican currencies.

Should the republics switch from a single monetary system to indigenous currencies as the economic community develops, the Soviet economy, or, rather, the economies of the republics, would face a host of major problems, most of which they have never encountered before. Some of them may be listed as follows:

1 the maintenance of a stable exchange rate of their currencies at a time when Soviet producers can offer no competitive goods to the world market except raw materials. Today, the leading hard-currency earners are Russia and Kazakhstan, and, potentially, because of cotton, the Central Asian republics; evidently, the exchange rates of currencies in the other republics would largely depend on the fluctuation of the Soviet currency;

2 the need to switch to settlements at world prices, which would entail drastic changes in pricing and payments schemes;

3 each republic would have to cope with the crisis on its own, with the technological requirements between producers limiting the freedom to choose the appropriate economic strategy;

4 the banking system will come under much greater technological strain, with much higher standards expected of it, and it will have to handle several types of currencies within the Soviet Union at the

same time.

In all likelihood, the existence of a rouble zone, allowing the convertibility of other currencies into the Russian rouble only, will be inevitable in the context of a community, even though the possibility of a new transferable rouble for use in mutual settlements cannot be ruled out. Such mechanisms would be able to work only in a relatively stable macroeconomic environment.

The option of the development (or disintegration) of a unified monetary system is very likely in the future, but all the above-mentioned problems may well occur even earlier, since the breakaway republics will most certainly introduce their own currencies.

A cherished dream of each republic is to gain full control over the hard-currency earnings from the export of goods produced on its territory and to have the right to borrow abroad on its own ('Programma ... ', 1991). Today the major part of hard-currency inflow is distributed centrally by the Union-Republican Foreign Exchange Committee. This is in charge of the funds gathered from the mandatory sales by producers to the state of 40 per cent of their export earnings at the official rate of exchange, in addition to that portion of hard currency which remains after they have set up hard-currency funds. The state spends a sizeable portion of its hard currency on foreign-debt servicing. However, in early April 1991 the Gosbank of the USSR opened an exchange market where producers could sell and buy hard currency at the market rate.

Permitting the republics to use hard currency as they wish is posing the following major problems to which no answers have yet been found:

1 the decentralization of hard-currency incomes, in particular accompanied by the decentralization of the banking system, complicates the transition to a convertible rouble as the common monetary unit and makes it extremely difficult to support the rouble's value against hard currencies;
2 the decentralization of hard-currency resources would call for the decentralization of the Soviet Union's foreign debt, necessitating the development of criteria acceptable to all republics. Here again, it is not clear how those republics which have no export capabilities will service their foreign debt; moreover the Soviet Union's creditors will hardly welcome the prospect of doing business simultaneously with 15 or more bad debtors;
3 much of Soviet industry requires supplies of imported raw materials, primary products and components. Because of this, falling Soviet exports in 1991 have caused output to drop by 10-12 per cent (an estimate of Gosplan experts). Considering that not all the republics can boast of great export capabilities, while all of them need hard currency, this development may add to the decline of production in the Soviet Union.

The fiscal system

This area of relationships between the union and the republics is currently arousing the greatest interest, since the critical state of Soviet finances, straining under the huge burden of the budget deficit, is one of the most serious obstacles in the way of market reforms and one of the more complex problems to be resolved.

Before 1990, the Soviet Union operated a centralized system of real-location of financial resources, whereby the USSR ministry of finance and the USSR state planning committee (Gosplan) were in a position to accumulate and subsequently distribute among the republics, regions, districts, industries and producers, the greater part of financial resources, either through the system of budgets or through the specialized funds of ministries and other government departments. A mechanism existed that functioned in much the same manner as the financial system of a large industrial organization where the management sees that its various divisions are funded consistently with due regard to priorities.

Such a system did not need taxes, so there were practically none. Through the instrumentality of individual prices, standard rates of contribution to the budget, and subsidies, the state was well-placed to regulate the finances of any organization. The republics would similarly set individual standard rates of contribution from turnover-tax revenues collected on their territory, and the overall size of subsidies (subventions).

The year 1990 saw the first changes in this inadequate, but still functioning, machinery. The major problem was that these changes occurred spontaneously, without a clear vision of a future arrangement and outside the context of general economic change. At first, by way of an experiment, the centre reached an agreement with Estonia on centralized transfer (from Estonia's budget to the centre) of a fixed portion of deductions from the producers' profits on the republic's territory. As a result, in the middle of 1990, Estonia stopped sending money to the centre altogether. In autumn of 1990, all the Baltic republics, in a unilateral move, decided to use all turnover tax revenues on their own,[3] and Russia decided to keep a larger proportion of these revenues.

In the autumn of 1990, a budget war broke out between the union and Russian governments, as the new leadership of the Russian federation supported the 'confederative' principle of forming the union budget from the contributions of the republics, an arrangement proposed earlier but rejected by the USSR Supreme Soviet (Parliament). The other republics approved of this approach. Once Russia had established control over its banking system in December 1990, ordering all tax revenues to be remitted to its own budget, the union government gave in and signed a budget agreement for 1991 on the terms laid down by Russia. The unbearable burden of social and defence spending, mistakes in budget planning, attempts to conceal the actual size of the deficit, the disintegration of the single system of financial control, and general economic decline (Aleksashenko and Yasin, 1990; Aleksashenko, 1991a) all influenced the situation in regard to the union and republican budgets. By the end of the first quarter of 1991, it was evident that the republics' revenues had fallen at least 33.3 per cent short of target, while the union received about 30 per cent of the expected amount (57 per cent from the republics' contributions, 26 per cent from incomes from international activity, 5.6 per cent from sales tax, etc.). The union budget deficit, as early as the first quarter of the year, totalled 27.1 billion roubles (Goskomstat SSSR, 1991). This happened even though both the union and Russian governments (no data is available for other republics) had not fully released funding for a number of programmes (23 per cent and 53 per cent of planned expenditures respectively) (Goskomstat SSSR, 1991; Goskomstat RSFSR, 1991), and there were no planned money flows to the pension and stabilization funds. Further, the tax-collection system has become highly decentralized and is not subordinated to the central authorities.

Addressing the Third Congress of People's Deputies of the Russian Federation, Boris El'tsin spoke of the need to end the budget crisis. Though his call was supported by the joint statement of the ten leaders, ('Sovmestnoe zayavlenie', 1991) it has not yet been decided exactly how to do this.

The fiscal system is playing a specific role in the execution of a macroeconomic stabilization policy in the Soviet Union (IMF et al., 1991, vol.1, p. 243), but, unfortunately, this fact is disregarded by the republican leaders in the Soviet Union, which hampers efforts to end the crisis. (A similar situation has taken shape in Yugoslavia.) Since this issue is of great importance to the future of the union, a closer look may be taken at its theoretical aspects.

A federation needs to work according to certain rules regarding the sharing of revenues and expenditures among various budget levels, so that the central authorities can control the situation and pursue an effective macroeconomic policy. Ideas of how to maximize the pay-off from resource allocation, in theoretical terms, (Oates, 1972) indicate that each level of government in the federation should receive its fair share of overall expenditures. Certain types of government spending, notably in defence, foreign affairs, international trade, inter-regional transport networks and telecommunications must all undoubtedly be incurred by the central government. Most of the other sectors, such as health, education, social security, public order, intra-regional transport, and regional infrastructures, which between them account for the best part of the budget, should be funded by regional and local authorities. To a certain extent, the pattern of spending needs to be complemented with arrangements designed to ensure the minimum levels of expenditure by certain services throughout the country's territory. This objective should be achieved by the central government through selective aid to lower levels of power (transfers).

Basically, the decentralization of a large proportion of social services should (though not necessarily) be accompanied by the distribution of revenues among various levels of power. In practice, most of the developed and developing countries rely on systems whereby regional and local governments, being responsible for a large proportion of social services, receive a sizeable portion of their resources from a higher authority. The choice between alternative funding arrangements for various levels of government depends on a wide variety of factors, which combine to produce a different effect in different countries under different circumstances. In macroeconomic terms, the following basic options can be identified.

At one end of the spectrum, we can see a confederative upward approach, whereby the lower government is responsible for delimiting the taxation base, tax rates and other essential elements of taxation, and collects the greater portion of taxes. Part of the tax revenues in this case goes to cover central government expenditures. This arrangement is expected to be used in Yugoslavia and many Soviet republics are strongly in favour of this approach. The approach, for all its political appeal, however, is seriously flawed: one shortcoming is the unequal distribution of the burden of spending among confederation members. This demerit is particularly evident in the widely differing opportunities of regions to collect taxes and in the prevailing macroeconomic situation. If, incorporating stringent and effective deficit-limitation measures by confederation members, this approach cannot be put into practice together with the required fiscal and monetary discipline, it would rob the central government of the chance to make fiscal policy an instrument in macroeconomic management.

A widespread approach in Western federations implies that various levels of government cover different parts of the tax base. The theory of fiscal federalism implies a variety of criteria for this arrangement (Oates, 1972; King, 1984; Shah, 1991). Normally, the following types of taxes should fall within the jurisdiction of the central government: (a) taxes on relatively changeable factors of production; (b) progressive taxes; (c) high cycling sensibility taxes; and (d) taxes which are difficult to collect at different levels of government. By this criterion, income taxes and foreign-trade taxes must be the exclusive concern of federal authorities. Furthermore, the criterion last mentioned above would also require federal jurisdiction to cover taxes derived from resources, such as the tax on oil or other minerals; normally, however, regional and local governments demand at least a share of such tax revenues. Taxes on goods and services, such as the value-added tax, the sales tax and excise duties, present greater difficulties. Such taxes, particularly in the transition period, are the most profitable form of taxation. Putting them under the jurisdiction of lower levels of government robs the federal budget of a major source of revenue and an effective instrument of macroeconomic regulation. In all these cases, the degree of autonomy enjoyed by the regional governments in determining the spread and rates of these taxes needs to be confined to a unified economic zone. It is best for property taxes on constant factors of production to be the domain of local authorities, as also various duties on local services. Normally, these taxes account for an insignificant portion of the overall consolidated budget revenues and can hardly be considered a major factor for macroeconomic regulation.

Another alternative way of sharing tax revenues, which is conducive to the autonomy of various levels of government, involves the joint use of the tax base. Using this approach, the central government establishes the tax base and other necessary conditions for collecting taxes by all means, including the tax rate for its own budget. Thereafter, regional, and in some cases, local governments add their taxes to the federal tax, increasing its rate. In terms of macroeconomic management, this approach is preferable with respect to delimiting the tax base because it implies greater opportunities for using tax instruments by central authorities, thereby making it possible to bring about financial stability. The uniform methods of determining the tax base in all the country's regions also guarantees the equal distribution of the tax burden, preventing attempts at tax evasion or the false transfer of resources. At the same time, efforts by the authorities at various levels to differentiate regional and local taxes are restricted by the uneven production factors and commodity flows to be found in a single economic zone.

The policy of reducing budget deficits is basic to macroeconomic management. The need for strict control over the balance of income and expenditure by governments at all levels is acknowledged by all federal states. The basic principles for such control are as follows:

1 central government regulations, covering the overall debt at all levels and with respect to ceilings on its growth;
2 the need for regional, and more, for local governments to obtain permission to allow their debts to grow; in strong federations, this kind of permission is given by the central government; in loose federations this is also done by the central government – in all cases with the concurrence of federation members;
3 new loans of sub-national governments, preferably of the central one, too, must be extended only for investment in production;
4 the budget deficits of sub-national governments cannot be financed by resources from the central banks of the republics, as this has an adverse impact on the financial system.

Today it is evident to almost everyone in the Soviet Union that political confrontation and strong decentralization, and even the centrifugal factor in the present developmental trends, are making it hard to build a fiscal system patterned on a classic model with a strong independent central budget. The prevailing view among political leaders now is that the functions of the union should be reduced to a minimum and its budget should be formed by the contributions of the republics. This issue is being debated chiefly at the level of sloganeering, without any earnest analysis of the financial set-up. The work to bring such an idea to fruition in 1991 called for solutions to several major problems. They included:

1 the coordination of the contents of the tax system and the overall size of the tax burden, agreements on tax matters, and a mechanism to prevent tax evasion;
2 a sharing by the republics of the revenues from the turnover tax when it is collected at the point of production, not at the point of consumption, and predominantly from end-products.[4] This arrangement calls for the development of a mechanism to enable a partial reallocation of revenues among the republics. Furthermore, the planned switch to a new monetary system will take time and money;
3 agreements on setting ceilings on the size of the union and republican budget deficits and methods of covering them;
4 arrangements to guarantee revenues for the union budget and fines on defaulting republics;
5 fixing the size of the contributions of the republics to the union budget; and
6 sharing receipts from external economic activities (customs tariffs and import and export taxes) between the republics, in the context of a unified customs space with a limited number of collection points of such receipts.

In addition to all the complexities of an economic nature, this problem has a political aspect. Indeed, if democratically elected, each level of power must have the opportunity to implement its ideas through its own fiscal policy (taxes and expenditures), being simultaneously responsible to its constituents for the effectiveness and efficiency of this policy. In case the above-described arrangement is put into effect, this kind of responsibility and independence will be negated.[5]

The search for solutions to these problems will consume much time and energy and call for concord and compromise. In my view, the present generation of political leaders is not ready for this; therefore, the likelihood of the country's disintegration will increase since it is impossible to resolve the budget crisis.

Yet it cannot be expected that once the Soviet Union is reconstituted into a community, the republics will be able to pursue a fully independent fiscal policy. As the community implies fixed exchange rates of currencies and freedom of capital movement, it will mean that the participating nations will lose a measure of their independence. Depending on institutional restrictions within the currency union, monetary policy may be formulated by the country's central bank, its currency being the leading one in the system, or by an agreement between central banks. The price of rejecting monetary independence will be an agreement among members at least to limit the financing of their budget deficits.

The important thing is to ban the financing of the government deficits of community members by domestic banks except for very short periods in cases of extreme need, when the money borrowed must be paid back within a year.

The experience of the countries which are part of the European monetary system serves to show that this kind of situation develops quite frequently. It should be said that even under stable conditions, a relatively large deficit piled up by some member of the currency union or confederation may have a serious unsettling impact on the behaviour of the other members. The following effects should be mentioned:

1 by drawing in a big way on the union's savings, community members with a large deficit are bound to increase the interest rate for the other community members;
2 later on, the accumulated deficit of a community member may precipitate a rapid growth in its debt, no matter whether domestic or foreign, and in the long run this will call for subsidies from the central bank – at a heavy cost for the rest of the union.

Another argument in favour of limits on the deficits which the members of the currency union or community may run up, is that the increased mobility of resources in a single economic zone and, consequently, the increased mobility of the tax base, makes it more difficult to realize sufficient tax-revenue targets and thus achieve a deficit-free budget.

Furthermore, acceptance of budget-deficit ceilings by community members must be backed by efforts to find the appropriate methods of the regional reallocation of financial resources. For instance, closer integration within the European Community is supplemented by a two-fold growth in the reform fund, with the weaker members of the Community pressing hard to ensure that further steps towards full currency union will be matched by further growth in these funds.

Regional support

The issue of economic support for the less-developed regions exists in any union of states, beginning with the global north-south problem. Given the economic, cultural and geographic diversity of conditions within the Soviet Union, action on this issue becomes of the utmost importance in the context of further reforms.

The economically least-developed parts of the Soviet Union are the Central Asian republics, which specialize predominantly in production of raw materials and cotton. In the old system, developmental differences were narrowed through the centralized redistribution of financial and physical resources and national economic planning. Following the signing of the budget agreement for 1991, the old system collapsed as the agreement provided for a regional support fund to be formed from the contributions of the republics. In practice, however, neither Russia nor the Ukraine nor Belorussia (the republics which bear the burden of expenditure on aid to other republics) have made any contribution whatsoever to the fund. Consequently, the Central Asian republics have not received a single rouble (Romanyuk, 1991) of the sum of some 7 to 7.5 billion roubles promised to them for this period.

A similar interrepublican redistribution fund is to be set up to pay compensation for retail price rises. However, the republics are not contributing to this fund either (Komin, 1991). Although the Central Asian republics demand that the promised transfers be made, the central government does not have the means to keep these promises.

Clearly, the issue of subventions is bound up with the organization of the budget system. In the case of a federation with a strong central budget, having a tax base of its own, the central government must provide for expenditures to narrow differences in the prevailing conditions among the federation's members by certain criteria (a common minimum of social services guaranteed to each individual). To this end, legislation on the federal-budget system should specify the types of transfers, their volumes and the terms on which they can be made.

In the case of a community, the instruments of support include the exchange-rate ratios and, again, special funds. As agreed, exchange-rate arrangements can be used to motivate export-oriented producers in countries which are receiving aid, thus improving their competitive position and protecting their market.

The following policies can be identified in the Soviet Union at this juncture:

1   preserving and modernizing the federal system (Central Asia and Belorussia);
2   switching to interrepublican credits under bilateral agreements (the Russian Federation); and
3   the refusal to participate in the work on this problem (the Baltic republics and, possibly, the Ukraine, which, however, has issued no official statements on this issue).

Since none of the republics which remain part of the union has yet announced the introduction of its own future monetary system, there have been no proposals for the use of agreed exchange rates. There is reason to believe that in the event of moves to this end, the resulting machinery would work in a diametrically opposite way compared with that of the EEC: the exchange rate of the currency used by the republic which is receiving support will rise rather than fall. This is because of the heavily monopolized economy with rigid technological factors involved in such deliveries.[6] What may prove profitable for a particular republic are latent transfers resulting from the increased exchange rate of its currency; but, evidently, even this does not obviate the need for special regional-development funds to be set up in a way acceptable to all the republics.

This problem is not being widely discussed in the Soviet Union today; it does not seem to be treated seriously.

Conclusions

The reform process in the Soviet Union has thrown into sharp relief the flaws of the old national-territorial structure of the state. Further changes in Soviet society in any area will be hampered by the outstanding problems of the internal arrangement of the country. The Soviet leadership's delayed realization of the importance of finding the answer to this problem between 1989 and 1991 has given rise to many ethnic conflicts, destroyed the unity of vital monetary and fiscal systems and is a major factor behind the loss of control over the macroeconomic situation.

Current debates over the future organization of the Soviet Union have thrown up three options: federation, confederation or community. However, in making a political choice, all specific aspects of the current situation in the USSR need to be taken into account, especially the economic crisis and market reforms.

A look at the record of reform in command economies will lead us to conclude that a tough financial policy is absolutely essential for ending the crisis and developing a new economic system. If we allow for the economic peculiarities of different kinds in the union and the republics, we shall clarify that such a policy can be properly executed either by the central government of a federation on the basis of a single monetary system, or by each republic using its own currency within the framework of a community. No interim arrangements – neither a confederation nor the popular theoretical structure proposed even in the draft union treaty, whereby each republic would itself decide what powers should be vested with the central government – can guarantee financial discipline and an end to the crisis.

These two alternatives – federation or community – are still possible today. However, it is necessary to emphasize that the second road (to community) does not require serious changes in political behaviour from the Soviet leaders. It does not force them to any flexibility or ability to reject their previous ideas. It only calls on them to continue their previous policy step by step, until it becomes quite clear that the economic crisis can be separately overcome.

In the long-term interest the preservation of a single monetary system is *strongly* desirable, as it can help the integration process in the future. Today, however, this position requires that leaders of the republics admit their mistakes and reach a consensus with the central *power*. This seems less likely today.

References

Aleksashenko, Sergei, (1991a) 'Reform of the Fiscal System in the Soviet Federation: The main Complexities and Possible Solutions', paper prepared for the Senior Policy Seminar on Intergovernmental Fiscal Relations and Macroeconomic Management in Large Countries, New Delhi, India, 26-28

February.

Aleksashenko, Sergei, (1991b) 'Fiscal Federalism in the Soviet Union: Is It Possible?' paper prepared for the Seminar on Fiscal Federalism in Economies in Transition, Paris, OECD, 2–3 April.

Aleksashenko, Sergei, (1991c) in *Nezavisimaya gazeta*, 6 April.

Aleksashenko, Sergei, and Yasin, Evgenii, (1990) in *Izvestiya* (Moscow issue), 30 December.

Biehl, Dieter, (1991) 'A Case Study of a Federal Country: Germany', paper prepared for the Senior Policy Seminar on Intergovernmental Fiscal Relations and Macroeconomic Management in Large Countries, New Delhi, India, 26-28 February.

'Draft Treaty ...' (1991) 'The Draft Treaty on the Union of Sovereign Republics', *Pravda*, 9 March 1991.

Fokin, V. (1991), *Nezavisimaya gazeta*, 30 April.

Goskomstat RSFSR (1991), *Rossiiskaya gazeta*, 30 April.

Goskomstat SSSR (1991), *Ekonomika i zhizn'*, No. 21.

Grinberg, R., and Legai, K., (1991), *Nezavisimaya gazeta*, 21 May.

Gygi, U. (1991) 'The Experience of Switzerland', paper prepared for the Seminar on Fiscal Federalism in Economies in Transition, Paris, OECD, 2–3 April.

IMF, IBRD, OECD and EBRD, (1991) *A Study of the Soviet Economy*, OECD Publication Service, Paris.

King, David, (1984) *Fiscal Tiers: the Economics of Multilevel Government*, Allen & Unwin, London.

Knight, Peter and Waxman, Roberta, (1991) 'Fiscal Federalism in the Soviet Union', paper prepared for the Senior Policy Seminar on Intergovernmental Fiscal Relations and Macroeconomic Management in Large Countries, New Delhi, India, 26-28 February.

Komin, A., (1991), *Pravda*, 23 May.

Malei, M., (1991) 'Special Road for Russia', *Rossiiskaya gazeta*, 16 March.

Matyukhin, G., (1991) *Rossiiskaya gazeta*, 30 April.

Oates, Wallace, (1972) *Fiscal Federalism*, Harcourt, Brace & Jovanovich, New York.

'Programma ...' (1991) 'Programma Pravitel'stva RSFSR po stabilizatsii ekonomiki i perekhodu k rynochnym otnosheniiam', *Rossiiskaya gazeta*, 21 May.

Romanyuk, V., (1991) *Izvestiya*, 16 May.

Shah, Anwar, (1991) 'Perspectives on the Design of Intergovernmental Fiscal Relations in Developing/Transition Economies', paper prepared for the Senior Policy Seminar on Intergovernmental Fiscal Relations and Macroeconomic Management in Large Countries, New Delhi, India, 26-28 February.

'Sovmestnoe zayavlenie ... ' (1991) *Pravda*, 26 April.

Vorontsov, V., (1991) *Rabochaya Tribuna*, 18 May.

Notes

1 The economic matters within the exclusive jurisdiction of the central government include only 'the approval and execution of the Union budget' and 'the conduct of external economic activities within the jurisdiction of the central government' (The Draft Treaty, 1991).

2 Even at this point of time, the stand of the central bank of Russia on any issue is diametrically opposite to the position of the USSR Gosbank, regardless of the economic aspects of their views.

3 Because of the peculiarities of organizing this tax, it is collected predominantly in industrial regions; the purpose of individual republic-wise rates of deductions was to narrow the developmental differences and redistribute resources.

4 The attempt to collect the sales tax at the point of retailing foundered. Revenues reached less than one-third of the planned amount and the rest ended up in the pockets of retailers (Vorontsov, 1991).

5 This argument was heard at the conference on 'Fiscal Federalism in Economies in Transition', organized by the OECD in April 1991.

6 Attempts to ignore these ties exacerbated the crisis trends in the countries of Eastern Europe that were once part of COMECON; the volume of their trade in 1991 was down to 37.5 per cent as compared to 50 per cent in 1990 (Grinberg and Legai, 1991).

8

Federalism and Marketization in the Soviet Union: Lessons from Economic Theory

Stuart Brown

The Soviet Union today faces two interrelated challenges: the revamping of its federalist system and the replacement of central planning with market institutions. Recently proposed Soviet reform programmes do not adequately capture the complex interaction between federal and economic restructuring. Can Western theory provide any additional insight?

While numerous strands of economic theory are potentially applicable, this paper isolates three diverse yet complementary approaches in the literature. The purpose here is to paint with broad brushstrokes. The construction of new models and the generation of specific results is postponed for future endeavours. The relative neglect of property ownership in this paper has no relation to its primacy in Soviet discourse. However, the focus here is on economic theory which has little to say about the consequences of redefining property relations.

The paper is organized as follows: In Section I, the theories of fiscal federalism and optimal currency areas are used to evaluate the efficiency of republic-specific stabilization, allocation and redistribution policies. Borrowing from the economic theory of clubs, Section II outlines a new conceptual approach to the dual problems of federalism and marketization in the Soviet Union. In Section III, game theoretic approaches to interrepublican negotiations with and without central authority involvement are reviewed as a means towards better understanding the struggle surrounding the draft union treaty. Finally, the relevance and limitations of these various approaches in the Soviet context are summarized in Section IV.

Section I: Fiscal federalism and Soviet restructuring

In this section Richard Musgrave's distinction between the stabilization, allocation and distributional functions of government in a federal setting is applied to the Soviet Union (Musgrave and Musgrave, 1984). The purpose is to review central propositions in the theory of fiscal federalism and explore their relevance to a multinational country requiring federal restructuring. The literature on optimal currency areas is also used to assess the welfare implications of republic-specific monetary and fiscal policies. Second, whether redistribution should be implemented largely by central versus local Soviet authorities is explored. Finally, what does the literature suggest about the proper division of public goods' provision between central and republican authorities?

Fiscal federalism: stabilization

THE SOVIET DEBATE

In recent years Soviet newspapers have been flooded with discussions on separate republican currencies (Kitaigorodskii, 1990; Ivanter, 1989; Ushanov, 1990). Originating in the Baltics, many such proposals have been influenced by political strivings for independence. The latter is considered meaningless without control over a minimum set of economic instruments, including the money supply. However, the case for independent republic monies has also been based on economic criteria. One argument is that regional *khozraschet* (self-sufficiency) is impossible when republics are powerless to maintain market equilibrium (Otsasson, 1990). Since the underlying reason for a growing disparity between local incomes and goods involves a breakdown in Soviet central macroeconomic management, the argument goes, to stabilize local economies republican governments have no choice but to introduce local 'certificates', and ultimately money, to defend local markets against excess demand pressures emanating from outside the republic. Certificate or coupon-money surrogates preclude money migration that lowers local goods' availability.[1]

In addition, by accelerating reform in one part of the country, some economists earlier maintained that an independent (Baltic) currency could expedite reform in the country as a whole. For example, because of its greater cultural and economic proximity to Western markets, the Baltic region could initiate an experiment in free economic zones using its own convertible currency, with exchange rates set in part so as to better stimulate exports and restrain imports. Arguably this would facilitate the ultimate external convertibility of the rouble.[2]

Orthodox Soviet opinion soundly rejects these claims and has developed its own counter-arguments. One position is that the introduction of local monies will aggravate autarkic tendencies, increase the transaction costs of interregional trade and aggravate the rouble's declining purchasing power. Second, it is argued that estimating the demand for money, especially with currency substitution and money migration, is much more difficult than estimating money demand under singular currency regimes (Kitaigorodskii, 1990). Adherents to this point of view argue that the solution lies in eliminating national inflation by restoring the proper balance between aggregate supply and demand; moreover the introduction of separate currencies will not render the Baltic states or others immune to this imbalance (Khandruev, 1990). Instead, there is no way to eliminate inflationary processes without coordinated action between central and republican authorities (Ivanter, 1989).

Third, such attempts to introduce additional monies goes against world trends toward monetary coordination and union following disenchantment with flexible rates. Fourth, for small republics to establish their own money diverts resources from consumption and accumulation (Vol'ukov, 1990) to say nothing about transaction costs in trading with neighbouring republics. Moreover, these observers see little role for regional currencies as a means of settlement in interregional transactions and ask who will determine and on what basis the exchange rates between such new currencies and the rouble (Ushanov, 1990). Finally, given a relative lack of resources and competitive products there, many are sceptical about separate regional currencies (say) in the Baltics including their role in facilitating eventual rouble convertibility (Petrakov, 1990).

THE FIVE HUNDRED DAYS' PLAN

In the summer of 1990, a working group created by the union and Russian parliaments and headed by academician Stanislav Shatalin drafted a radical economic reform plan. The document, *Perekhod k rynku* (*Transition to the Market*, hereafter the '500 days' plan') touched upon every major aspect of the transition from central planning.[3] The plan takes the regional devolution of power as *de facto* and envisions a new social contract among sovereign republics, each of which earns exclusive ownership rights and management prerogatives to property located on its territory. '500 days' starts with the premise that republican law dominates union law within each republic. Republics bear the principal responsibility for local economic development.

While the 500 days' plan clearly regards republican sovereignty as the essential cornerstone of a revamped Soviet federation, the plan nevertheless insists that republics concur on certain fundamental rules. Among these is the centralization of monetary policy and the maintenance of the rouble as the sole currency on Soviet territory. Although the document is vague on this point, this decision was presumably intended to ensure an unimpeded interrepublican flow of finance for efficiency, without which national unity would be deemed impossible.

According to the plan, monetary policy is to be controlled by a board of governors of the 'reserve system' (*Rezervnaya sistema Soyuza*). The Soviet President is to appoint the chairman while each republic will appoint its own representative to the board. The reserve system board is to determine monetary policy for the country as a whole. The central banks of the individual republics are to be members of the reserve system and are to subordinate their emission and regulatory functions to decisions of the union reserve. Republics will be charged with supervising commercial banks on their own territories. Republican ministries of finance will determine the rules regulating the issuance and circulation of government securities and management of the government debt.

The exact division of union- and republic-level authority over monetary and fiscal policy is not clearly outlined in the 500 days' plan. For example, republican central banks will be charged with administering the republics' income, expenditures and debt. Financing state debt using reserve system reserves is apparently prohibited, but in special situations loans of up to 12 months for union-level or republican budgets from the union reserve may be approved. While the republican banks are prohibited from financing the republic's budget deficit through the direct purchase of government bonds, both the republican central banks and the union reserve system can require commercial banks to purchase government bonds. Based on these guidelines, it is plausible that government banks could conceal bond purchases through commercial banks, encouraging an uncontrollable explosion of internal debt and a resulting credit expansion.

OPTIMAL CURRENCY AREAS – WESTERN PERSPECTIVE

Given the conflict between republican desires to introduce independent currencies and the 500 days' plan's insistence on the maintenance of the rouble as the sole unit of exchange throughout the Soviet Union, what can Western economic theory suggest about the proper locale of a stabilization policy in a federation?

Four possible patterns of stabilization exist: centralized monetary and fiscal policy, decentralized monetary and fiscal policy, centralized monetary and decentralized fiscal policy, and decentralized monetary and centralized fiscal policy. The Soviet Union today is an example of the first category, the properties of which are well-known. The second category resembles a strictly confederal arrangement and is not discussed here. Instead, the discussion focuses on the latter two possibilities.

According to Western theory, a (stable valued) money functions as a pure public good via its properties of non-rival consumption and non-excludability. Moreover, money's utility expands with the domain over which it is used: the more people use a certain money, the lower are its transaction costs. Furthermore, central monetary control eliminates the inflation-prone tendency for local authorities to capture larger shares of national resources through competitive money creation (Oates, 1972). These arguments are in line with the unified currency and monetary policies prescribed by the 500 days' plan.

But this way of framing the problem circumvents an issue raised initially by Robert Mundell: namely, what constitutes an optimal currency area? (Mundell, 1961). Identifying national sovereignty with a singular money begs the question whether multiple intranational monies can be second-best when (say) the country's central bank fails to demonstrate the requisite monetary discipline.[4] Alternatively, is the argument for multiple monies compelling enough to support political independence for particular regions?

The economics' literature offers several criteria which might help determine whether the present Soviet Union, or alternatively certain sub-regions, constitute optimal currency areas. An examination of the principal arguments in this literature is useful in assessing the *economic* basis for individual Soviet republics, or sub-groups of them, adopting independent currencies.[5]

The argument for separate currencies gains tentative support from Mundell's insight that flexible exchange rates between multiple monies represent second-best responses to geographical factor immobility and price inflexibility. In particular, whenever there are countries containing regions each characterized by different industrial structures, a shift in demand from one set of products to another alters the interregional structure of demand. To offset the ensuing employment consequences in one region, the central bank expands the growth rate of the money supply but at the cost of exacerbating inflationary pressures in the other (high demand) region. Mundell's conclusion is that the transaction costs of conversion and valuation implicit in a multiple currency world must be compared with the advantages of employing two separate currencies. Despite being an aggregate supply-constrained economy, the Soviet Union exhibits significant variations in regional unemployment. For example, unemployment in Central Asia significantly exceeds that in the western Soviet Union, due in part to more rapid population growth. The potential benefits from two separate currencies in these two areas is therefore understandable.

According to Mundell, transaction costs aside, currency areas should be governed by the use of a single money whenever factor mobility can substitute for changes in real exchange rates. In contrast, when factor mobility is weak, a flexible exchange rate may be preferable to facilitate the necessary change in interregional terms of trade.[6]

Following Mundell, others have offered alternative criteria for determining the domain of optimal currency areas. For example, Ronald McKinnon (1963) suggests that if a country (region) is highly open, fixed exchange rates (i.e. a single money) may reconcile the internal and external balance more efficiently than flexible exchange rates (McKinnon, p. 717). Others have emphasized relative product diversity in conjunction with labour mobility in determining the optimality of a currency area. In particular, export diversification 'serves, *ex ante*, to forestall the need for frequent changes in the terms of trade and, therefore, for frequent changes in national exchange rates' (Kenen, 1969, p. 49).

In the Soviet Union the degree of factor mobility among republics should not be overestimated. Cultural factors such as language and family unity and logistical matters such as insufficient housing both create a considerable gulf separating the Tadzhik and Estonian labour markets, for instance. A study by Mitchneck found that while Soviet migration flows do respond to factors such as distance, investment and services similar to those in other countries, industrial employment opportunities have little impact on migration. High job security provides a likely explanation (Mitchneck, 1991). This may change as the Soviet economy moves to a more demand-constrained system. At present, however, significant impediments to labour mobility between major areas of the country (e.g. from Central Asia to Russia or even within Russia itself) and an inflexible wage system reinforce the argument for differentiated monetary policies.

An increasingly emphasized theme in the optimal currency literature is that transaction costs aside, having one's own currency is preferable even when the latter is perfectly fixed to some other currency; revenue via seigniorage (a tax on money balances) accrues which would otherwise be paid to another country if one of them holds a 'foreign money' or to a central government of which one of them is a sub-region (Fischer, 1982).[7]

Stressing the inflation tax, Canzoneri and Rogers (1990) define optimal currency areas as regimes in which the advantages of 'tax smoothing' made possible by multiple currencies outweigh the associated transaction costs. Arguing that optimal tax rates – defined as a taxation regime that distributes the total taxation required to finance an exogenous level of government spending across two instruments in such a way as to equate the marginal disutility of each tax – 'depend upon characteristics of the activities being taxed, including collection costs' which may well vary across different regions, 'regions that require the same inflation tax may form an optimal currency area'.

For example, seigniorage is an especially important form of revenue collection in regions with extensive black markets whose profits are by definition difficult to tax by conventional means. Although it is impossible to measure what percentage of economic activity occurs outside legal avenues, it is nonetheless clear that the extent of black-market activities is much greater in certain republics, notably Georgia and Armenia. Because of difficulties in collecting sufficient revenue through other channels, such republics might find seigniorage a valuable revenue source.

The benefits of control over seigniorage, however, must be weighed against higher transaction costs. Given the high integration among Soviet republics and their isolation from the world economy, emphasis on the transaction cost aspect of multiple monies seems relevant. In the RSFSR in 1988, for instance, imports (domestic and foreign) accounted for 15 per cent of consumption, while exports made up 12 per cent of production. For other republics the share of interrepublic imports and exports was even higher, averaging about 25 per cent of consumption and production of total material production respectively, and making up close to 40 per cent of consumption and production of industrial goods in republics such as Georgia, Lithuania, Moldova, Armenia, Turkmenistan and Estonia (*Ekonomicheskoe i sotsial'noe razvitie soyuznykh respublik*, 1990).[8] It must be kept in mind that integration with the global economy is trivial for most Soviet republics. Even would-be secessionist republics, unless prevented, will be forced to rely disproportionately on trade with other Soviet republics for the foreseeable future (Van Arkadie and Karlsson, 1992, Chapter 7). It must be added, however, that much of interrepublic trade is inefficient. The trend towards or away from further integration among Soviet republics as they move collectively toward a market economy is therefore difficult to predict.

Complicating this picture is the desire to accelerate integration in the global economy. In part, this presupposes the gradual introduction of currency convertibility. Economists in the regional peripheries of the Soviet Union cannot be faulted for their impatience either over Moscow's sluggish actions to facilitate rouble convertibility or over the centre's exchange-rate policy which serves to discourage exports. The problem is that republics advocating their own monies vary greatly in the product diversity and competitiveness that buttresses currency convertibility. The Russian republic, for instance, is rich in exportable resources such as gold, diamonds and timber, which could be sold as needed to support a newly convertible currency. In contrast, the Georgian republic, which lacks significant energy deposits and whose most prominent export is sub-tropical agricultural products, would face stiff competition for the limited European market from traditional European Community suppliers such as Turkey and Israel, making Georgia a much weaker candidate for a convertible currency.

Meanwhile, the more immediate issue involves the allocation of foreign exchange (hard currency) between republican and union governments. The disparities among Soviet Union republics with respect to valuta produced relative to used are significant (Brown and Belkindas, 1990, 1991). Indeed, such differences are even more pronounced with respect to oblasts, most notably among those areas in Western Siberia which shoulder the country's main valuta-generating burden relative to regions specializing in uncompetitive manufactures (Granberg and Rubinshtein, 1989, p. 26). Given that valuta in the Soviet Union holds the key to relative prosperity, is the latter's unequal regional distribution sufficient cause for taking the creation of an independent money seriously in certain republics?

As noted above, factor mobility across Soviet republics tends to be low and republic priorities are strongly influenced both by cultural factors and by relative degrees of development. The tendency for regions to specialize in certain industries also implies that as the Soviet Union moves toward a market economy, the inevitable adjustment shocks caused by shifts in demand and structural change will be concentrated in specific republics. A severe drop in demand for cotton, for example, would devastate Uzbekistan's monoculture economy. Forty-two per cent of the Russian republic's northwest region's industrial output is concentrated in the machine-building sector (*PlanEcon*, 15 January 1991), leaving it highly vulnerable to decreased demand for outmoded Soviet machinery as factories strive to become internationally competitive. Entire Soviet towns have been constructed around a single industry or even factory: for instance, the city of Tolyatti produces Zhiguli cars while certain Siberian towns are completely devoted to the petroleum industry.

More generally, the choice between fixed and flexible exchange rates and the spatial definition of optimal currency areas will depend on a complex interaction between a region's industrial structure, the types of economic disturbances that predominate (real versus monetary, supply versus demand, external versus internal), and the nature of the regional government's loss function, which influences the response to various shocks (Genberg, 1988). The interaction of these factors will determine the actual insulation properties of fixed versus flexible exchange rates in a particular situation (Argy and De Grauwe, 1990; Tyson and Kenen, 1980).

Soviet economists despairingly repeat that the republics are planning to implement their own monies at the very time when Europe is adopting a single currency. It is worth keeping in mind, however, that the economic and cultural gulf separating (say) Turkmenistan and Latvia is considerably greater than that between (say) the UK and Germany. Nevertheless, until recently the UK's desire for macroeconomic autonomy outweighed its interest in the European monetary union. Given the economic and cultural differences among Soviet republics, distinct monetary policies would theoretically provide them with powerful tools with which to pursue disparate policy objectives.

FISCAL DECENTRALIZATION AS A SUBSTITUTE FOR MULTIPLE MONIES
Arguably, these varied objectives could be amply met through autonomous regional fiscal policy. When initial conditions, preferences, or shocks differ across regions, fiscal policy independence adds policy flexibility that may eliminate the need for a decentralized monetary policy (Masson and Melitz, 1990 pp. 24–5). Particularly in the presence of substantial factor immobility, separate regional fiscal policies can influence regional levels of employment, investment and real wages: 'There is nothing especially exotic about an economy that does not use its own money' (Fischer, 1982, p. 298).[9]

However, one danger is that republican governments would borrow excessively, assuming that the central bank would monetize their debt. Regional governments would tend to overspend, since they would not have to internalize the effects of the resulting financial imbalance on other regions' welfare (Canzoneri and Diba, 1991). A concern is that localities will compete through fiscal and other incentives to attract investments; such policies can be seen as begger-thy-neighbour from the country's perspective.

At present, the Soviet Union is experiencing a variation on this localist theme. Unlike the union-level government, Soviet republics do not have access to credits from international financial markets.[10] Meanwhile, the republics have forced the central government to monetize their debt through policies of revenue diversion. In the first quarter of 1991, the central banks of the 15 republics remitted only one-third of required payments to the union budget. The republics chose to retain (and spend) tax payments earmarked by the central government for its own expenditure. As a result, the central government has obtained huge credits from the USSR Gosbank in a money-creating move. In such a second-best world an argument can be made for multiple currencies. Pressure would be placed on republic governments to balance their budgets or print their own money. Exchange rates would regulate the resulting interrepublican money imbalances.

Overspending by local governments is not the only argument against autonomous regional fiscal policies. A country (region) may find it advantageous to 'forego the right to issue its own currency and alter its exchange rate in order to participate in a major fiscal system' (Kenen, 1969, p. 47). A larger fiscal system permits funds to be redistributed to moderate the effects of regionally-concentrated shocks. This risk-sharing property of an integrated currency and fiscal system allows the deficit region (country) to smooth its adjustment process by drawing on the resources of surplus regions. Furthermore, such transfer can become a built-in automatic component of the federal tax structure (Sachs and Sala-I-Martin, 1991).

Such a mechanism, however, can only be effective if federal tax rates are high relative to regional ones, permitting significant federal tax reduction during a localized recession. The United States relies on this type of arrangement. An alternate method, however, of reducing region-specific shocks is to borrow on international capital markets. Since the European Community's federal tax is only roughly 0.5 per cent of GDP, its member countries, who are long-standing creditworthy borrowers, can continue to turn to international capital markets for stabilization purposes despite being members of a united currency area. The Soviet Union closely resembles the United States case, in that Soviet republics, like the American states, are not recognized international borrowers. Since Soviet republican governments are generally not considered creditworthy, the argument for a risk-pooling federal revenue system is strong.[11]

Such risk-pooling, however, is only advantageous if the costs of participating do not exceed the perceived value of diminished risk. Given the current Soviet federal revenue crisis and declining economic performance, the ability of central fiscal policy to alleviate regional shocks is doubtful. The republics have witnessed the inability of the union government to deal effectively with the aftermath of the Chernobyl accident, the Armenian earthquake or the ecological disaster surrounding the Aral Sea. Thus, at the union-level, the argument that a centralized fiscal policy cushions regional shocks is shaky indeed.

However, risk-pooling may be an operative factor in interrepublican relations. An 'Agreement on Economic, Scientific-Technical, and Cultural Cooperation' signed by the leaders of the four Central Asian republics and Kazakhstan in June 1990, for instance, called for the establishment of a joint fund to save the Aral Sea and to help those living in the vicinity as well as the negotiation of mutual accords on economic cooperation, financial, health, education and agricultural policy (Goble, 1990). Similarly, the three Baltic republics have signed accords calling for interregional economic cooperation. Increasingly, priority is being given to concluding interrepublic cooperation agreements (especially supply contracts) which bypass Moscow. Such limited-participation risk-pooling arrangements may prove to be increasingly popular among coalitions of republics with common cultures, economic goals or complementary industrial structures.

Fiscal federalism: redistribution

Should a redistribution policy be the purview of regional (local) or central governments? A theoretical problem with local jurisdiction over redistribution, even among a population generally committed to strong egalitarianism, is that wealthier citizens will migrate to regions with less progressive income programmes while the poor will do the opposite. Such responses can devastate regional productivity and income (Oates, 1972, pp. 7–8). The argument for vesting control over redistribution in the central government relates to lower mobility across national boundaries relative to intranational mobility.

Thus, entrusting local authorities with redistribution would appear most persuasive where serious impediments to interregional mobility within one nation render differential local redistribution standards more enforceable. Given the reluctance to relocate among many groups in Soviet society for fear of loosening familial ties or suffering the fate of minorities in republics engulfed by ethnic chauvinism, not to mention chronic housing shortages throughout the Soviet Union, there would appear to be more scope than usual for local control over redistribution policy.

Increasing ethnic identification within Soviet republics and sub-republic units theoretically might also garner additional support for local redistribution while discouraging interregional redistribution. That is, individuals may prefer helping the poor in their immediate communities rather than elsewhere. When transferring income from the rich to the poor locally, redistribution arguably enhances the welfare of both groups; hence, a first-best solution requires differing redistributive programmes in each jurisdiction (Pauly, 1970). Meanwhile, 'Who's feeding whom?' suggests strong anti-egalitarian sentiment on interregional financial flows (Brown and Belkindas, 1990).

Acknowledging the desire of republics to control redistribution within their borders, the 500 days' plan calls for most social programmes to be both planned and eventually financed by republics. The plan seeks to avoid the appearance of 'levelling' – the incentive-destroying Soviet policy of equal compensation regardless of work performed – through large-scale central redistribution. Nonetheless, the plan advocates retaining some redistributive powers in the centre. The 500 days' plan realistically assumes that given wide income disparities among republics, combined with the peculiarities of Soviet revenue collection that deprives certain poor republics of necessary financial resources, local redistribution must be supplemented with cross-republic transfers. Observers in Central Asia argue that one of the bases for a new union treaty should be the greater equalization of 'starting positions'. To some degree, union authorities and other republics concur as uneven development is partially due to confiscatory central taxation policies (Mirsaidov, 1990, p. 25). And it has been pointed out that common minimum standards for public services in a federation can be justified on efficiency grounds (Shah, 1991, p. 13). But the 500 days' plan is equally correct in recognizing the limits to richer republics' tolerance of cross-republic redistribution. The recent 'Who's feeding whom?' controversy embodies a widespread perception that most Soviet republics contribute more resources to the national economy than they receive in return. Such perceptions clearly reduce the support for fiscal redistribution. This contradiction is a potential threat to the stability of any new federal arrangement (Brown, 1991).

The 500 days' plan's proposed union-level stabilization fund epitomizes the plan's approach to balancing these conflicting interests. The stabilization fund is to be created to assist enterprises suffering through macroeconomic instability during the period of transition to a market economy. While this union-level fund will presumably provide a minimum amount of aid, individual republics will have the option of creating their own stabilization funds (*Perekhod k rynku,* 1990). The plan also calls for a universal floor for unemployment benefits and minimum wages while permitting individual republics to target supplementary funds toward these areas. Thus the plan gives the republics significant leeway in creating their own redistribution policies. The level at which funding for republic welfare programmes will be provided, however, is not made clear in the plan.

Fiscal federalism: allocation

In market economies, a clear delineation exists between public and private goods. At the same time the distribution of property among federal, state and municipal levels is clearly delineated. In the Soviet Union, the bulk of goods are produced in the state sector, and the distribution of state property among various levels of government is currently the subject of intense political manoeuvring and negotiation. All other questions of governmental jurisdiction await the resolution of this overriding problem.

Once a compromise is struck on property ownership, which level of government should produce goods to maximize allocative efficiency? The strongest case for central management arises with pure public goods, where the entire nation benefits from consumption and excludability is impossible to enforce. A classic example is national defence. Were local governments to finance such production, interregional externalities would aggravate the free-rider problem. Localities would seek to benefit from adjacent local production, leading all localities, hence the nation, to underproduce the good. In contrast, considering the value of a marginal unit to the nation, the centre is more likely to produce an efficient output level. Both the 500 days' plan and the draft union treaty appear to emphasize this principle. For example, the centre is entrusted with defence and runs the integrated interrepublic transportation and communication networks in coordination with the republics. A worker at Ukrainian Gosplan refers to this principle as applying to 'production complexes and sectors, which are of decisive importance for ensuring the functioning of the USSR economy as an organic unity of independent economies of the Union republics' (Baramykov and Nevelev, 1990, p. 20).

An important issue arises, however, when certain public goods are consumed only in certain localities because of a preference differentiation by ethnicity or geography. People select their residences at least in part based on their preferences for the amount and quality of local public services (Tiebout, 1956). In principle, public goods should be financed by the people consuming them. Thus, if central provision ignores variations in local tastes, efficiency is sacrificed. Depending on scale economies, the degree of preference diversity within a federation, and the deadweight loss from taxation-induced mobility, 'a public good that is best provided centrally in one country may be better provided by decentralized levels of government in another' (Oates, 1972, p. 31). In general:

for a given population size, the welfare gain from the decentralized provision of a particular local public good becomes greater as the diversity in individual demands within the country as a whole increases and as each geographical grouping of consumers becomes more homogeneous in terms of their demands for the good. (Oates, 1972, p. 37)

One public good which may be more efficiently produced locally is food subsidies. On 2 April 1991 the central government-determined retail prices of many food products rose two to three times in an effort to reduce government expenditure on retail subsidies. There is evidence, however, that optimally, subsidy policies should differ among republics. In Tadzhikistan, for example, while the increase in bread prices provoked bitter resentment, the rise in meat prices caused little stir. Meat is rarely available in state stores in Tadzhikistan and is not *halal* (not slaughtered according to Islamic prescriptions). Thus, Tadzhiks, accustomed to purchasing meat at above-state prices at local bazaars, paid little mind to increased state-meat prices. In Moscow, on the other hand, where farmers' market prices are three times those in Tadzhikistan, and *halal* is not an issue, the tripling of state-meat prices causes a much greater impact (Carley, 1991). This evidence suggests that differentiated meat- and bread-subsidy policies, catering to local customs and conditions, might prove more efficient.

Another example of desired republican autonomy is greater control over foreign-trade policy. Republican governments seek the ability to implement their own foreign direct investment and export stimulation programmes (Masol, 1990, p. 27). This would permit greater access to foreign exchange which in the current Soviet climate holds the key to advanced technology, higher productivity and an enhanced standard of living. An Uzbek central committee first secretary remarks that his republic does not even know where and how much cotton is shipped abroad. At the same time he suggests that his republic should retain the ability to control the dispersement of foreign-exchange revenue:

> We must not allow a situation in which every oblast, receiving foreign currency for cotton, buys passenger cars, video equipment, and telefaxes, while the most acute problems of public health, education, processing of agricultural products, and so forth are not solved. (Karimov, 1990, p. 23)

Republican demands for greater control over economic policy are often vaguely formulated and do not grapple with coordination issues. For example, consider the following rather vague statement: '... a sovereign Soviet Ukraine must possess broader rights in pursuing its own financial, credit, and taxation policy. This will allow us to take fuller account of the particular features of the development of individual regions, and provide economic encouragement to priority development of particular sectors' (Masol, 1990, pp. 27–8). In an exception to the general under-appreciation of coordination, in the spring of 1991, Russia, Ukraine and Belorussia announced that representatives would soon meet to agree on a coordinated increase in the retail prices of essential goods. For budgetary and other reasons unrelated to any lack of acknowledgement of coordination issues, certain other republics have declined to respect all-union legislation on price ceilings implemented in April 1991.

Fiscal federalism: revenue collection

The above examination of stability, allocation, and redistribution issues relates to the expenditure side of fiscal policy. The efficient division of fiscal authority between federal and regional governments, however, is also dependent on the distribution of revenue-collection authority. International experience suggests that balancing the allocation of tax and expenditure authority between the different levels of a federation is far more effective than employing intergovernmental transfers to balance regional budgets (Shah, 1991).

In the Soviet case, however, numerous factors complicate the prospects of achieving regional revenue and expenditure balance. The centrally-administered Soviet taxation system is a major roadblock. For example, an elaborate, non-uniform array of turnover (sales) taxes separate consumer (retail) and producer (wholesale) prices. Because turnover tax is highest for final consumer manufacturers, it disproportionately augments revenue in republics consuming such manufacture. In contrast, raw-material producers that predominate in certain republics generate little turnover tax. Revenues in these republics' budgets suffer accordingly.

An additional issue complicating the division of revenue-collection authority is the large amount of 'fiscal-type' taxation and expenditure that occur outside government budgets. Much enterprise income is diverted into extra-budgetary centralized funds controlled by industrial branch ministries. Branch ministries have been major players in the regional distribution of funds in what amounts to government subsidized investment.

In addition to such complications to balancing revenues and expenditure, a clear, satisfactory division of federal, republic and regional revenue-collection authority has yet to be mapped out. According to the 1977 Soviet constitution, all decision-making power concerning taxes is explicitly granted to the federal government. Since 1989, however, the USSR Supreme Soviet has passed two laws, 'On the Basic Principles of Economic Relations of the USSR and the Union and Autonomous Republics' and 'On the General Principles for Local Self-Government and Local Economy in the USSR' (*Izvestiya*, 15 April 1990, pp. 1–2) which grant limited taxation powers to lower regional governments. The republics, however, have rejected these laws as not providing sufficient revenue-raising autonomy.

The call for a one channel taxation system in several proposed Soviet plans and its *de facto* occurrence in several republics raises certain difficult policy questions. For example, the absence of an autonomous central revenue base eliminates the possibility of macroeconomic fiscal policy. It also opens the door to individual bargaining between the centre and the republics over financial contributions to the centre. One possible outcome of such an arrangement is reflected in the current exacerbation of the central Soviet budget deficit.

Fiscal federalism: institution building

The Musgrave division of the functions of government between stabilization, redistribution and allocation is traditionally described in a narrow manner, considering only the provision of public and private goods in the usual sense. This restricted definition, however, fails to account for the most important federalist issue facing the Soviet Union and other centrally planned economies today: the allocation of institution-building (constitution) authority:

> The fact that resources are also required to establish and maintain institutions and decision-making rules is not explicitly taken into account. In order to be able to apply economic analysis not only to the provision function, but also to the constitution function, the three Musgravian notions have to be extended: *Allocation* aims at the efficient use of resources not only for producing private and public goods, but also for establishing and managing institutions, and for controlling the jurisdiction of public institutions and the rights of private agents. *Distribution* refers no longer only to income and wealth, but also to the fair and equitable assignment of powers, authority and responsibilities to public institutions on the one hand and of rights to private agents on the other. *Stabilization* finally is extended to comprise also stability of society and steady development of its political system. (Biehl, 1991)

At what level should economic institution building be conducted in the Soviet Union? On the one hand, the USSR's vast diversity of cultures and levels of development suggest that regional governments, catering to the specific needs of a given locality, would be best suited to designing economic reform programmes. The Soviet Union's relatively low factor mobility provides a significant degree of market segmentation, suggesting that independent reform programmes might be successfully conducted without requiring the introduction of separate monies or spurring significant labour migration. Could regional Soviet authorities, for example, successfully conduct independent privatization, price reform and banking policies? To what extent is the devolution of institution-building authority efficient and desirable?

While recognizing the need for decreased central control, Soviet reformers arguably have not demonstrated the requisite appreciation of the macroeconomic consequences from competing reform experiments in different republics. In contrast, the imposition of one uniform reform strategy for the Soviet Union overall runs the risk that this single reform blueprint is flawed. The larger the number of reform experiments *ceteris paribus* the greater the likelihood that one will prove effective and worthy of emulation (Biehl, 1991, pp. 9–10; Summers, 1990).

Various republics, including Estonia and Lithuania, have implemented certain pricing measures which contradict centrally directed norms. For instance, Estonia raised the price of vodka on its territory by several times in early 1990. In contrast, after the 2 April 1991 centrally-imposed price rises which trebled the price of flour, Tadzhikistan was searching for a means to reinstate bread subsidies at the regional level (Carley, 1991).

Given the vastly varied cultures and regional economic potentials existing in the Soviet Union, an argument can be made that the regional pacing of price deregulation would allow for the greater control of inflation since regions could monitor local supply and demand conditions and set price ceilings accordingly. Barring interrepublic customs barriers, however, variations in pricing policies will be difficult to sustain. Thus, a republic which subsidizes consumer goods will find that a significant portion of those subsidy payments go straight into the pockets of the black market, while the goods are consumed in neighbouring republics. If republics choose to erect customs barriers to protect regional pricing regimes, the Soviet money supply would be effectively divided, raising the transaction costs of interrepublican trade. Because it can only succeed if markets are isolated, regional price reform is problematic. Other types of institution-building, such as a privatization policy, face potentially fewer obstacles if conducted at the regional level. For example, while Armenia has taken great steps towards privatizing the majority of its agricultural land, a working group of the Uzbek council of ministers stresses the importance of irrigated cultivation and the associated need to revive cooperative ownership and utilization of *kolkhoz* property: ' ... neither the republic's current socioeconomic conditions nor its historical traditions allow us to pose the question of introducing private land ownership' (Uzbek SSR Council of Ministers, 1990, p. 85).

Section II: Club theory approach to federalism and marketization

Richard Cooper is exactly right in suggesting that regional blocs make most economic sense in a world of public goods. Aside from transportation costs, the prices of private goods generally should be equalized throughout the world. For example, it is generally preferable for national and world welfare to lower tariffs uniformly than to establish preferential trade arrangements. Regional as opposed to global integration is justified, however, when strong differences in preferences and values dictate significant variations in the types of public goods provided. Most profoundly, differences in public goods' provision should reflect fundamental variations in their approach to property relations, risk-bearing and other systemic features as well as particular types of public services (Cooper, 1986). Thus, the 'optimal combination of communities or regions for an integrated area' may involve a grouping of several countries or alternatively, sub-divisions of a single country (ibid., p. 124).

This way of viewing integration moves beyond and in some sense rejects Jack Viner's notion of customs unions as trade creating-trade diverting entities and Robert Mundell's trade-off between transaction costs and macroeconomic autonomy (optimal currency areas) (Cooper, 1986, p. 126). Instead this perspective leads directly to a notion of 'clubs'. Communities unite in regional blocs to attain distinct public goods, including certain redistribution schemes, 'a regulatory framework for economic and social transactions' and a broader ideological commitment to a particular social system and nationalism (ibid., p. 126).[12]

Given the extreme income and cultural heterogeneity of the Soviet Union, indeed even within single republics, the most applicable branch of club theory deals with discriminatory clubs in which *heterogeneous* agents jointly consume not only a shared good, but also the attributes of the other members. In such a club:

> Each member has a fixed vector of characteristics that is made available to the other members according to his utilization rate of the club. Heavier users provide the club with a larger amount of their attributes than less heavy users. The total available quantity of any membership attribute depends upon the aggregate utilization rates of all members and the amount of that attribute associated with each member. By varying the utilization rate, a member determines his or her consumption of the other members' characteristics as well as that of the shared good; a jointness in consumption exists. Members' characteristics may be viewed by the other members as generating either an increase ... or a decrease ... in utility. (Cornes and Sandler, 1986, p. 184)

In the following discussion we posit that the public good which a would-be club of Soviet republics shares is the transition process to a market economy. The 500 days' plan and other market transition proposals assume that all republics agree at least upon the desirability of the transition to a market economy. In order for this transition to be achieved, however, republics must agree to implement concrete, coordinated steps toward this goal. In theory, the most effective means to achieve such cooperation is to shatter the existing federal system, establish republic sovereignty and then allow the independent republics to recontract. Given the current independence-oriented mindset in the republics, voluntary entry and exit are crucial in any recontracting process. Moreover, the ultimate federal (confederal) system should be sufficiently flexible to accommodate as much diversity in membership terms as possible (Kux, 1990a, p. 7).

The applicability of club theory to the Soviet Union can best be understood by confining our analysis to the interactions of two regions: the Baltic republics and Russia.[13] These regions are distinct in many respects but most obviously in their physical endowments and economic cultures. The bulk of the Soviet Union's most critical energy and metal resources are concentrated in Russia. In contrast, as Moscow's blockade of Lithuania dramatized, the Baltics are conspicuous in their relative lack of such endowments. The Baltic republics, however, are home to the most Western-oriented Soviet citizens, with historical market-economy experience. With their arguably greater acceptance of entrepreneurialism and associated risk-taking, relatively high labour skills and favourable port access, the Baltics are good candidates for leading an experiment in rapid marketization or for luring foreign capital via free economic zones, especially if they facilitated access to the Soviet heartland. Finally, the Baltics bring a tradition of non-communal agriculture which improves the chances for successful land privatization there (Aganbegyan, 1990, p. 55).

The Russians, to the contrary, are often depicted as craving stability and income equality; the hostility directed at Russian cooperatives and private shops corroborates this suspicion. An historical distrust of foreign commercial presences combined with an almost total lack of market experience, also strongly suggest that Russia is ill-fit to play a vanguard role in the USSR's marketization process. Despite the virtually unanimous passage of the 500 days' plan by the Russian Supreme Soviet, the average Russian remains ambivalent and sceptical about embarking on a transition process which will surely involve great social dislocation.

Given the disparate attributes of the Russian and Baltic peoples, it is logical that by pooling each side's advantages, a mutually-beneficial alliance in a pursuit of a market economy could be forged. Alliance stability tends to rest on the superiority of a collective good (Olson and Zeckhauser, 1966, p. 269) as well as on an efficient intra-alliance taxing arrangement (Sandler, 1975). The following scenario of Baltic–Russian club formation illustrates the type of multiregional club which could form among multiple combinations of Soviet regions.

Assume that Russia produces two goods – energy and the public good (the transition process) – while the Baltics produce a consumer tradeable as well as the public good. By assumption, Russia is less efficient in producing the public good than are the Baltics; meanwhile, energy (along with entrepreneurialism) is a necessary input in the production of the public good. In the absence of (cheap) energy, the Baltics would have to allocate resources away from the production of the public good in order to produce an exportable consumer good to finance necessary (but now more expensive) energy imports.

With their comparative advantage in producing the public good, the Baltics' welfare is raised when the availability of cheap Russian energy allows them to specialize in public good production. Russia, in return, will eventually benefit from 'spill-ins' from Baltic production of the collective good (the market transition). These spill-ins would allow a reallocation of resources away from the public good to the 'private' good (oil) in line with Russia's comparative advantage. Russia's welfare would thus be raised despite higher Russian taxes (defined as the opportunity cost of selling the Baltic republics energy cheaply rather than at world-market prices). Such an arrangement would presumably further benefit Russia by allowing it selectively to appropriate positive aspects of the Baltic market-transition process while remaining largely isolated from many (particularly ill) effects of the transitional learning process. Thus, the Baltics would essentially serve as Russia's filter – allowing the Russian republic to 'preview' the effects of potential market-transition policies.

In our scenario of emancipated Soviet republics recontracting with each other, in principle the next step would be to examine the potential participation of the remaining republics in the Baltic–Russian 'club'. Incentives to accept specific additional members into the alliance would be based on the notion that (differential) 'tolls' regulate the use of a club: 'Some members with desirable traits may be paid to join, since they generate enough positive characteristics to offset any crowding caused by their presence' (Cornes and Sandler, 1986, pp. 184–5). Others, who offer little in the way of unique attributes but threaten to increase 'congestion' by absorbing a disproportionate percentage of club resources (such as all-union funds), may be refused admission. The potential contribution (or cost) of each Soviet republic's participation in the alliance would be judged based on its unique attributes.

As described, a recontracting among Soviet republics based on a concept of 'clubs' involves no central authority. This appears consistent with direct trade arrangements developing among the Soviet republics today and accords well with premises about the efficacy of informal cooperation among state governments ('To Form a More Perfect Union?', *Harvard Law Review*, 1989). However, it is not difficult to imagine a role for a central authority, particularly during a transformation as immense as the projected Soviet transition to a market system. For one thing, a central authority can serve to arbitrate conflicts among the republics and enforce contracts. Moreover, it is critical that at least minimum coordination exists with respect to price, tax, antimonopoly and privatization policies and to avoid unprofitable interregional competition for foreign capital. Such coordination presumably requires an active central government.

As discussed in the section on optimal currency areas, the choice of stabilization (and exchange-rate) policy is partly a function of industrial structure, the nature of disturbances that tend to impact particular regions as well as the nature of the government's loss function. That discussion centred on the pros and cons for republics of fixed versus flexible exchange rates (single versus multiple monies), including insulation from external shocks.

In our club model, while the question of exchange rates between the Baltic and Russia is not considered, the assumption is that Russia is partly insulated from an external disturbance through some unspecified mechanism, while the Baltic is not. The trade-off for both parties shifts from macroeconomic stability within the union versus republican policy autonomy to the returns to learning by doing versus the social and political cost of direct exposure to world economic forces.

A further implicit cost to avoiding such direct exposure is that the discipline imposed on internal government policy by world economic conditions is less immediate, which may aggravate the extent of internal disturbances resulting from inadvisable public policy (Currie, forthcoming). Given the different economic structures and loss functions between the two regions, they approach this trade-off differently. Thus, it is not a question of gradualism versus shock therapy for the Soviet Union, but whether either may be more appropriate for particular regions of the country.

In short, the challenge is to establish a union which requires a sharing of resources and responsibilities but which can also accommodate varied interests. While the conception outlined reflects the spirit of Gorbachev's notion of 'a differentiation of federal ties ... taking into account the specifics of the region, each people, their culture and traditions' (quoted in Kux, 1990a, p. 7), it is strictly relevant for the transition period to a market economy. Once that transition is completed, there is nothing to restrict subsequent recontracting.

Section III: Game-theoretic approaches to interrepublic bargaining

As the Soviet economic and constitutional crises deepened during 1990, relations between Moscow and the republics grew increasingly strained. Subordinating a comprehensive re-examination of Soviet federalism to economic restructuring, Gorbachev had intended to forestall separatist trends while preventing conservative forces from reasserting their traditional prerogatives. Meanwhile, a deteriorating economy combined with glasnost was reawakening historic interethnic strife. Resurfacing nationalist forces began to challenge the principles of Soviet federalism contained in the country's 1922 constitution.[14]

Such is the difficult environment in which Gorbachev has proposed a draft union treaty designed to refashion economic relations among the Soviet Union's constituent republics. While certain Soviet republics have declined to sign any union treaty, others have accepted such a treaty in principle. Some republics are willing to accept a loose confederation whose members are independent states. The 23 April 1991 document signed by Gorbachev and the leaders of nine republics appears to concede that even if a central power (Moscow) remains, several republics may leave the union. The remaining republics tentatively agree to interact on the basis of certain shared principles, including the mutual provision of most-favoured-nation status. Such status implies a quasi-customs union in which transactions are conducted in roubles at internal, regulated prices. Those republics which decline to participate would presumably trade in hard currency at world market prices. Both the April agreement and the subsequent anti-crisis economic coalition of ten republics highlight the endogeneity of federal structures and coalition formation. This foreshadows continued, complex bargaining among republics as each struggles for the maximal attainment of its goals.

Such an environment, eminently strategic in structure, provides an ideal basis for the application of game theory. This section examines bargaining among constituent regions of a federation. A series of game-theoretic, political-economy-type models have been constructed to address particular features of the current negotiations surrounding a new union treaty in the Soviet Union (Asilis and Brown, 1991a, 1991b, and 1991c). These models distinguish between various types of 'centres': no central planner, a benign arbitrator (with no motives beyond securing efficient allocation within the union) and an 'emperor' (i.e. itself a strategic actor, motivated to maintain the system). Based on these models, an assessment can be made of conditions under which interrepublican agreements arbitrated or coordinated by Moscow can yield efficient outcomes, and, consequently, would be preferable to pure interrepublican bargaining (without central arbitration). This approach also allows for the potential impact of foreign players (Asilis and Brown, 1991b).

Efficiency and stability of decentralized versus centrally arbitrated regional reform in the Soviet Union: the non-interventionist case

A formal description of interrepublic negotiations is highly complex because of the multiple dimensions involved. These include the large number of union republics (not to mention sub-republic entities), heterogeneous preferences among the republics regarding the outlines of a new federalist regime, disparities in the perceived costs of participation in federal arrangements, the large asymmetries in size and factor endowments among the republics, and the sheer uncertainty concerning the multiple shapes a new Soviet federation could take. Differing degrees of risk aversion among republics also yield important implications about the various types of coalition arrangements.[15]

Negotiations among Soviet republics over the transition to a new regime are best modelled within non-cooperative bargaining environments. Such environments can be described in terms of the following variables: 1) number of players; 2) fixed versus time-varying set of players; 3) the object over which bargaining occurs; 4) reservation value (outside option value or threat point);[16] 5) information structure: complete versus incomplete; 6) symmetric versus asymmetric players; 7) time horizon: static versus dynamic; 8) risk sensitivity; 9) efficient versus inefficient bargaining schemes; and 10) decentralized bargaining versus bargaining by arbitration. The types of outcomes which are obtained depend on which of the above assumptions are made. The non-cooperative bargaining model most appropriate for capturing Soviet reality is one that is dynamic and allows for (a minimum of) 15 asymmetric players operating under incomplete information.

The reasons why incomplete information is the only relevant environment include: 1) information concerning how well Soviet republics perform, individually and collectively, is unclear. This largely stems from the peculiar value principles (hence, prices) under Soviet central planning; 2) potential improvements in economic performance will be a function not only of the eventual (market-based) system but also of external factors such as the international terms of trade, foreign country commercial and aid policies, and the outside perception of sustainability of any regime change in the Soviet Union, factors all of which entail uncertainty; 3) besides uncertainty based in country-wide systemic properties, some information can be considered private to individual republics. For example, republic authorities would probably know with greater certainty the production possibilities of the enterprises located on their territory. In part, this reflects proximity. More fundamentally, local enterprises and popularly elected republic authorities probably view themselves more as natural allies in the scramble over natural resources, as compared with the all-union authorities who must balance competing sectional and regional demands.

In an incomplete informational environment, special mechanisms must be introduced to yield an efficient bargaining process (Myerson and Satterthwaite, 1983). Asilis and Brown (1991c) model two groups of republics who act as both buyers and sellers of unification. The cost of group B (A) supplying unification to group A (B) corresponds to the value to group B (A) from secession (i.e., the opportunity cost of unification).

This model generates the following result: if the pay-off (e.g. GNP growth per capita or some alternative welfare measure) obtained under unification by any republic in the worst state of the world (such as extremely adverse terms-of-trade shocks) is less than the pay-off obtained under secession in the most favourable state of the world (e.g. highly favourable wealth effect, such as oil discovery or oil-price decreases for a net oil importer) then no efficient bargaining process among republics exists. This points to inefficiency in the bargaining process among union republics and motivates the search for new institutional arrangements.

Which mechanisms exist, if any, that would implement efficient arrangements among Soviet republics? We show that an arbiter, to whom individual republics report concerning their private information, achieves interrepublican agreement efficiently under reasonable conditions. The arbiter's role is straightforward. Both republic groups involved in each sale of unification agree to announce their private information to the arbitrator simultaneously. The arbitrator's sole role is to facilitate information exchange between groups of republics; it reaps no individual pay-off. It is shown that truthful revelation by both groups constitutes a Nash equilibrium and that this type of mechanism is always efficient.[17]

This finding is important because it illustrates that given the characteristics of the Soviet bargaining environment – asymmetric bargaining positions and incomplete information – efficient bargaining outcomes among republic groups can be achieved only through a central arbitrator who facilitates informational exchange. Certain republics, such as Moldova, are insisting that negotiations among republics be conducted without any central authority, the 'fifteen plus zero' formula (Socor, 1991). This is also the spirit of the five previous meetings in Tallinn among representatives exclusively from republic and sub-republic levels. Our findings, however, show that because of incomplete information, such unarbitrated talks will yield inefficient bargaining results.

We also link asymmetric bargaining power among Soviet republics to differing degrees of risk aversion. In particular, assuming that smaller republics (in general exhibiting a less varied spectrum of natural resources as compared to their larger counterparts) are relatively risk averse, then crucial equity implications obtain for Soviet government policy.[18] For instance, if the centre structures interrepublican negotiations by partitioning republics into two groups – large and small – then by virtue of the smaller republics' higher relative risk aversion and the two-player nature of the bargaining, the negotiations will favour the larger republics. The result is that any policy that increases the probability of unification by encouraging information disclosure or increased communication across republics (directly or indirectly through Moscow) yields a non-egalitarian equilibrium bargaining result.

Efficiency and stability of interrepublican coalitional arrangements

The model discussed above portrays simple regional (republican) government recontracting over the terms of trade (Asilis and Brown, 1991a). Given the increasing probability of actual secession in the Soviet Union, the issue shifts from the equity/efficiency of interrepublican recontracting to the potential alliances among republics and the central government.

First, a social planner, whose sole charge is to maximize the sum of republic utilities (welfare), is introduced into the model (Asilis and Brown, 1991c). The presence of such a social planner implies a confederal arrangement in which the taxation and expenditure authority is delegated to the central government by regional authorities. An arrangement advocated by El'tsin, for example, supports a loose confederation or league of states based on direct treaties among republics (Kux, 1990b, p. 19).

The social planner is charged in one case with solving the unconstrained problem of permitting individual republics to secede or remain in the union based solely on each republic's utility. In another (constrained) case, the social planner must choose whether or not the simultaneous secession of all republics or, alternatively, the maintenance of the existing union, is socially optimal.

Second, we model the (arguably more realistic) case in which a central planner supplants the (altruistic) social planner and becomes an 'emperor' who interacts strategically with the republics. The purpose of this characterization is to ascribe some independent agenda to the central authority. Specifically, the centre is concerned foremost with maintaining the 'empire' and a particular social system – call it socialism. The republics must decide whether to initiate actions intended to break away from the union (governed by central authority and planning) or work towards the consolidation of the present regime.

The 'emperor' scenario with its strategic manoeuvring between centre and republics provides an apt model of current trends in the Soviet Union. In 1990, for example, Estonia, a republic which is openly pushing for independence, became the first Soviet republic to introduce a 'one-channel' budget system which requires all enterprises to pay tax to the republic budget. Estonia intended to pay a lump-sum to the all-union budget for federal services. Moscow counteracted this Estonian move toward 'confederal' relations by insisting on a transfer of 341 million roubles for 1990, roughly twice the amount that Estonia had previously contributed. When Estonia refused to pay, Moscow cut the republic's fish product and feed-grain subsidies, forcing Estonian authorities to raise prices. The deadlock was finally broken in October 1990 when Estonia agreed to pay 250 million roubles to Moscow. Other instances of republic-centre interaction, such as the 'banking war' and Latvia's unilateral offer to pay $400 million toward Soviet foreign-debt service, also demonstrate the increased role of strategic manoeuvring.

In the model, a combination of the republic's wealth (ω), degree of risk-aversion or perhaps more accurately, entrepreneurism (θ), and 'love of freedom' (β) determines each republic's actions. In determining the types of interrepublican coalitions that may arise in support or opposition to the central government, we need empirical proxies for these coefficients. Multiple indicators are used to assign these values to individual republics which are then ranked accordingly.

The 'wealth' variable ω should capture the resource feasibility of a given republic mounting a secessionist campaign. Values for the β variable which capture the republics' 'love of freedom' convey not only a theoretical desire to break away from central planning (and the current Soviet Union), but also the willingness to back this desire with concrete steps and resources. One factor that may lower this value below what it otherwise would be is intrarepublic ethnic tension; the latter strengthens Moscow's leverage within the republic as the would-be protector of minorities.

The third value considered here is relative risk aversion or entrepreneurism (θ). It is crucial to emphasize that θ applies to estimates of overall risk aversion for the representative individual in a given republic *independent* of the desire and commitment to achieve independence. This can be compared through a variety of measures, including the per capita amount of private labour activity or cooperatives or private plots as a share of total agricultural output.

The willingness of non-coordinated republics to commit resources towards either supporting or thwarting the central authority's survival is a product of a complex interaction between given republics' ω, β, and θ values. The resulting actions are examined in the context of two possible states of the world:
 – the continuance of central planning;
 – the destruction of central planning ('freedom').
Each of these states may be further characterized as sustaining a union of republics or allowing secession. The state of the world achieved will be the one towards which the majority of resources have been committed by all regions combined, i.e. the balance of resource allocations in support of central planning or freedom made by each individual region.

Given a specific definition of a republic's expected utility (see Asilis and Brown, 1991c), the model shows that the optimal support/oppose action for the individual non-coordinating republic varies as follows:

1 A republic with a strong love of freedom and low risk aversion will oppose the central planner.
2 A republic with a strong love of freedom but high risk aversion will support the centre.
3 A republic with a weak love of freedom and low risk aversion will oppose the centre.
4 A republic with a weak love of freedom and high risk aversion will support the central planner.

It follows that in an uncoordinated environment, low risk aversion is a necessary condition for a freedom-loving republic to support the centre's downfall, whereas high risk aversion is a necessary condition for a centre-loving republic to support the centre. The inefficiency of uncoordinated arrangements is demonstrated by the fact that in this situation, even if all republics are freedom-loving but are risk averse, then all republics will find it individually optimal to support the centre. This paradox bears witness to the potential gains to coordination.

Club formation and coalitional equilibria among republics and the centre

Once we allow for interrepublic coordination in the context of strategic bargaining by both republican and central agents, the possibility of coalitions among republics arises. A coalitional equilibrium can be defined as an arrangement (the actual amount of investment in support of or in opposition to the centre) which is feasible to each republic and such that no republic has the incentive to either deviate unilaterally, nor in conjunction with other republics, within or without its coalition. The object of every coalition is to maximize the utilities of its member republics.

An innovative model is designed to help analyse the nature of coalitional arrangements, and specifically questions of efficiency within coalition formation. The republics' underlying ω, β and θ endowments in principle interact to generate a number of possible formations: the maintenance of a federation of 15 republics or multiple possible sub-sets of republic coalitions. The model is additionally capable of depicting the (anticipated significant) variations in the powers republics across different coalitions cede to the centre as well as in the specific parameters of the new system they (collectively) wish to build.

The scenarios generated by the model will not only provide the potential characteristics of republic coalitions that may form, but will also suggest the means by which Western economic assistance may influence the coalitional choices made by the Soviet republics. External elements, including the application of Western export credits, can influence the Soviet republics' choice of coalition arrangements. Thus, the West's economic policies should aim to promote the types of coalition outcomes which are regarded as desirable.[19]

Section IV: Conclusion

Were the Soviet Union a stable federation, the system directors could worry about the proper sequencing of market-type reforms. Were the Soviet Union instead already a mixed market economy with a predominance of private property, intellectual effort would be focused on reallocating expenditure and taxation authority among various levels of government. In the absence of both a stable federation and a market economy, the processes of Soviet marketization and federalization will be jointly determined. This paper applies economic theory to this dual challenge.

The central thread uniting the Soviet republics is support for marketization. However, the specific strategies and tactics employed to achieve this common goal evidently vary among the republics and, indeed, along sub-republic lines. Meanwhile, they begin this transition with very limited common bonding which might be provided (say) by pride in Soviet super-power status, support for the principle of risk-sharing and a guaranteed minimum living standard, or a commitment to certain existing institutions. The resulting instability of the existing federation based on a virtual central monopoly of property and decision-making violates the underlying requirement of federalism in market economies – common adherence to a system of values and institutions. Is general allegiance to a future of markets and a shared history enough to bind these disparate states together?

The theories and models discussed in this paper bring varied strengths and weaknesses to the task of helping to resolve the Soviet federal dilemma. For example, the theory of fiscal federalism, combined with the optimum currency literature, places in broad focus the efficiency and equity implications of the specific delimitations of national and sub-national governmental authority. In contrast, these theories are less useful on dynamic issues of transition. And they are weak in addressing the consequences of acute heterogeneity within a population; the elasticity of responses to changes in governmental policy are unlikely to be geographically uniform within large multicultural states.

To be useful to Soviet reformers, the theory of fiscal federalism must be stretched beyond an environment of well-defined fiscal structures to incorporate the task of institution-building. In erecting institutions, the central challenge lies in realizing a feasible balance between macroeconomic stability within the union and sufficient republican autonomy. One tentative conclusion is that such a balance is easier to attain in certain areas like property reform and social policy compared to other attempts at policy devolution such as stabilization and price reform.

The debate over who should control monetary and fiscal policies strikes to the heart of this tension between stability and autonomy. Given vast cultural diversity, limited labour mobility, disparate industrial structures with a correspondingly greater likelihood of regionally concentrated shocks, the inefficient nature of goods integration and the absence of a capital market, the case against separate republican monies within the Soviet Union cannot be as easily dismissed as it would be in more homogenous and integrated countries. Nevertheless, the transaction costs of multiple Soviet currencies would probably be high and serve to reinforce growing political divisions.

With the adoption of one common money, the importance of independent fiscal policies increases in the eyes of republican authorities. However, in the current political environment, higher spending in hopes of central bank monetization would be tempting for republican governments. This has beggar-thy-neighbour qualities and risks macroeconomic disaster. Thus, stability requires strictly balanced republican budgets or enforceable limits on fiscal deficits.

Nevertheless, 'while some centralization of fiscal decision-making is required in a currency area, the need is much less than for monetary policy' (Tower and Willett, 1976, p. 25). In terms of allocative and redistributive functions, a much greater devolution of expenditure and taxation authority should be countenanced within the Soviet Union as compared to most states. Given marked variations in regional preferences including over fundamental systemic properties, combined with limited factor mobility, it is efficient to allow republic provision of most public goods. Furthermore, given strong interethnic misunderstanding and even hostility, republican governments should be granted more control over redistribution policy among their own citizens than is customary elsewhere. Nevertheless, given the strong variations in revenue capacities among the Soviet republics, a commitment to minimum levelling would be impossible without some redistribution from richer to poorer regions.

The case for differentiated reform programmes need not presuppose republican monopoly over local reform. Rather, a differentiated federal targeting of republican economic programmes is arguably first-best given the centre's theoretical ability to internalize coordination concerns. For example, some coordination of republican price and taxation reforms would appear essential. However, with imperfect information and issues of strategic behaviour that affect federal government credibility, a second-best approach of differentiated reform programmes conducted at the republican level, supplemented perhaps with federal guarantees, may be preferable.

The merit of applying club theory to the Soviet Union – discriminatory club theory in particular – is its explicit recognition of the constraints that a multinational Soviet Union places on the transition process. Accordingly, it stresses a system of recontracting among republics, similar to the broad conception underlying the Shatalin plan, but, in contrast to the latter, one which highlights the diversity of strengths and weaknesses that each republic brings to the common goal or public good – the transition to a market economy. While the theory of fiscal federalism presupposes greater stability and political legitimacy than appears to be present in the Soviet Union today, club theory provides a formal framework for analysing the dynamic problem of cooperation among disparate agents united by a common transitional target. In certain ways it captures the essence of recent agreements struck among Moscow and a majority of Soviet Union republics.

The stability of such an arrangement depends both on the merit of the collective good – the proper design of marketization strategy – and the efficiency of the intra-alliance taxing scheme. In our model the taxing scheme rests on the superior endowment of energy and non-energy raw materials in some republics and the cultural endowments of greater entrepreneurism in others. Other taxing arrangements can certainly be envisioned.

In applying the theory of clubs to the Soviet Union, three overriding questions surface. First, is it feasible to design a geographically differentiated transition strategy in which the 'front lines' serve as shock absorbers or filters that to some degree moderate the initial ill effects of the learning process? Or is there no alternative to a uniform application of shock therapy? Second, what kind of an exclusion mechanism can be imposed that resolves the 'free rider' dilemma? Third, what role does the centre play?

The issue of regional filters is complex and worthy of future study. In an important sense, such a phenomenon existed in the CMEA system as part of these countries' state monopoly of foreign trade. A major objective of this system was to insulate its members from adverse world shocks. A potential byproduct of such arrangements, however, is to mask evolving opportunity costs and thus the suggested need and pull for structural change. As East European experience shows, ignoring such signals can sacrifice long-term growth in return for temporary stability (Brown, 1991). The issue, then, is whether the controlled exposure to direct foreign competition in our framework, with some republics serving as a partial buffer, will effectively facilitate the transition to a market system in the remaining republics.

A variety of potential exclusion mechanisms for internalizing benefits, hence consolidating a club, can be entertained. One possibility has been suggested in the agreement among nine republics and Gorbachev. Here 'most-favoured-nation' status is granted to the nine and denied to the remaining republics. The latter presumably will be required to trade at world market prices and in hard currency rather than at intraclub prices. The stability of this arrangement is questionable, given the desire of Russia and other raw-material-producing republics to export these goods at higher world-market prices. A second possible exclusion mechanism would be a complete embargo on trade with non-signatories. Finally, positive spillovers to non-participants in such an arrangement might be precluded by adopting specific production technologies requiring components only available within the club.

All such arrangements provide examples in which members would find it costly to deviate from club conventions. In the absence of such standards, which effectively segment markets and exclude free riders, clubs are less likely to form and/or be sustained. A further obstacle to their formation is that the individual benefit that club membership ostensibly yields is itself subject to uncertainty. Finally, moral hazard and enforceability problems abound, with all members serving simultaneously as principles with respect to others' assignments and agents with respect to their own assignment within the club.

Reference has already been made to the potential coordinating role that the centre can play. The centre can also establish credible rules of the game, including federal guarantees for minimum social benefits and foreign investment. For example, foreign investors may hesitate to commit funds in one republic for fear that a subsequent action by another republic could be detrimental. Such would be the case if the latter republic provided some sort of export subsidy to its firms which could then undercut an enterprise in which a Western firm had invested. Such extra uncertainty and risk raises the premium above the world opportunity cost for foreign investment in the country. Federal guarantees to would-be investors which apply uniform standards across the country would serve to lower this premium and lure a greater quantity of foreign funds than arguably would be the case with interrepublican competition for foreign capital. However, in the simple model of club theory sketched in this paper, the stability of the arrangement attributable to a centre's coordination role is not formally explored.

The advantage of the bargaining, game-theoretic approach outlined in this paper over alternative frameworks is the former's focus on endogenous outcomes of complex interactions among the republics. The difficulty of predicting such outcomes reflects the general equilibrium character of the solutions to activities involving interacting agents who differ along many dimensions. Therefore, this approach allows us to consider many alternative configurations following from varying assumptions about the nature of the agents – in this case, Soviet republics. For example, multiple coalitions, including customs-union type arrangements, could form out of a break-up of the Soviet Union. The allocations of political and economic functions can differ among such formations.

The role of the centre may also be radically different across the resulting sub-groupings or within a single revamped Soviet Union. For example, will central authorities resemble the benign social planner paradigm in which the centre functions essentially as an elicitor and/or coordinator of information or enforcer of system-wide rules established by consensus? Or alternatively, will the centre be imbued with substantial regulatory powers and wield its own strategic agenda? Such an agenda may involve efforts to maintain elements of the existing system as well as to control the reform programme, including what it decides to devolve to lower administrative levels.

The coalitions of republics emerging from this strategic bargaining environment, including their internal patterns of assigned rights and responsibilities, are also sensitive to various types of centre subsidy and taxation schemes, as well as foreign-country aid or other policies. The distinctive quality of the bargaining approach is that it does not impose an exogenous structure on outcomes, such as requiring all union republics to remain within the federation.

In conclusion, the Soviet Union today faces the unenviable task of restructuring the federation while altering its economic system. By suggesting how certain Western models can yield insights to aid in this enormous intellectual challenge, this paper aims to contribute a richer conceptual framework and spark more creative thinking on the combined problem of federalism and marketization.

References

Aganbegyan, Abel, (1990) *FBIS*, 27 September.

Aleksashenko, Sergei, (1991) 'Reform of the Fiscal System in the Soviet Federation: The Main Complexities and Possible Solutions', paper prepared for the Senior Policy Seminar on Intergovernmental Fiscal Relations and Macroeconomic Management in Large Countries, New Delhi, India, 26–28 February.

Argy, Victor, and Paul De Grauwe, (eds) (1990) *Choosing an Exchange Rate Regime: The Challenge for Smaller Industrial Countries*, Washington, DC: International Monetary Fund.

Asilis, Carlos M., and Stuart S. Brown, (1990) 'Efficiency and Stability of

Decentralized versus Centrally Arbitrated Regional Reform in the Soviet Union: The Non-interventionist Case', working paper #90-22, Department of Economics, Georgetown University, December.

Asilis, Carlos M., and Stuart S. Brown, (1991a) 'Efficiency and Stability of Decentralised versus Centrally Arbitrated Regional Reform in the Soviet Union,' Stockholm Institute of Soviet and East European Economics, Working Paper No. 24.

Asilis, Carlos M., and Stuart S. Brown, (1991b) 'Western Aid and Soviet Reform: the Role of Coordination', Stockholm Institute of Soviet and East European Economics, Working Paper No. 25.

Asilis, Carlos M., and Stuart S. Brown, (1991c) 'Coalitional Formation in a Reforming Federal CPE', Stockholm Institute of Soviet and East European Economics, Working Paper No. 26.

Baramykov, Ye. and Nevelev, A. (1990) 'Development of Interrepublic Relations Under Conditions of Expanded Economic Independence of the Union Republics', *Ekonomika Sovetskoy Ukrainy*, May, No. 5; *JPRS–UEA–90–028*, 15 August, pp. 17–27.

Biehl, Dieter (1991) 'Intergovernmental Fiscal Relations and Macroeconomic Management – Possible Lessons from a Federal Case: Germany', draft of paper prepared for World Bank Seminar, New Delhi, 26–28 February.

Brada, Josef C. (1988) 'Interpreting the Soviet Subsidization of Eastern Europe', *International Organization*, 42, 4, Autumn, pp. 639–558.

Brown, Stuart S. (1990) 'Theoretical Approaches to Regional Economic Reform in the Soviet Union', draft, Georgetown University.

Brown, Stuart S. (1991) 'Trade-Theoretic Approaches to Soviet Regional Autonomy', Final Report to the National Council for Soviet and East European Research, 27 May.

Brown, Stuart S. (forthcoming) 'The Rise and Fall of Soviet Protectionism', in Peter Hauslohner and David Cameron (eds) *Political Control of the Soviet Economy*, Cambridge University Press.

Brown, Stuart S. and Misha V. Belkindas (1990) 'Who's Feeding Whom?: A Balance of Payments Approach to Soviet Interrepublican Relations', manuscript, Georgetown University.

Brown, Stuart S. and Misha V. Belkindas (1991) 'Who Owes Whom?: An Examination of Soviet Interrepublican Commodity Flows', manuscript, Georgetown University.

Buchanan, James M., and Roger L. Faith (1987) 'Secession and the Limits of Taxation: Toward a Theory of Internal Exit', *The American Economic Review*, Vol. 77, No. 5, December, pp. 1023–31.

Canzoneri, Matthew B., and Behzad Diba (1991) 'Fiscal Deficits, Financial Integration and a Central Bank for Europe', Georgetown University Department of Economics, Working Paper 91–07, revised May.

Canzoneri, Matthew B., and Carol Ann Rogers (1990) 'Is the European Community an Optimal Currency Area? Optimal Tax Smoothing versus the Cost of Multiple Currencies', *American Economic Review*, June.

Carley, Jo (1991) 'Tajiks Find Rise in Bread Prices Hard to Swallow', *The Financial Times*, 2 April.

Cooper, Richard (1986) *Economic Policy in an Interdependent World*, Cambridge, MA: MIT Press.

Cornes, Richard and Todd Sandler (1986) *The Theory of Externalities, Public Goods, and Club Goods*, Cambridge: Cambridge University Press.

Currie, David (forthcoming) 'European Monetary Union: An Analysis of Regime Change', *Economic Journal.*

Ekonomicheskoe i sotsial'noe razvitie soyuznykh respublik, (1990) Moscow.

Fischer, Stanley (1982) 'Seigniorage and the Case for a National Money', *Journal of Political Economy,* Vol. 90, No. 21, pp. 295–313.

Genberg, Hans (1988) *Exchange Rate Management and Macroeconomic Policy: A National Perspective,* The Graduate Institute of International Studies, July.

Goble, Paul (1990) 'Central Asians Form Political Bloc', Radio Liberty, *Report on the USSR,* 13 July.

Granberg, A (1990) 'They Say That Russia is Undermining Our Union ... ', *Ekonomika i zhizn',* September, No. 39; in *JPRS–UEA–90–043,* 11 December, pp. 95–7.

Granberg, A. G., and Aleksandr Rubinshtein (1984) 'Siberia's Participation in the External Economic Ties', *Foreign Trade,* No. 8, pp. 26–30.

Ivanter, V.(1989) 'Regional'nye den'gi', *Pravitel'stvennyi vestnik,* No. 21, October, pp. 6–7.

Karimov, I. A. (1990) 'Not to Be Taken by Surprise', *Pravda vostoka,* 27 May; in *JPRS–UEA–90–31,* 30 August 1990, pp. 22–5.

Kenen, Peter B. (1969) 'The Theory of Optimum Currency Areas: An Elective View', in Robert Mundell and Alexander Swoboda (eds) *Monetary Problems of the International Economy,* Chicago: University of Chicago Press.

Khandruev, M. (1990) 'U kogo klyuchi ot ekonomiki', *Ekonomika i zhizn',* No. 11, March, p. 15.

Kitaigorodskii, I. (1990) 'Regional'nye den'gi', *Ekonomika i zhizn',* No. 2, January, pp. 4–5.

Knight, Peter T., and Roberta J. Waxman (1991) 'Fiscal Federalism in the Soviet Union', background paper prepared for Senior Policy Seminar on Intergovernmental Fiscal Relations and Macroeconomic Management in Large Countries, New Delhi, India, 26–28 February.

Kux, Stephan (1990a) 'Soviet Federalism', *Problems of Communism,* Vol. 39, March–April, pp. 1–19.

Kux, Stephan (1990b) *Soviet Federalism: A Comparative Perspective,* Occasional Paper Series, 18, Boulder: Westview Press.

McKinnon, Ronald I. (1963) 'Optimal Currency Areas', *The American Economic Review,* No. 4, September.

Mankiw, N. Gregory (1987) 'The Optimal Collection of Seigniorage: Theory and Evidence', *Journal of Monetary Economics,* No. 20, pp. 327–41.

Masol, V. A. (1991) 'On the Political, Social, Economic and Ecological Situation of the Ukraine', *Pravda Ukrainy,* 27 May 1990; *JPRS–UEA–90–031,* 30 August 1991, pp. 25–36.

Masson, Paul and Jacques Melitz (1990) 'Fiscal Policy Independence in a European Monetary Union', paper prepared for a conference at the Deutsche Bundesbank, Frankfurt, 21–23 February.

Material'no tekhnicheskoe obespechenie narodnogo khozyaistva SSSR, (1988) Moscow.

Mikhailov, L. (1990) 'Natsional'nyi dokhod: proizvedennyi i ispol'zovannyi', *Ekonomika i zhizn',* No. 10, March.

Mirsaidov, Sh. R. (1990) 'Economic Independence: Ways of Achieving It', *Ekonomika i zhizn',* May; *JPRS–UEA–90–030,* 1990, pp. 23–31.

Mitchneck, Beth A. (1991) 'Geographical and Economic Determinants of Interregional Migration in the USSR, 1968–1985', *Soviet Geography,* pp. 168–89.

Mundell, Robert (1961) 'A Theory of Optimal Currency Areas', *The American Economic Review,* September, pp. 657–65.

Musgrave, Richard A. and Peggy B. Musgrave (1984) *Public Finance in Theory and Practice,* McGraw-Hill.

Myerson, R. and M. Satterthwaite (1983) 'Efficient Mechanisms for Bilateral

Trading', *Journal of Economic Theory*, vol. 28, pp. 265-81.

Oates, Wallace E. (1972) *Fiscal Federalism*, New York: Harcourt Brace Jovanovich.

Olson, Mancur Jr. and Richard Zeckhauser (1966) 'An Economic Theory of Alliances', *Review of Economic Statistics*, Vol. 48, No. 3, August, pp. 266–79.

Otsasson, R. (1990) interview in *Izvestiya*, *FBIS–SOV–90–018*, 26 January.

Passel, Peter (1990) 'In Domestic Soviet Trade, Russia Has the Most Chips', *New York Times*, 7 October, section 3, p. 3.

Pauly, Mark V. (1970) 'Optimality of Public Goods and Local Governments: A General Theoretical Analysis', *Journal of Political Economy*, May–June.

Perekhod k rynku, (1990), August, Moscow.

Petrakov, Nikolay (1990) interviewed by Oleg Poptsov, *Moscow News*, No. 33, 26 August–2 September, (in English).

PlanEcon Report, (1991) 15 January.

Sachs, Jeffrey and Xavier Sala-I-Martin (1991) 'Federal Fiscal Policy and Optimum Currency Area', paper given at Establishing a Central Bank: A CEPR/CGES/IMF Conference, Georgetown University, 1–2 May.

Sandler, Todd (1975) 'The Economic Theory of Alliances: Realigned', Craig Liske, et al. *Comparative Public Policy: Issues, Theories and Methods*, New York: Wiley Halsted Press, pp. 223–39.

Shah, Answar (1991) 'Perspectives on the Design of Intergovernmental Fiscal Relations in Developing/Transition Economies', Senior Policy Seminar on Intergovernmental Fiscal Relations and Macroeconomic Management in Large Countries, New Delhi, India, 26–28 February.

Sheehy, Ann (1990) 'The Draft Union Treaty: A Preliminary Assessment', *Report on the USSR*, 21 December, pp. 1–6.

Socor, Vladimir (1991) 'Political Power Passes to Democratic Forces', in Radio Liberty, *Report on the USSR*, 4 January.

Summers, Lawrence H. (1990) 'Soviet Federalism', *Challenge*, September–October, pp. 15–16.

Ter–Minassian, T. (1991) speaking notes for the session on 'Macroeconomic Management Issues in Federal Systems', EDI Seminar on Intergovernmental Fiscal Relations.

Tiebout, Charles M. (1956) 'A Pure Theory of Local Expenditures', *Journal of Political Economy*, Vol. 64, No. 5, October, pp. 416–24.

'To Form a More Perfect Union? Federalism and Interstate Cooperation', (1989) *Harvard Law Review*, Vol. 102:842, pp. 843–63.

Tower, Edward and Thomas D. Willett (1976) *The Theory of Optimum Currency Areas and Exchange Rate Flexibility*, Special Papers in International Economics, No. 11, May, Department of Economics, Princeton University.

Tyson, Laura and Peter Kenen (1980) in E. Neuberger and L. D. Tyson (eds) *The Impact of International Economic Disturbances on the Soviet Union and Eastern Europe*, New York: Pergamon.

Ushanov, P. (1990) 'Pribaltika: sobstvennye den'gi', *Ekonomika i zhizn'*, No. 20, May, p. 3.

Uzbek SSR Council of Ministers Working Group, (1990) 'Basic Directions Toward Stabilizing the Uzbek Economy and Principles for Entering into a Market Economy', *Selskaya pravda*, 17 October; *JPRS–UEA–90–041*, 5 December, pp. 82–91.

Van Arkadie, Brian and Mats Karlsson (1992) *Economic Survey of the Baltic States*, Pinter, London.

Vestnik statistiki, (1990) No. 3.

Vestnik statistiki, (1990) No. 4.

Vol'ukov, A. (1990) 'Krony, Laty, Lity: Ne nanesut li oni udara po rublyu?', *Pravda*, 14 May, p. 2.

Notes

1 It is worth noting that this argument reverses traditional arguments that favour a small country using a foreign money to impose discipline on domestic authorities. The difference here is that the foreign money (the rouble) is itself not properly controlled.

2 Current discussions in the Baltics tend to emphasize the danger of surplus roubles 'buying up' (convertible) Estonian kroons (say), sabotaging the experiment in an independent money.

3 While formally rejected by the union government, the plan was accepted in principle by the Russian parliament and remains the standard against which all competing economic plans are judged.

4 While fairly uncommon, multiple monies within a single political entity is not unprecedented. For example, while part of the Russian Empire, Finland introduced the Finnish mark in 1860. The Finnish bank controlled its own financial and credit system independently of Russia's financial ministry. Finland also maintained an independent customs department.

5 Mundell himself concedes that multiple currencies may be politically unfeasible 'except in areas where national sovereignty is being given up'. (Mundell, 1961, pp. 663–4). In fact, the situation in the Soviet Union is sufficiently volatile to either represent an exception to this conventional rule or leave open the emergence of a loose federation or confederation in which coexisting monies would be possible.

6 More generally, the received wisdom of the literature on exchange-rate regimes is that whether flexible or fixed rates are preferable depends on numerous structural parameters of given economies and the nature of disturbances (Genberg, 1988, pp. 10–23).

7 In the case of fixed rates, the country using its own money can collect seigniorage but only at a rate that is determined by the foreign country's inflation rate, as opposed to the optimal rate which could be achieved through flexible rates (and its own inflation rate). The optimal rate of inflation and seigniorage will vary by country (see e.g. Mankiw, 1987).

8 European Community calculations corroborate Goskomstat's statistics and confirm the relative openness of the Soviet republics in comparison to the EC member states. Excluding the RSFSR, the EC found that Soviet republic trade turnover ranges between 30 per cent and 60 per cent of GNP, while corresponding ratios within the EC are 20 per cent to 30 per cent for the largest member states. Only in smaller states with very open economies, such as The Netherlands, does the ratio of trade to GNP reach 60 per cent.

9 While Fischer is concerned here with whether one nation should use the currency of another, his discussion is equally applicable, at least from an economic perspective, to the issue of separate regional currencies within a nation.

10 Indeed the creditworthiness of the union government has come under significant scrutiny lately.

11 It has also been argued that independent regional fiscal policies are problematic in that multiplier effects are small due to large interregional spillover effects and because local government debt tends to be held externally – that is, in other regions of the country. Hence, the concern is that local governments need to be more concerned about the future debt servicing; this, in turn, limits the desire to deficit finance for stabilization purposes (Oates, 1972, p. 28).

12 For an application of club theory to the Council for Mutual Economic Assistance, see Brada, 1988.

13 It is legitimate to argue that Russia is much too big and diffuse to be treated as one integrated region. In fact, we can persuasively focus on centre oblasti in Siberia (say) for this exercise with greater justification. However, at this stage the problem is more tractable if we deal at the level of union republics.

14 Although there have been several Soviet constitutions (the present being from 1977), the 1922 constitution which formally created the Soviet Union remains the fundamental legal document outlining the relationship between republics and the centre.

15 By risk aversion among republics is meant the relative risk aversion of a representative individual resident of the republic. (See text below for further elaboration.)

16 An outside option is a position which a republic can assume if no interrepublican agreement is reached. If negotiations fail to yield an agreement on transition to a new federal arrangement, then each republic will resort to its highest or most favourable feasible 'outside option'.

17 A Nash equilibrium is a string of actions such that the action chosen by each player is optimal, given the actions chosen by others.

18 This analysis assumes the domination of policy preferences over political structures. However, where the desire for political independence dominates economic criteria – e.g. in the Baltic republics – our assumptions, e.g. that smaller republics are more risk averse, and the associated results, may no longer hold.

19 Using a somewhat different model of interrepublic interaction in the Soviet Union, Asilis and Brown (1991b) explain why a Marshall or Grand Bargain-type plan should be rejected in favour of the superior and less expensive alternatives of Western assistance.

PART IV
HOW TO FACE THE FUTURE

9

A Critique of Soviet Reform Plans

Anders Åslund

The Soviet government, the republican governments and Soviet economists are preoccupied with writing reform plans. Since the 'Abalkin Plan' was published in October 1989 (*Ekonomicheskaya gazeta*, No. 43, 1989), a large number of reform plans, partial or comprehensive, have been drawn up and many have been published. The purpose of this paper is not to discuss them in detail, but rather to bring out the major weaknesses of the most important programmes. We shall focus on the programmes, that is their declared intentions, leaving the implementation aside.

The choice of which programmes to focus upon is clear-cut. First of all, the current union government programme stands out as a guideline. Its present form is the draft of Prime Minister Valentin Pavlov's 'Anti-crisis Programme' ('Programma deistvii', 1991), which was presented to the USSR Supreme Soviet on 22 April 1991 (*Izvestiya*, 23 April 1991), though it was explicitly introduced as a further elaboration of the 'Basic Guidelines on Economic Stabilization and Transition to a Market Economy' ('Osnovnye', 1990), which in turn were presented as President Mikhail Gorbachev's programme and adopted by the USSR Supreme Soviet on 19 October 1990. The natural contrast to the government programme remains the 500-day or Shatalin Programme of August 1990 (*Perekhod*, 1990). I shall also pay some attention to the rather short programme of the RSFSR government which was adopted on 12 May 1991 by the RSFSR Supreme Soviet. In many ways, it is a sequel to the 500-day programme, but there are significant differences and it is clearly designed for the RSFSR, omitting concerns unique to the Union.[1]

My intention is to contrast these programmes with the mainstream of the Western and East European literature on systemic change in socialist economies. All of a sudden, a substantial literature of this kind has emerged. On a number of points a broad consensus prevails among Western and East European economists.[2] First, 'the transition must be achieved rapidly if it is to stand a chance of success' (Dornbusch, 1991, Summary). Second, the transition must imply a comprehensive switch to a fully-fledged market economy with a strict macroeconomic stabilization policy, together with a comprehensive domestic and external liberalization. The domestic liberalization should comprise the freedom of entrepreneurship, production, sales, purchases and pricing. Foreign trade needs to be liberalized which requires a unified exchange rate. Differences remain on whether the exchange rate should remain floating or be fixed in order to serve as an anchor for the stabilization (Lipton and Sachs, 1990a; Blanchard et al., 1991).[3] Some issues, notably privatization, are still subject to extensive dispute, and no obvious road to success has emerged so far.[4] Moreover, the details of the future society with all its institutions are far from elaboration.

Given these assumptions, what are the major shortcomings of the principal reform programmes that have emerged in the USSR to date? I have tried to select the most crucial issues, by scrutinizing the key elements in a systemic change, starting with political preconditions, and continuing with intellectual comprehension, stabilization, liberalization and overall issues, though admittedly my choice must be considered subjective. I shall focus entirely on the initial stage of systemic change and avoid problems that become evident later on, such as structural changes and ensuing unemployment, as well as the vital but controversial issue of the means of privatization.[5] Thus I pinpoint nine factors that appear to me to be the major stumbling-blocks for the switch to a new economic system in the short term:

- neglect of democracy;
- relations between the centre and the republics;
- inability to conceptualize a market economy;
- unfounded belief in gradual transition;
- the budget deficit;
- gradual price liberalization;
- faith in import substitution;
- excessive confidence in the capabilities of the state apparatus; and
- failure to understand the costs of transition.

As is evident from these formulations, I focus on the instruments of actions rather than the consequences of action or non-action (such as inflation or shortages).

Neglect of democracy

An outstanding lesson from East-Central Europe is that no comprehensive economic change was possible before democratization. With characteristic vagueness, President Gorbachev evaded this point when declaring his commitment in Oslo: 'to stabilize the democratic process on the basis of broad social contract and a new state constitution of our Union as a true, free and voluntary federation' (*Izvestiya*, 7 June 1991). As opinion polls show, the bitter truth is that Gorbachev is highly unpopular in his own country and would lose a democratic election. The lesson the Soviet nomenclature seems to have drawn from the revolutions of 1989 in East-Central Europe is that any roundtable agreement or coalition government will quickly put an end to their days in power. Therefore, they are extremely reluctant to accept any real democratization. Since the Shatalin Programme, after all, was drafted with Gorbachev's consent, it is naturally coy about the importance of democratizing the political system. Many economic programmes tend to forego this point as a purely political matter.

Nor do truly democratic sentiments run particularly deep among Soviet economists. There is a widespread belief among the Soviet intelligentsia that workers and peasants are not 'mature enough' for democracy. In early 1991, it had become commonplace within a large part of the Communist party establishment to speak of South Korea, Taiwan, Singapore, Spain under General Franco and Chile under General Pinochet as suitable models for 'a gradual transition to a market economy'.[6] However, this reasoning is seriously flawed. None of these states had a command economy or a Communist establishment to begin with; they had predominantly private ownership and a market economy. There the issue was the need to deregulate and liberalize the economy.

Why is democracy so important for the change of economic system in a formerly socialist state? First, it is a question of credibility. Nobody can be less credible as a marketeer and privatizer than a party that was created in order to abolish the market economy and confiscate private property. Second, legitimacy is vital, because the change of system will inevitably be very costly. Thus it is important to offer the population a leadership it can trust and support. Otherwise, mass discontent leading to serious social unrest is likely. Third, it is a question of interests. The Communist establishment represents all the vested interests of the old system. It is implausible that the CPSU can succeed in breaking these vested interests, and even if it could it would be much more difficult for it than for any other party in power. Fourth, economics must gain superiority over politics. Enterprise directors are more accustomed to listening to political demands than to economic ones, because they were politically appointed. Even if they are told to pursue economic objectives, they are wise enough to know that in the end they will be judged by their political loyalty.

In practice, the consequences of these limitations were well clarified by the abortive attempts by General Jaruzelski to undertake authoritarian reforms in Poland from 1982.[7] Rather than turning to capitalist dictatorships in a wishful manner, the Soviets should focus on the experiences of Poland, which Egor Gaidar (1990, 1991) in particular has given appropriate attention. Poland has long been the politically and economically most complex Communist country after the USSR: it was the largest European Communist country and its level of economic development and economic structure were reasonably similar to those of the USSR. Their cultural affinity is significant, although both Poles and Russians prefer to deny that.

Thus, the evidence suggests that capitalist countries can enjoy good economic development for a long period under dictatorship, though only at an intermediary level of economic development. However, for Communist countries, democratization seems to be an absolute condition for a successful change of economic system. This is something few Soviet economists seem to realize.

One frequent line of argument is that the Soviet military and policy apparatus are so strong that no systemic change can be carried out against their wishes. This argument can be countered in several ways. The military may be co-opted, persuaded or defeated. Still, the eventual outcome in all three cases should be democratization, though it seems plausible that time is needed to cajole the military in one way or the other.

Powers must be delimited between the centre and the republics

There must be a clear division of powers between the union and the republics. In a series of draft union treaties the centre has gone ever further in the devolution of powers to the republics, but the problem is that no functioning agreement has been reached to date. This is hardly because of any lack of understanding, but merely a result of a prolonged political struggle over power between the centre and the republics.

One effect of this dispute has been the 'war of laws' which implies that there is no agreement on jurisdiction between the republics and the centre. As a result, nobody can know which law applies – if any. More frequently than not, there are two conflicting laws on vital economic issues that apply in the same territory. Without law, there can be no property rights and without these there can be no real economic stabilization or development.

Another consequence of disagreements between the centre, the republics and the local organs is that tax revenues are dwindling. Since all three levels claim the right to collect the same taxes, it has frequently become possible not to pay to any level. Significantly, the union budget received only 40 per cent of anticipated revenues during the first quarter of 1991. The rest, it seems, was not absorbed by other organs, but simply not collected (*Ekonomika i zhizn'*, No. 21, 1991, p. 1).

Obviously, no economic order can be introduced before the basic issue of jurisdiction is resolved at least provisionally. Most of the points raised in favour of democratization are also valid here. The government of whatever territorial unit we discuss must be considered legitimate by the vast majority of the population concerned, if it should be possible to undertake a far-reaching economic change.

Inability to conceptualize a market economy

Even reasonably knowledgeable Soviet reformers have great difficulty understanding what a market economy actually entails. It seems that travelling abroad is necessary but not sufficient to give reformers such insights.

The preamble of the Shatalin Programme presents a relief in this regard. It clearly sets out the right of man to property, to economic activity, and to free consumer choice and of the right of enterprises to the freedom of economic activity. However, it also grants citizens the right to 'just prices', increasing incomes and social guarantees, implying that many prices should remain regulated (*Perekhod*, 1990, pp. 5-12). While the basic principles of the Shatalin Programme are essentially market-oriented, substantial state intervention is envisaged when details are discussed. One of the worst lapses occurs in the section on social guarantees and wages, where a far-reaching regulation of wages is outlined, and a guaranteed minimum income superseding the average per capita income is suggested (ibid., pp. 100-6). Admittedly, these regulations are contradicted by the ensuing section on the labour market, but it is this inconsistency in thinking that is the problem. Similarly, after having declared that peasants should have the right to claim their share of the land and to leave a state or collective farm, the Shatalin Programme suggests that the resources for the next few years are only sufficient for 150-180,000 peasant farms, implying that peasant farms are to be both formed and equipped by the state (*Perekhod*, 1990, pp. 172-4).

In the government programme, a proper concept of a market economy is noticeably absent. The 'Basic Guidelines' restate a number of principles from the Shatalin Programme, though they are somewhat diluted: maximum freedom for economic activity, full responsibility of economic organizations, competition among producers, free price formation, refutation of the state to participate directly in economic activities (with exceptions) and an open economy ('Osnovnye', 1990, p. 1). However, the basic economic rights are connected with enterprises rather than individuals, and the rights of individuals and private enterprise are not specified. Evidently, the reason for this confusion is political or ideological, but regardless of the cause, such foggy language impedes the proliferation of an understanding of the market.

Still, the situation has improved. The most lucid and advanced legal document on the rights of entrepreneurship to date is the 'Law on the General Basis of Enterpreneurship of Citizens in the USSR', adopted by the USSR Supreme Soviet on 2 April 1991. For the first time, private (*chastnoe*) enterprise as well as hired labour were legally recognized without any particular limitations. Moreover, this law heralded the principles of 'equality between all forms of ownership, the freedom to dispose of ownership and the choice of sphere of activity' (*Izvestiya*, 10 April 1991). Thus, freedom of private enterprise has been legislated in the USSR.

Even so, President Gorbachev and the CPSU are only prepared to embrace private ownership in very limited forms.[8] Pavlov's 'Anti-crisis Programme' simply bypasses basic principles and is characterized by an extraordinary confusion between principles pertaining to a market and a command economy. Gorbachev made a typical statement on the principles of the reformed economy in Oslo: 'the intensification of economic reform in the direction of the creation of a mixed market economy based on a new system of ownership relations' (*Izvestiya*, 7 June 1991).

It is difficult enough to conceive of a market economy if you try, but Gorbachev and the Soviet government insist on confusing the principles by talking of a 'mixed' economy rather than embracing private enterprise. Similarly, the frequent references to the unique nature of Russia, implying that private enterprise is alien to the nation, further undermine attempts to move in the direction of a market economy.

A clear declaration of the need for guaranteed property rights of private ownership and a free market, followed by all legal and preferably constitutional guarantees, is required if a change of system is to gain credibility. The government must prove its commitments to capitalism. In short, capitalism has to be declared and to become a basis of the new rule, as it was in the East-Central European countries before they launched a true shift to a new economic system.

An unfounded belief in gradual transition

In the USSR, there is a nearly universal belief in the necessity of gradualism in the transition to a market economy. Indeed, this was the outstanding shortcoming of the Shatalin Programme. Although it favoured a swift transition to a market economy over 500 days, it suggested that various measures should be introduced at different times, mostly without providing any grounds for the sequencing; nor was it possible to discern any economic logic in the proposed timing of events. On the contrary, both prior experiences of stabilization and systemic changes elsewhere, notably in Poland, and the dominant current of economic theory suggest that a swift and comprehensive change, comprising as many simultaneous measures as possible, is most likely to minimize the social costs of transition (Blanchard et al., 1991). Naturally, the transition will last for years and be muddled by political upsets, but the aim should be to see it through as quickly and consistently as possible.

One ground for the Soviet appreciation of gradualism is common sense. The cost of transition appears to be less if the change occurs in small steps. This belief is partly inspired by lingering notions of central planning. It is far too common to aspire to plan oneself out of the old system rather than to formulate a general strategy.

Another argument for gradualism, primarily used by former Deputy Prime Minister Leonid Abalkin, is that the Bolsheviks had pursued fast changes and that it would be wrong to do the same as they had done in reverse. This is an untenable argument. Current decision-makers should not avoid policies simply because they are reminiscent of the Bolsheviks. Obviously, the needs of any particular situation must be considered on their own merits.

In fact, gradualism is probably preferred simply because it is the ordinary way of administration – taking one decision after the other without considering any coordination. Furthermore, the Russian mentality is widely perceived as conservative and resistant to change. If any alteration is required, it had better be gradual. These sentiments are reinforced by all members of the old establishment who want a minimum of change. Progressive proponents of gradualism would be well advised to scrutinize the actual reasons for gradualism seen by conservatives and draw their own conclusions.

A refreshing exception is the RSFSR programme for economic stabilization and transition to a market economy. It states in all clarity: 'There is one conclusion: a gradual transition from a planned to a market economy is impossible.' However, by the next page, it has lapsed into a contradiction: 'To move gradually to a market mechanism of price formation' ('Programma Pravitel'stva', 1991, pp. 2-3).

The budget deficit must be eliminated

A major conclusion of the general stabilization theory is that when inflationary expectations are high, it is vital to pursue policies which reduce them drastically. One such standard device is to eliminate the budget deficit. It could also be argued that in formerly Communist countries, it would be preferable to have a certain budget surplus, as few instruments of a monetary policy exist or can function at the outset. The Shatalin Programme, though somewhat ambiguous, was basically in favour of a swift elimination of the budget deficit (*Perekhod*, 1990, pp. 44, 86-8). Still, it made the elimination of the budget deficit a top priority, together with control of the money supply.

The Soviet government, on the contrary, has continuously stated that it would be irresponsible to cut the budget deficit so much as to harm social programmes (*Pravitel'stvennaya*, 1990). Considering that the actual decline in the national income in 1991 was feared to be 15-20 per cent (*Pravitel'stvennaya*, 1990, p. 6), this argument sounds nothing but populist. Such a fall in the national income would have a far greater social impact than social benefits amounting to a couple of per cent of the GNP. The real reason was probably that it is very difficult to cut expenditures, especially for a weak government representing the vested interests of the old system.

Consequently, raising social benefits appeared politically more important than reducing the budget deficit. Thus the budget deficit was allowed to rise to possibly 20 per cent of the GNP, because social programmes and subsidies that have been considered politically necessary have grown extraordinarily (Åslund, 1991c). Typically, the anti-crisis programme suggests that the union and the republics should elaborate 'extraordinary budgets' without suggesting any target for the budget deficits ('Programma deistvii', 1991). A clear target must be formulated; and it must be above most other considerations, if any stabilization is to take place.

All sides seemed anxious not to cut defence expenditures significantly. The Shatalin group wanted to reduce defence expenditures by a mere 10 per cent and the government by about 7 per cent (Åslund, 1991b, pp. 214-15). Apparently, both sides were so afraid of the military-industrial complex that they did not dare to demand the necessary cuts from the

exaggerated defence budget.[9] Hardly any disbursements seem as super-
fluous as the huge defence expenditures. The USSR wanted to maintain
virtually the same level, although its defence commitment for Eastern
Europe had been abandoned; much of its armaments production would
go straight to scrap, because of the disarmament agreements; no apparent threat to Soviet territory was at hand.

The budget deficit must essentially be reduced through massive cuts,
because in the transition to a market economy, traditional state revenues
are bound to fall (McKinnon, 1990, p. 133). The profit tax rate has fallen
to 35 per cent of enterprise taxes, while it used to amount to 55-60 per
cent; turnover tax revenues have been very high and cannot be maintained
at such a level when prices become deregulated and much of trade
becomes privatized; the foreign trade tax revenues must fall with the liberalization of trade.

The first response of reformers has been to call for higher taxation for
individuals. Thus, Grigorii Yavlinskii proposed taxation on individual property, higher landtax rates and gift taxes and individual tax declarations on
a quarterly basis in March 1990 (Yavlinskii, 1990, p. 32). This response
approaches the issue from the wrong direction. Instead, reformers must
realize that the country will have to make do with small state revenues in
the transition period for a number of good reasons. First, the state budget
has traditionally been far too large, with expenditures amounting to
slightly over 50 per cent of GNP. Second, the state apparatus is in no shape
to handle large sums of money efficiently. It is better for the efficiency of
the society as a whole that the money stays with the citizens. Third, it is
vital to avoid the Soviet economy developing into a mafia economy and
the best method of prevention is a maximum of liberalization: the fewer
limitations there are, the fewer the opportunities to extort bribes. Fourth,
since unemployment is likely to rise sharply in the wake of systemic change,
it is important to stimulate supply and the creation of private viable jobs
as much as possible. Therefore, taxes and tax regulations limiting supplies
should be kept at a minimum. Fifth, it will take a long time to develop a
tax-revenue administration in any case. Sixth, for a market economy with
such a relatively low level of economic development, it would seem normal
to have a tax burden of some 30 per cent of the GNP to judge by the experiences of successful market economies around the world.

Price liberalization should be comprehensive

The current Soviet price structure is utterly distorted in all aspects. Any
partial alteration will only lead to new distortions, which in turn will cause
distortions in the real economy. If prices on only some goods are set free,
substitutes will be exposed to an exaggerated demand. Since the original
price structure is highly distorted, considerable shifts in relative prices will
occur whenever some prices are liberalized. Repetitive sharp swings in relative prices are highly disruptive, both to enterprises and to macroeconomic
stability. The domestic price structure has no relation to relative prices on

the world market, obstructing any liberalization of foreign trade before virtually full-price liberalization. The extraordinary degree of distortions of relative prices is a strong argument for a greater extent of free prices than is mostly the case in mature market economies. As long as a new free-price structure has not been established, no enterprise can know what its true costs are – which is a perennial argument against any bankruptcy. Potential investors will be dissuaded if there is no way of knowing or guessing future prices and costs.

Even so, every programme under consideration is in favour of a gradual liberalization of prices and justifies this with social considerations. A typically slippery formulation is to be found in the anti-crisis programme: 'to pursue a gradual reduction in the sphere of administrative regulations, with the intention of completing the transition to *primarily* free price formation by 1 October 1992' (my emphasis; 'Programma deistvii', 1991). The confusion on this point in the RSFSR Programme has already been cited. The Shatalin Programme was most gradualist on prices (*Perekhod*, 1990, pp. 93-8). Economists and politicians are giving in to popular pressures on the price issue, since the population at large seems to believe that the gradual liberalization of prices will bring about fewer social costs.

A lasting belief in import substitution

Currently, there is little understanding for protectionism in economic theory; and where it exists it is limited to particular cases, preparing for an outward-oriented economic strategy (Sachs, 1989, p. 16). There is hardly any defence left for import substitution: that is, the importation of capital goods for the domestic production behind high customs walls, but it remains the Soviet attitude. The traditional Soviet system was highly protectionist and a mercantilist attitude to foreign trade seems to have survived. It is widely considered preferable to allow foreign investment and to import equipment than to liberalize foreign trade. The anti-crisis programme calls for 'measures to develop import-substituting production and technology' (Programma deistvii, 1991) even though it also calls for the introduction of internal convertibility. Effectively, it wants to maintain extensive quotas and tariffs.

Although the Shatalin Programme advocates economic openness in words, the foreign-trade regime that it outlines is surprisingly similar to the government programme. Although the concept of import substitution is not used, the programme insists on the 'necessity of strict state regulation' of foreign trade, while the attitude to foreign investment is rather more positive (*Perekhod*, 1990, pp. 124-31).

Presumably, this dislike of free trade is a combination of the Soviet tradition of isolation and the huge size of the country. Foreign trade is also perceived as a speculative source of high private incomes and the black-market exchange rate is rightly considered to undervalue the rouble grossly. However, these arguments are essentially of a political and populist nature. With its high degree of monopolization and distorted relative prices, the USSR is in great need of outside competition to bring about a swift improvement.

Excessive confidence in the capabilities of the state apparatus

The steady stream of demands directed to the state illustrates how weak a notion people have of what a market economy is about. The government programmes in particular are full of specific requests to the state apparatus. Typically, the government is supposed to 'pursue an active policy to develop entrepreneurship' ('Programma deistvii', 1991) while it would be more appropriate to demand liberalization instead. All kinds of specific state actions are proposed, primarily in the fields of social and structural policy.

Not only would it be inappropriate for the state to undertake all kinds of activities, it would be impossible. The state apparatus has long been both overextended and overstrained and it has been severely reduced during perestroika – by about half its employees at central levels. It is also demoralized because bureaucrats and the old nomenclature are incessantly criticized in the media. Nor do civil servants know what to do in the new system, not least since the legal system is patchy and rudimentary. Their salaries tend to be fixed and thus decline in a time of inflation. The change of system requires completely new abilities and different state organizations.

The conclusion is that the Soviet Union should adopt much more liberal conditions than usually exist in the West. Demands on the state should be reduced to a bare minimum – to the essential issues, such as law and order, basic state institutions, providing fiscal and monetary balance, an infrastructure and a social safety net. State revenues should be reduced accordingly, which will happen more or less automatically. Naturally, this will imply that a pretty wild capitalism will develop, reminiscent of Charles Dickens' Britain in the 1840s or a wild west economy. But currently the most likely alternatives seem to be lasting misery or a mafia economy worse than in southern Italy, which would provide far more limited benefits.

Failure to comprehend the high costs of transition

Two important lessons may be drawn from the initial transition in East-Central Europe. First, the previous level of economic development has turned out to be very low indeed, as only few had understood. Second, great structural changes are required, involving huge social costs, although it is an open question how large these costs will be (Lipton and Sachs, 1990a).

Regardless of how big each of these factors will be, the country will experience a shock. In order to make that acceptable, the people must be prepared psychologically. The Polish and Czechoslovak governments did a great deal to inform their populations about the imminent severe hardships. Hence, their populations accepted the consequences with surprising calm. The East Germans on the contrary have felt cheated, since the impending grand future suggested to them turned out to be more distant.

In the last few years, populism has prevailed in Soviet politics. It has resulted in a reluctance to allow price rises and decisions to expand social programmes without any real source of financing. Although the current anti-crisis programme expresses great worry over the economic situation, it fails to clarify the severity of the economic situation, in particular since it contains virtually no figures. Thus the government is stuck in populism. It needs a source of legitimacy to overcome this tendency.

Poland offers an illuminating example of how fast the necessary transition can be. The Polish roundtable agreement of April 1989 was highly populist, because the Communists were still in power and the democratic opposition just added up its demands. However, in October 1989, one month after the non-Communist government had taken office, it presented a programme which possessed all the clarity one could ask for, spelling out all the harsh measures that were necessary for an economic recovery and systemic change (*Rzeczpospolita*, 12 October 1989).

Conclusions: political reform is a precondition for systemic change

The concerns I have focused upon may be divided into two groups of problems, political and intellectual, though some issues involve both aspects. Unequivocally political matters are the neglect of democracy, the conflict between the centre and the republics, the lenience towards the budget deficit and the hesitance about price liberalization. In fact, they may be grouped into two main problems: the democratization of the Soviet Union and the new federal structure – and partial dissolution – of the Soviet Union. These are clearly the crucial initial issues to solve – at least provisionally – before a true systemic change can be unleashed.

Yet, surprisingly, many problems are primarily caused by a lack of intellectual comprehension: policy-makers do not understand what a market economy is; they believe in a gradual transition, in import substitution and in the bountiful capability of the state apparatus. They fail to realize just how economically backward their country really is. Also, the policy-makers' inability to recognize the economic importance of democracy is to a great extent an intellectual deficiency. On the one hand, this may arouse optimism, because none of these issues are all that difficult to understand. On the other hand, it makes plain how scarce economic knowledge and market-oriented thinking are in the USSR. Even if these foremost issues are being solved, there are a great many others below the surface which are bound to cause trouble as soon as any detailed economic programme is implemented.

A long-term problem is the shortage of all kinds of skills specific to a market economy. Initially, the lack of general conceptualization may be the predominant problem, but later on the poor knowledge of ordinary legal and auditing practices and management and marketing skills will become major stumbling-blocks.

It may seem strange that I have not called any economic issues difficult, but the reason rests in the very definition of our query – to investigate what factors within the commonly agreed economic framework hamper the initiation of systemic change. Privatization, inflation, unemployment and structural changes are later worries. It is also apparent that a great many ideas have already been tested and the lessons learned in East-Central Europe. The USSR stands to benefit from these lessons. Its leaders should look realistically into the Polish drama rather than wishfully at the East Asian fairy-tale. It is at least as important to learn from other people's mistakes as from their successes.

Hopefully, these observations have also cast some light on the role of President Gorbachev. To judge from his behaviour and statements during 1990, he has been steadfast on three issues. First, he has avoided arranging any democratic election involving himself, thus skipping true democratization, since he realized that he would lose. Second, he has been dragging his feet on the union issue and it remains uncertain how far he has actually travelled. Third, he has insisted on 'the socialist choice' and resisted mass privatization. As I have argued above, all these positions must be abandoned, if true change of the economic system is to take place. Gorbachev may shift his position on these issues as on so many prior points, but he has already maintained this stand for so long that his credibility is limited.

The parallel with General Jaruzelski seems apt. He could stay on only as President with limited powers (and not as party leader) and for a short period. Admittedly, Jaruzelski did not block the systemic changes, but he was a much weaker personality than Gorbachev.

This reasoning leads us to focus upon democratization as the most crucial precondition to systemic change, while there are also strong arguments in favour of a solution of the union-republic relationship as a vital precondition. It should be comparatively easier to find economic leaders who realize what is necessary; and an economic programme can casily be adopted from the Polish experiences. Therefore, the two political preconditions seem decisive, though they in turn are naturally influenced by economic and social developments.

References

Aganbegyan, Abel G. (1990) 'Programma stabilizatsii ekonomiki i perekhoda k rynku (proekt)', mimeo., 11 September.

Åslund, Anders (1991a) 'Principles of Privatisation for Formerly Socialist Countries', Stockholm Institute of Soviet and East European Economics, Working Paper No. 18.

Åslund, Anders (1991b) *Gorbachev's Struggle for Economic Reform*, 2nd ed., Pinter, London.

Åslund, Anders (1991c) 'Gorbachev, *Perestroyka*, and Economic Crisis', *Problems of Communism*, 40, No. 1, January-April, pp. 18-41.

Åslund, Anders (1991d) 'Four Key Reforms: the East European Experiment Phase

II', *The American Enterprise*, 2, No. 4, July-August, pp. 48-55.

Blanchard, Olivier, Rudiger Dornbusch, Paul Krugman, Richard Layard and Lawrence Summers (1991) *Reform in Eastern Europe*, MIT Press, London.

Bush, Keith (1991) 'Pavlov's Anticrisis Program', *Report on the USSR*, Radio Liberty, 17 May, pp. 1-6.

Commission of the European Communities (1990) 'Stabilization, Liberalization and Devolution: Assessment of the Economic Situation and Reform Process in the Soviet Union', *European Economy*, No. 45, December.

Dewatripont, Mathias, and Gérard Roland (1991) 'The Virtues of Gradualism and Legitimacy in the Transition to a Market Economy', CEPR Discussion Paper No. 538.

Dornbusch, Rudiger (1991) 'Priorities of Economic Reform in Eastern Europe and the Soviet Union', CEPR Occasional Paper No. 5.

Gaidar, Egor T. (1990) 'Trudnyi vybor', *Kommunist*, 67, No. 2, January, pp. 23-34.

Gaidar, Egor T. (1991) 'V nachale novoi fazy', *Kommunist*, 68, No. 2, January, pp. 8-19.

Galbraith, John Kenneth (1990) 'The Rush to Capitalism', *The New York Review of Books*, 25 October, pp. 51-2.

Grosfeld, Irena (1990) 'Prospects for Privatization in Poland', *European Economy*, No. 43, March, pp. 139-50.

Hanson, Philip (1990) 'Property Rights in the New Phase of Reforms', *Soviet Economy*, 6, No. 2, pp. 95-124.

Hanson, Philip (1991) 'Soviet Economic Reform: Perestroika or "Catastroika" ', *World Policy Journal*, 8, No. 2, Spring, pp. 289-318.

Hare, Paul, and Irena Grosfeld (1991) 'Privatization in Hungary, Poland and Czechoslovakia', CEPR Discussion Paper No. 544.

Hewett, Ed A. (1989) 'Perestroika – "Plus": The Abalkin Reforms', *PlanEcon Report*, 1 December.

Hewett, Ed A. (1990/91) 'The New Soviet Plan', *Foreign Affairs*, 69, No. 5, Winter, pp. 146-67.

IMF, IBRD, OECD and EBRD (1990) *The Economy of the USSR. Summary and Recommendations*, Washington, DC, 19 December.

IMF, IBRD, OECD and EBRD (1991) *A Study of the Soviet Economy*, Vol. 1, Paris.

Kornai, Janos (1990) *The Road to a Free Economy*, Norton, New York.

Lipton, David, and Jeffrey Sachs (1990a) 'Creating a Market in Eastern Europe: The Case of Poland', *Brookings Papers on Economic Activity*, No. 1, pp. 75-147.

Lipton, David, and Jeffrey Sachs (1990b) 'Privatization in Eastern Europe: The Case of Poland', *Brookings Papers on Economic Activity*, No. 2, pp. 293-341.

McKinnon, Ronald I. (1990) 'Stabilising the Ruble', *Communist Economies*, 2, No. 2, pp. 131-42.

Olson, Mancur (1982) *The Rise and Decline of Nations*, Yale UP, London.

'Osnovnye napravleniya po stabilizatsioi narodnogo khozyaistva i perekhodu k rynochnoi ekonomike' (1990) *Pravda*, 18 October, pp. 1-4.

Perekhod k rynku. Kontseptsiya i Programma (1990) Moscow, August (the programme of the Shatalin group).

Pravitel'stvennaya programma formirovaniya struktury i mekhanizma reguliruemoi rynochnoi ekonomiki. Proekt (1990) Moscow, September (the government programme).

'Programma deistvii Kabineta Ministrov SSSR po vyvodu ekonomiki iz krizisa (proekt)', (1991) *Delovoi mir*, 16-17 April (the government anti-crisis programme).

'Programma Pravitel'stva RSFSR po stabilizatsii ekonomiki i perekhodu k rynochnym otnosheniyam' (1991) mimeo., Moscow, May (the RSFSR government programme).

Sachs, Jeffrey D. (1989) (ed.), *Developing Country Debt and the World Economy*, University of Chicago Press, Chicago.

Yavlinskii, Grigorii A. (1990) 'Program of Economic Reform: Popular Support, Stabilization, Restructuring', in Aven, P.O., S.S. Shatalin, and F. Schmidt-Beck (eds.), 'Economic Reform and Integration', proceedings of 1-3 March, IIASA, CP-90-004, pp. 27-38.

Notes

1 For a discussion of the government programme of September 1990 (*Pravitel'stvennaya*, 1990), the 500-day programme, the Aganbegyan compromise (Aganbegyan, 1990) and the President's programme ('Osnovnye', 1990) see Hewett (1990/91), Åslund (1991bc), EC (1990) or IMF et al. (1991). The anti-crisis programme has been discussed in Bush (1991).

2 See Kornai (1990), Lipton and Sachs (1990a), Dornbusch (1991), EC (1990), IMF et al. (1990) or Blanchard et al. (1991). For a more universal argument for rapid change, see Olson (1982). I share the essence of these views, as should be evident from the rest of this paper.

3 There are still people who argue for gradualism. However, the arguments are not very convincing. One group led by John Kenneth Galbraith (1990) has simply failed to realize the depth of the crisis. Another argument forwarded by Mathias Dewatripont and Gérard Roland (1991) assumes the knowledge of costs, which means implicitly the existence of relevant prices and statistics, and that the very stability of society is not in danger. Their argument seems to be valid for structural changes in a stable Western economy but not for the transition process. A third group simply refuses to accept the cost of transition and thinks that it will be less if the transition is protracted – an argument for which the mainstream finds no evidence.

4 For a discussion, see Grosfeld (1990), Hare and Grosfeld (1991), Sachs and Lipton (1990b) and Åslund (1991a).

5 I have discussed these issues in Åslund (1991d).

6 Arkadii Volskii, Chairman of the Scientific-Industrial Union has mentioned Japan, South Korea and Taiwan (*Ekonomika i zhizn'*, No. 11, March 1991, p. 6). Kazakhstan's President Nursultan Nazarbaev has embraced Singapore, South Korea and the Asian dragons in general (*Izvestiya*, 11 May 1991), while the first party secretary of Moscow, Yurii Prokof'ev has gone furthest, naming Spain under Franco and Chile under Pinochet (*The Financial Times*, 6 February 1991).

7 Philip Hanson (1991, p. 311) arrives at the same conclusion with somewhat different arguments.

8 Gorbachev's worst statements are to be found in *Pravda*, 1 and 2 December 1990, where he declared that he would never accept the private ownership of land.

9 I have been informed that there was a secret part of the Shatalin plan, suggesting larger defence cuts, but if it exists, it seems more significant to me that it has remained both secret and neglected.

10

The Role of the State in Transitional Postcommunist Economies: the Experience of Economic Reforms in the 1980s and 1990s and Problems in the Foreseeable Future

Alexander Bim

It has to be stressed from the beginning that the author of the present article does not belong to those supporting the recently widely circulating view that a realization of the so-called 'anti-étatist' (or 'non-state') model of development is a necessary choice for the Soviet society. These kinds of views are a manifestation of an absolutely understandable negative reaction to the total étatization of social life, which is so characteristic of totalitarianism; this reaction, however, is superficial and shallow. The level of a society's civilization, the efficiency of its economy and the degree of social satisfaction of its citizens are defined not by the weakness of the state, but by the correlation between the type and particular features of the state on the one hand, and the whole spectrum of the interests of the society and its individual members on the other.

As Egor T. Gaidar has pointed out, within the framework of a market economy the state is a real social institution, capable of using its powers (and actually using them) to regulate the economic activity of producers to control the purchasing power of money, etc. (Gaidar, 1990, pp. 11-15).

In the Soviet Union, representatives of both the ruling élite and democratic groups seem to be united on one matter: during the transition from the administrative command economy to the market system, the role of the state is – and will be in the foreseeable future – extremely important. This has a symbolic meaning. The emergence of fully-fledged subjects of the market economy will not diminish the importance of the state as the main actor, in the process of reforms (institutional, structural, financial), especially in the first stages of transition. On the contrary, the very emergence and effective functioning of the above-mentioned structures under Soviet conditions is possible only as a result of a purposeful policy on the part of the state. A proper understanding of these outlined problems is extremely important. In spite of the apparent politicization of everything remotely connected with the state, it is possible to outline a certain circle of problems of interrelations between the state and the economy, integral to the formal appearance of structures of power and even to their concrete political substance.

At the same time, the choice of strategy regarding the role of the state in the economy is of extreme importance. Basically, there are three theoretically possible variants (see also Bim, 1990, p. 599):

- the classic Marxist-Leninist variant, realized in practice in the USSR and Soviet-model countries. It implies state dominance not only in political but also in economic life through the dominance of the state property. It is paradoxical, but this variant, in spite of its obviously utopian and reactionary nature, has still convinced supporters, surprisingly, even among some people who call themselves 'pragmatists';[1]
- the social-democratic strategy, which implies a multiplicity of property forms and the existence of a developed market with an essentially prominent role of the state (which is by no means a supreme owner) in regulating economic and – especially – social processes;
- the liberal strategy, signifying limited state participation in the formation and development of the economy, within which market relations constitute the basic regulator in the whole complex of production, innovation, exchange and distribution relations.

The choice between the second and the third variant is not just a matter of political discussions. It is a question of content, direction and, if one may say so, of intensiveness of the sociopolitical functions of the state. Consequently, it is a question about the structures which are to fulfil these functions. The social-democratic variant obviously demands structures on a larger scale responsible for the planning and implementation of social policy. This variant, the most likely one, will put definite limits on a scale of destatization and privatization of property, which implies the existence of some kind of bodies to manage state property. The liberal strategy, on the contrary, will permit sharp reductions on the scale of the present departmental-hierarchical systems.

Let us now formulate two basic principles:

Principle one. One should not a priori accept this or that model; otherwise it is difficult to avoid tendentiousness and a repetition of the mistakes of the Marxists, who absolutized abstract constructions and schemes. International experience is somewhat difficult to relate to Soviet conditions, though basically actual experience is the only reliable guide. I believe we must apply *an absolutely pragmatic approach to the problem of the economic role of the state.* It should only be given those particular functions which objectively demand fulfilment by political structures in order to dismantle the system of the administrative-command economy and undertake the transition to a normal and healthy one.

Principle two. It is necessary to avoid absolutizing dates and rates of destatization – as well as dates and rates of stabilization measures and market-type reforms.[2] *It is much more important to ensure the proper objectives and conditions of reforms, achieving meaningful results during the whole period of the unavoidably long process of transition.*

In this short paper it is obviously impossible to undertake a detailed analysis of the whole complex of problems relating to the role of the state in the course of reforms in postcommunist economies. Avoiding too much detail (in most cases well-known to specialists) I have therefore attempted to generalize the experience and to ascertain the most important tendencies and challenges that are imminent.

Main socioeconomic functions of the state during the transitional period: a conceptual framework

In my former works (Bim, 1989, 1990), I have already argued that the state has to fulfil the following functions under conditions of its democratization and development of market relations in the economy:

– reforming property forms and property relations, and the creation of a market environment in the economy;
– ensuring economic and social rights, and freedom of individuals;
– targeting socioeconomic development;
– ensuring social stability (preventing violent and antagonistic social conflicts).

Let us now consider some problems in the realization of these functions.

Reform of property relations and property forms and the creation of a market environment

At present Soviet society has reached a level of socio-psychological maturity, when broad masses of the population recognize that a necessary condition for the further development of the country is that real economic independence of individuals is guaranteed on the basis of the multiplicity of property forms. There are also opponents of this idea. But regardless of personal interests and economic competition over different property, the pluralism of property forms is also correctly regarded as one of the main social guarantees of the real freedom of individuals in a renewed society.

There are reasons to believe that in public consciousness, as well as in legislation and governmental reform projects, a gradual process of development of quite a rational programme of destatization and privatization is under way (for more information see Yasin, 1991, pp. 99-111). I believe that in the near future the following problems will prove to be the most difficult for a practical realization:

First, popular paternalistic and egalitarian stereotypes must be overcome, as well as the negative attitude of the pauperized majority of the population towards entrepreneurship and a broad-scale differentiation of individuals in terms of income and property. In the Soviet Union this problem will obviously be considerably more serious than in most other post-communist economies.

Second, natural aspirations must be transcended of the state and communist party bureaucracy to block privatization or to create various pseudo-new organizational and economic structures that are in reality a camouflage for the same state property and departmental-hierarchical system. Examples are the so-called 'state concerns', 'state joint-stock companies' and 'commercial' banks, which are being created now. They cannot be regarded as effective forms of destatization.

Third, the dangerous tendency of the merging of the old and new political élite, first of all at the republican and local levels, with the new commercial structures must be checked. We can hardly accept the forms of cooperation between government and commercial banks, insurance companies, stock and commodity exchanges, suggested by the RSFSR Council of Ministers, i.e. the introduction of government officials (state controllers) onto the boards of these companies ('Programma pravitel'stva RSFSR', 1991, p. 12). This is an obvious exaggeration of the role of the administrative apparatus in economic regulation. The functions and prerogatives of the state and its bodies should be limited and 'distanced' from defining micro-proportions of the economy. The latter should be done by market structures. The government should rather avoid intervening here or establishing direct controls. Effective measures to stop the convergence of state and commercial institutions (which unfortunately is developing intensively now, and which is nothing less but a new form of super-monopolism) are in order.

Fourth, concrete schemes and mechanisms must be elaborated and implemented in order to ensure an optimal proportion of main forms of privatization. They should vary for different sectors of the economy and at the same time be mutually coordinated. The main forms are: leasing and buy-out; the distribution and realization of individual investment cheques; and the free sales of shares.

Ensuring economic and social rights (social security net)

The key element of a new model of social security – and perhaps of the social policy in general – is the establishment of such a combination of forms and methods, which correspond both to the democratic state and to the new property structure (Bim, 1990, p. 602). I believe that the implementation of a social security programme functions now has to take the following realities into account:

For a majority of the Soviet population, essential changes occurred around the end of the 1980s and the early 1990s with regard to social guarantees. It became of primary importance for the state to ensure at least a minimal acceptable level of supply of goods and services in the consumer market, and provide for a reasonably stable functioning of this market. The importance of the state ensuring a minimal level of money income has decreased dramatically as a result of the emptiness of the consumer market. After Prime Minister Valentin Pavlov's 'price reform' of 2 April 1991, the situation changed slightly. The better organized social groups started fighting for increased wages, which did not help to alleviate the poverty of the market.

While some guaranteed payments and benefits (for example, some new pensions) exceed the requisite minimal level, others are below the minimum, which corresponds to the minimal socially acceptable level of consumption. According to my estimate, the differences in guaranteed incomes have grown considerably, which cannot be justified under present conditions.

A very important type of social guarantee, property rights, is utterly underdeveloped. In my opinion, property rights should be properly sanctioned and defended by law. This will be one of the methods of regulating the new structure of ownership and state support to the owners. Various forms of insurance payments should be among the most important of these guarantees.

There is a problem of the delimitation of the functions and responsibilities between the central and the republican governments in the sphere of social security. If the union state survives in some form, then the basic social guarantees, and notably the ensuring of a minimal consumption level, should be provided to all citizens by the central authorities. Any extension of these guarantees is a natural right of the republics and regions, as long as a modification does not violate anybody's legal rights.

Inflation causes a number of special requirements to be met by the mechanism of social security. The latter should not contribute to the acceleration of the prices-incomes spiral. The economic practices of populism, which are a characteristic feature of many post-totalitarian (but not yet really democratic) regimes, is nothing less than an invitation to hyperinflation.

The following principle is to be firmly pursued: under market conditions the state guarantees only the minimal level of consumption, that is minimal wages for workers and minimal income for those unable to work. This principle is conditioned by the necessity to pursue a hard anti-inflationary policy, as well as by new criteria of social justice which are to be accepted by the society. In this connection, it is reasonable to support income indexation only for those people who are otherwise unable to increase their incomes without such help. A more generous approach would signify a lack of understanding of the requirements of a stabilization policy.

Targeting socioeconomic development

Obviously we cannot be satisfied with the targeting of socioeconomic development in the course of Soviet reforms of the late 1980s and early 1990s. Partly this can be attributed to the general paralysis of power, partly to a poor conceptual basis of economical stabilization and reform sequencing.

Let us try to identify some typical shortcomings of the main current reform programmes. Reform proposals of the central government (for example, 'Programma deistvii', 1991) include a number of reasonable measures necessary for economic stabilization and the transition to a market system. These are, foremost, price liberalization, cuts in budgetary expenditures, destatization and the demonopolization of the economy. However, these generally correct ideas are not supported by the mechanisms necessary to bring them into practice. Many provisions of these proposals are merely declarative. Therefore, we cannot regard these documents as a fully-fledged reform programme.

The government programmes say nothing about an active use of administrative mechanisms nor about the reconstruction of the fundamentals of the command economy, but many measures presented in detail pertain in fact to a command economy. This is particularly true of the sections on the 'normalization of economic ties' and the social provisions for the people.

Our conclusion is that a very serious contradiction exists in the Ryzhkov-Pavlov programmes between the declarative and vague nature of stabilization and market-type measures, on the one hand, and the many centralized administrative and organizational measures, on the other. It is the latter which currently constitute a basis for practical actions of the all-union government. Obviously, communist governments are incapable of finding a satisfactory solution for this fundamental problem of current reforms: namely the new role and functions of the state under conditions of transition to a civilized economy.

If the present regime does not cease to exist, the following problems will continue to play a primary role:

1 Growing inflationary processes pose a danger of hyperinflation. International experience demonstrates that governments which do not enjoy popular support are usually incapable of undertaking effective anti-inflationary measures (strengthen the national currency, undertake drastic cuts in budgetary expenditures, liberalize prices and regulate incomes).
2 Destatization and privatization policies will be slow and inconsistent, since the state apparatus will by all means try to retain control over property.
3 Demonopolization policies will just be formalities, because of a lack of any meaningful support to potentially competitive commercial structures.
4 Structural and investment policies will be weak as a result of the weakness of the regime and the lack of viable economic mechanisms.

5 The emphasis will be maintained on state institutions as the main regulators of economic activity, predominantly through administrative measures.[3] The consequences will be a deepening recession and the conservation of the ineffective structure of production.

6 The integration of the Soviet economy into the world economic system will be hindered for the above-mentioned economic and political reasons. The country will also have difficulties in receiving as well as properly using assistance from developed countries and international organizations.

At the same time, we must avoid harbouring any illusions about the potency of the reform programmes of republics and democratic opposition forces. First of all, the republics are struggling for the extension of their rights but have only vague ideas on how functions should be delimited between them and the centre. This results in risks of prolonged confusion and chaos.

Second, there is a danger that the republics will reproduce stereotypes of the command economy at republican level. The republics often overemphasize administrative actions, and the main battles between the republics and the centre concern the transfer of the union property into republican jurisdiction.

Third, a curious thing is that the republics demand independence and at the same time want the centre to take the most important decisions. The position of Kazakhstan is a typical example (see Beng, 1991). While developing a republican economic reform programme, the republican leadership leaves to the centre the liberalization of prices, the stabilization of financial systems, and privatization policies: that is, the politically hardest decisions. Though this approach is right, what remains of the declared economic independence and sovereignty?

Fourth, the republican programmes and the programmes of democratic forces not only disregard truly anti-inflationary measures, but inversely in their struggle against the centre they contribute to the further acceleration of the inflationary spiral with the excessive expansion of social programmes.

Finally, the opposition programmes, being too declarative, lack the most important element: normally concrete mechanisms of realization. This is a manifestation of the low professional level of the authors of these programmes. The lack of professionalism is a general, serious problem in the Soviet Union. Only a few professionals are ready to become reform leaders at different levels of government. There are too many amateurs both in politics and economics. At the same time there is a growing recognition that democracy means primarily professional government and administration in the name of the majority (Shevtsova, 1991). I strongly support the idea, promoted by many Western experts, that at present the most valuable help the West could give the Soviet Union is technical assistance (training of specialists) (Åslund, 1991b, p. 33).

Ensuring social stability (preventing violent antagonistic social conflicts)

The social situation in the Soviet Union in 1990 and 1991 clearly demonstrates that this function is not being fulfilled in a satisfactory way. In fact, all the above-mentioned functions should contribute to this purpose but since they are being poorly implemented, they prove ineffective.

To ensure adequate social stability it is necessary that:

– the state rebuilds its ability to regulate the whole complex of economic and political processes, reaching a relative unity on the distribution of authority between different administrative levels;
– a forecasting of the socioeconomic situation develops with the identification of negative processes and preventive measures against their causes;
– reforms do not lead to the prolonged worsening of living standards for broad strata of the population.

The necessary conditions for the implementing of this function are simultaneously the necessary conditions for maintaining an organizational role for the state, and thus for the peaceful and democratic development of social reforms.

The state, the interests of individuals and social coalitions

Would the reader forgive me the following truism: a state may exist and function only if its policies essentially reflect broad public interests. In this connection I should like to emphasize two particular features of Gorbachev´s perestroika.

First of all, the democratization of society and the attempts towards the transition to a market economy imply a profound reorientation of many individual and group interests, and the breaking-up of the existing system of social coalitions. This process demands adequate reactions by the state. Let us now consider two examples.

A fundamental social contract existed in the totalitarian economy. It was based on paternalistic-egalitarian stereotypes and entailed a contract between the ruling bureaucracy and the majority of employees. The employees accepted an irrational organization of production and labour, a low level of consumption 'in exchange for' a minimal differentiation of incomes and an excessive equalization of social guarantees. At present the situation has changed dramatically. The state (represented by its leadership) has made several attempts to stop serving the interests of the undemanding pauperized masses, but the position of employees has not been changed. Therefore attacks against reformers in 1990 and 1991 (first evident in 1989 in the miners' strike) were not surprising. The reformers had broken the fundamental social contract, but they had failed to change the position of the state.

Another social contract existed between the communist party and the state élite on the one hand, and the economic bureaucracy, primarily the managers of enterprises, on the other. This contract was extremely complex. The state limited the economic initiatives of enterprise managers with its plans and norms, but without the possession of information on production possibilities, the state left managers substantial room for manoeuvre and even for a specific 'dictate from below'. For decades the state supported unviable enterprises and created privileges for managers and a relative stability of their social status. The managers, in turn, were conscientious promoters of state interests in labour collectives.

Also in this sphere, perestroika destroyed the existing *status quo*. The managers obtained some formal freedom of action, but lost the vital guarantee of support for the functioning of their enterprises on the basis of the centralized distribution of resources. Moreover, they were practically left on their own to deal with social demands from labour collectives. At the same time the distribution of consumer goods collapsed and the recession deepened, while cooperatives and other non-state enterprises emerged with high wages and prices. Still, there are a number of aspects of transition to new property forms which would permit the solution of at least some of the state managers' problems. There is an obvious contradiction: the state itself is alienating a powerful pro-state coalition but it still expects support from the members of this coalition. Alternatively they may find a solution themselves. This is not a realistic basis for maintaining cooperation. Little wonder that managers of many enterprises react very negatively to any attempt to reform economic relations and structures.

The second characteristic feature of Gorbachev´s reform is that the state has not made any serious attempt to establish a new social base, a social coalition to support market-type reforms. It has initiated the destruction of old social contracts and the fall of old ideological and psychological stereotypes, while it has fostered the broad public acceptance of the view 'we can no longer live like that'.

In my view, there was no need to undertake actions which had such an outcome. The mistakes and miscalculations of perestroika which are now discussed and are often interpreted as reasons for the deepening crisis and slow reform process, are of a particular nature. The basic reason is the neglect of the real interests of big social groups and the inability to mobilize their interests in favour of reforms. Consequently, powerful social coalitions have been activated against reforms and the focus of public debate has shifted from economic problems to political struggle.

The experience of European postcommunist countries demonstrates that a change of political regime and the acceleration of the reform process gives a certain credit to the new political and intellectual élite. But this issue is extremely complicated and support is not endless. Also, it has proved to be easier to undertake stringent stabilization measures, as a result of which all social groups suffer more or less equally (though the failure in the Polish presidential elections in December 1990 of Prime Minister Tadeusz Mazowecki proves that severe stabilization measures are not easily forgiven) than to undertake decisive actions towards the economic and social differentiation of society with the destatization and privatization of property.

Even to a greater extent than the other reforms, the privatization process demands that special attention be paid to the whole complex of social interests. It is difficult to agree, therefore, with attempts to treat them as if they were of a purely economic nature.

Assessing the ways and means of privatization from this perspective, we have all the reasons to believe that only those solutions may be regarded as optimal which permit the involvement of the majority of citizens in the creation of a new structure of property and property relations. People´s enterprises and other forms of collective ownership, therefore, are more attractive not because they incur higher economic efficiency (international experience proves that this is not so), nor because they might somehow be related to 'socialist choice'. Leased and collective enterprises may become the transitional devices in the shift from total étatization of property to full-blooded market structures, permitting the people gradually to pass this difficult transformation, while ensuring the maximum possible individual participation. This seems to be the only feasible way to make the inevitable process of social stratification more stable and fair.

We have to consider free distribution through the so-called coupon privatization as a perfectly possible and, perhaps, reasonable method in the near future, not because somebody would like to prevent the state budget from receiving revenues from privatization, nor because a free distribution of property offers few incentives for hard work. It is simply a matter of choice: whether to pay a certain price for the formation of a large social coalition in favour of market reforms, or once again to succumb to the temptation to maximize state revenues in the short term, disregarding the political effects. Thus, the establishment of viable and interested pro-reform coalitions is the most important general precondition for the overall success of reforms. It is dangerous to underestimate this point. It will be of vital importance throughout the lengthy transition period. Attempts to establish pro-reform social coalitions should not take extreme forms. There are many examples of excessive attention being paid to satisfy the demands of various social, regional and professional coalitions in the name of political stability, thus endangering the achievement of strategic state goals.

The danger of a revolution of social expectations is characteristic of the first stages of post-totalitarianism: social pressures aiming at social concessions are contagious. To a certain degree this has already manifested itself in Poland and the Eastern parts of the FRG. In the USSR the escalation of the social demands of the workers contains a dangerous potential not only for the present regime, but even for market reforms as such.

In spite of all the attractions of the neoclassical liberal model of the state and the various shortcomings of the social democratic model which have manifested themselves in some Western countries, one thing is clear: reforms cannot be treated as purely economic. Different elements of social strategy are not an end in themselves, but the social orientation of market reforms is extremely important in order to render the restoration of totalitarianism and the command economy impossible.

On the national-state organization: economic aspects

This problem is obviously of a more political than economic nature. I firmly believe that at present it has no simple solution. A stable, lasting resolution of this problem will only be the result of a long historical process, including the development of a fully-fledged market. Nevertheless, we have to try to find a reasonable compromise.

At present, disintegration processes in multi-ethnic states are creating obstacles to economic reforms.[4] In Yugoslavia a sensible economic programme was launched by Prime Minister Ante Markovich in 1990, but it was undermined by the centrifugal tendencies of the republics. In the USSR, though, the radical forces that have come to power in some republics are pushing the central government towards more coherent reformist actions. In the Soviet Union many hopes are currently turned on multilateral negotiations between the republics; but does not the stress on these negotiations imply an admission of how difficult it is to reach any mutually acceptable agreement?

Key issues are the preservation of a single economic space and reasonable 'monocentrism' as well as the extension of the economic prerogatives of the republics. For example, in 1991 the union budget lost a normal tax base, as no agreement on federal tax was reached. Sometimes republics break already-signed agreements by refusing to make the agreed contributions to the union budget and union funds. There are also examples of withdrawals of previously given concessions. Therefore current declarations and agreements are no guarantees against serious problems. Clear delimitations of functions, rights and responsibilities between the union and its subjects would considerably facilitate the process. The conclusion of the union treaty is a coordinating process, which can bring meaningful results.

Contrary to current declarations and agreements, there are still active attempts to identify the centre with the union. The central government´s threats to impose severe sanctions against republics unwilling to sign the union treaty have been repeated time and again, also against republics prone to stay in the union. It is difficult to understand how these sanctions could be implemented.

There are, however, certain hopes of a comprehensive union agreement. There is the joint declaration of the President of the USSR and leaders of nine republics (23 April 1991). It would be constructive to establish a new union of willing republics, although it would be difficult. At the same time it has to be finally and unambiguously recognized: some republics (e.g. Lithuania and Georgia) should be left alone. Efforts should be concentrated on the complicated problems of delimitation and the development of normal and civilized cooperation rather than pushing them to join the union which is now impossible. In this case there will be no need to use any sanctions.

Problems of replacing administrative-command management bodies with institutions for the state regulation of a market economy

The concept of the establishment and functioning of state institutions for market regulation has to be developed from scratch. The research efforts undertaken so far on the so-called organizational structure of management in various Soviet scientific centres were focused on the administrative-command economy. Usually this kind of research did not go beyond the development of sectoral and regional management schemes and new types of associations and enterprises. Political and social aspects were ignored. These studies may be used as a basic starting point only to a very limited extent.

The international experience of the delimitation of the functions, rights and responsibilities in economic regulation among different levels of government and various governmental bodies is much more important. Basically, it is a reasonable idea about a parallel development of new bodies and the reformation or liquidation of the old ones. At the same time, state management should undergo a radical modernization.

It is dangerous to ignore the existence of old state structures while changing the organization and establishing new structures. Otherwise the process of transformation cannot be synchronized. What is going on with the branch ministries, for example? In the past they were proponents of state monopolism and performers of the administrative-command system; now they have almost lost their power. However, the extension of enterprise rights was not accepted by the branch ministries as an impetus to search for new functions in a mixed economic system. On the contrary, the branch ministries shrank into themselves, melancholically remembering their lost power, nurturing the mood of uncertainty (which they would also like to pass on to other social groups) and blaming the current reforms and reform leaders for an absence of positive perspectives. All the above-mentioned is essentially true of the apparatus of central economic bodies.

It has been decided to establish a whole row of new central economic bodies – the State Property Fund, an Economic Stabilization Fund, an Anti-Monopoly Committee, a Committee for Assistance to Small Businesses, etc. These bodies and their functions have a direct relation to the powers and activities of branch ministries and other governmental bodies. How will the problem be solved? By supplanting the latter or through 'peaceful coexistence'? Coexistence would mean the preservation of old economic relations and would weaken new structures. Currently, this appears plausible as there are still a large number of branch ministers in the cabinet and several of the old bulwarks of the command economy have been little but renamed. The State Planning Committee has become the Ministry for Economy and Forecasting; the State Committee for Material Supplies has become the Ministry for Material Resources. Practically all the new market-oriented bodies have been refused ministerial status.

Within the structure of a mixed economy, an essential part of the functions of the ministries must be transferred to enterprises, their associations, and other market structures such as commercial banks and exchanges. However, the long practice of the centralization of financial resources has led to their concentration in the ministries and their subordinate bodies. Enterprises have to undertake the transition to new legal forms with insufficient financial resources. Often they have to give an abnormally large share of their profits to the ministries. There is an urgent need for a clear, unambiguous solution to this problem. The liquidation of the old sectorial structures, including the ministries, must be accelerated and their funds transferred to potentially viable enterprises, new state bodies for market regulation, or to authorities (i.e. Soviets) at various levels.

It is necessary to establish institutions for the regulation of the market. They are decisive for the conditions under which new independent enterprises are to operate. For example, the declared freezing – till the end of 1991 – of established economic ties among enterprises, obligatory state orders and the existing price practices will most probably impede the introduction of market relations. The State Contractual system, which is supposed to be negotiated by the State Committee for Material Provision, the State Agricultural Committee, and the Ministry of Trade will hardly be related to market forces.

Closing remarks

I have tried to show the complexity of theoretical, methodological, political and practical problems, linking the reform of the state system with economic reform in postcommunist countries. The fall of communist regimes and political democratization are the most important but not the only factors of consistent economic reforms.

Reforms in the USSR and East European countries have to be, I believe, of a clearly pragmatic nature, without a priori presumptions and preferences favouring any particular model. On this basis it would be reasonable to define the functions of the state in the economic sphere and in corresponding institutional structures.

This chapter deals with tendencies which manifested themselves in the late 1980s and early 1990s. Essential functions of the state are the transformation of property forms and property relations, a proper selection of targets for economic policy and the construction of a social security system. The social orientation of reforms is the most important condition for their success. The social orientation should include the establishment of 'pro-reformist' social coalitions which can become the driving forces of transition to a market economy.

The danger of a 'revolution of social expectations' needs to be unambiguously stressed. This 'revolution' may lead to a revival of traditions of social pressures and demands to meet any social claim at any price.

References

Åslund, Anders, (1991a) 'The Soviet Economic Crisis: an Abortive Search of a Solution', Stockholm Institute of Soviet and East European Economics, Working Paper No. 16.

Åslund, Anders, (1991b) 'The Soviet Economic Crisis: Causes and Dimensions', Stockholm Institute of Soviet and East European Economics, Working Paper No. 17.

Beng, Ch. Ya., (1991) 'Kazakhstanskii eksperiment', *Izvestiya*, 11 May.

Bim, Alexander, (1989) *Reforma khozyaistvennogo upravleniya; zadachi, opyt, problemy*, Nauka, Moscow.

Bim, Alexander, (1990) 'Sotsial'no-ekonomicheskaya rol' gosudarstva v sovremennoi perestroike ekonomiki', *Ekonomika i matematicheskie metody*, No. 4, pp. 599-609.

Bovin, Alexander, (1991) 'Krizis sotsializma i natsional'nyi vopros', *Izvestiya*, 11 May.

Gaidar, Egor T., (1990) *Ekonomicheskie reformy i ierarkhicheskie struktury*, Nauka, Moscow.

Hansson, Philip, (1986) 'Superministries: The State of Play', *Radio Liberty Research*, RL 167/86, 21 April.

Hewett, Ed A., (1988) *Reforming the Soviet Economy*, Brookings, Washington, DC.

Kurashvili, Boris P., (1987) *Ocherk teorii gosudarstvennogo upravleniya*, Nauka, Moscow.

Pajestka, J., (1986) 'Observations on the future of the economic reform in Poland', *Oecon. Pol*, No. 2.

Parsons, T., (1982) *On Institutions and Social Evolution*, Chicago.

Petrakov, Nikolai, Alexander Bim, Yurii Borozdin, Andrei Vavilov and Vilen Perlamutrov, (1991) 'Ekonomicheskaya programma Rossii', *Nezavisimaya Gazeta*, 12 May.

Petrakov, Nikolai, Alexander Bim, Yurii Borozdin and Vilen Perlamutrov, (1991) 'Ekonomika strany i politika Kabineta (Est'li u pravitel'stva antikriziznaya programma?)', *Business World (Delovoi Mir)*, 14 May.

'Programma deistvii Kabineta Ministrov SSSR po vyvodu ekonomiki iz krizisa', (1991) mimeo., April, Moscow.

'Programma pravitel'stva RSFSR po stabilizatsii ekonomiki i perekhodu k rynochnym otnosheniyam', (1991), mimeo., 22 April, Moscow.

Sconfield, A., (1984) *In defense of the mixed economy*, Oxford.

Shevtsova, Lilya, (1991) 'Volya k vlasti. O novoi rasstanovke politicheskikh sil, ikh vliyanii i protivoborstve', *Izvestiya*, 25 May.

State, Finance and Industry: A Comparative Analysis of Post-war Trends in Six Advanced Industrial Economies, (1986), Brighton.

Stigler, George, (1986) *The Theory of Economic Regulation: The Essence of Stigler*, Stanford, California.

Williamson, Oliver E., (1975) *Markets and Hierarchies*, Free Press, London.

Zala, J., (1971) 'Central intention and planning', *Acta Oeconomica*, Vol. 7, Nos. 3/4.

Yasin, Evgenii, (1991) 'Razgosudarstvlenie i privatizatsiya', *Kommunist*, No. 5, pp. 99-111.

Notes

1   The position of the government of the RSFSR on this problem is rather contradictory ('Programma pravitel'stva RSFSR', 1991, p. 14). Supporting the idea of destatization, the authors of the programme at the same time declare that they 'will resist dispersal of big capital'. In reality this means nothing less than ensuring the possession of the 'commanding heights' for state capital.

2   It is difficult to agree with the idea that a gradual transition from a planned economy to a market one is impossible. This approach is supported even by some authoritative experts (Åslund, 1991b, p. 30). But what does 'gradual approach' actually mean? The current Soviet economic crisis, which is usually mentioned as an argument for the impossibility of gradual transition to the market, is not caused by 'graduality' as such. The reasons are the unacceptable miscalculations and inconsistency of state economic policy, and in fact, the absence of real reforms.

3   This was clearly indicated, in particular, in: 'Programma deistvii', 1991'; Petrakov, Bim, Borozdin and Perlamutrov (1991).

4   These processes obviously have their reasons and explanations. The rationale for absolutizing the aspirations of peoples for sovereignty is that these aspirations include a natural negative reaction to totalitarianism (Bovin, 1991). It is impossible to ignore it; however, it is also dangerous to ignore the limitations of this approach from an economic point of view.

11

Ulterior Property Rights and Privatization: even God cannot Change the Past

Leonid Grigoriev

Privatization looks a most complicated integral part of the transition from a command to a market economy. We see the process as a clear assigning of property rights to non-state subjects by one or another method. The real goal of privatization is an effective market economy. Restrictions on the methods and speed of the process are by nature political and social. At a certain level large-scale privatization would help to set new market rules of the game, especially competition, and to create the new entrepreneurial class.

The experience of privatization in East European countries in 1989-91 have given plenty of examples of complexities. Social costs happened to be much higher than expected and associated structural crises more severe. Privatization basically lagged behind stabilization and price liberalization. The process will take five to six years even in East Germany and much more time in other countries of the region. A clear political goal, public support and the efforts of legitimate governments were not enough to speed up the process or avoid disputes over the methods of privatization, especially in the case of the state industrial enterprises.

Privatization became an integral part of radical market-oriented reforms in East European countries from the very beginning in 1989-90, but with one exception, the USSR. New political forces came to power in East European countries to start systemic changes and especially to change the ownership structure. The political goal of perestroika in the USSR was different from the systemic changes in neighbouring countries. Until 1990 the forces that led the evolution of Soviet society sought to revitalize the centrally planned system by introducing market elements or industrial democracy. It was the obvious contrast to other East European countries which had undertaken the same unsuccessful experiments in the 1970s and 1980s. So the old bureaucracy tried to reform the command system without real systemic changes which would jeopardize its social status. It prolonged the period of seeking and redefining the true purpose of reforms in the USSR.

The case of the Soviet Union was and remains quite different to other countries of the region. Systemic changes in the USSR developed but by other ways and means, led by other political and social forces. The purpose of this chapter is to describe the real path of the country's transformation and the political and social lessons of reforms in 1989-91. Spontaneous privatization in the USSR also has different features in comparison to neighbouring countries. Studying the programme of social and psychological feasibility of privatization in the USSR gives a certain explanation to the laws of privatization of the USSR and Russia approved in early July 1991 (*Izvestiya*, 8 August 1991, p. 3; *Ekonomika i zhizn'*, No. 31, 1991).

The lessons of 1989-91

Public discussion and the policy of the union government until the autumn of 1989 were concentrated mainly on macroeconomics, structural policy and industrial democracy. From the summer of 1989 some attempts were made to draw the master plan of market-oriented reforms made by the Ryzhkov-Abalkin government. These programmes were focused on price policy, stabilization and to a minor extent on destatization (*razgosudarstvlenie*). Decentralization of decision-making led to wage-price pressure, barter trade, repressed inflation and the budget crisis not expected by the government but easily predicted on the basis of East European experience. The rising strength of republican authorities resulted in a shift of power of economic decision-making from the union gosplan to republican gosplans, but not to enterprises. Besides, a crisis of the old federal structure and national problems complicated all issues of ownership in the country.

No programme of 1990-91 and none of the main political leaders gave a clear definition of the purpose of systemic changes in the USSR or privatization in particular. The market economy was proclaimed a political goal of the central government in the autumn of 1989, but no major programme of transformation has been put in action by the summer of 1991. The term 'private property' came into practical use in one of the presidential speeches only in August 1990 (*Pravda*, 19 August 1990, p. 2). Destatization and privatization have been extensively discussed by Soviet economists since September 1990. But only the 500 days' plan considered it as an important political goal for the government and put this part of the transformation plan into its regular place. Still, at least until May-June 1991, all official programmes of reform (and legal acts introduced) reflected the lack of vision of the emerging society. The main objective of privatization – the creation of a competitive market economy – was overshadowed by other political goals and problems: social justice, the redistribution of real political power and control over enterprises between central authorities and republics. Bureaucracy, monopolies and injustice seemed to be the main problems absorbing the reformers, who hoped to promote greater economic efficiency and social justice. Specific details of privatization, such as prices, goals and speed, were largely left unresolved.

The central government had lost a lot of time pondering over radical market reform before the social interests of different strata were defined, though it was not ready or competent enough to move in this direction anyway. Privatization had become an increasingly difficult task both socially and politically (Vanous, 1990, p. 4). National and republican movements were characterized by negative attitudes to the old system and the central authorities, but less by positive goals such as a market economy.

At the first stage of the turn to a market economy (autumn of 1989–spring of 1990) privatization was not discussed publicly at all. At that time supporters of a market economy were mostly concerned about the low quality of the first versions of the law on joint stock companies, for example (Grigoriev, 1990a). Several articles on the significance and problems of privatization were first drafted in February (by Yavlinskii et al., 1990; Aleksashenko and Grigoriev, 1991). Assessments of the situation by Western and East European economists and their programme suggestions of that time (Bauer, 1990; Dhanji and Milanovic, 1990; Grosfeld, 1990; Hinds, 1990; Nuti, 1990; Vanous, 1990; Yarrow, 1986 and 1990) were known to only a handful of Soviet economists.

Official programmes were mostly concentrated on the corporatization and destatization, at least until August 1990. Only in the 500 days' plan and the parallel governmental programmes did privatization find its regular place. The 500 days' plan concentrated on two types of privatization: the slow and the quick ones (Hewett, 1990, p. 152). It reflects the attempt to consider this process as a double-purpose weapon: both an instrument for systematic transformation and for stabilization (*Perekhod k rynku*, 1990, Chapters 1 and 4). Dispute over the fate of the 500 days' plan in the autumn of 1990 gave very specific impulses to the process of privatization, changing its meaning both for the central government and for the public and probably rendering privatization inevitable.

Public debates on the road to the market economy led to the more substantial concerns about the type of privatization. A lot of popular academic economists and journalists were afraid of nomenclature privatization for political reasons. Numerous articles claimed that the only just procedure is the free distribution of national assets by one or another system, mainly by vouchers (Belova, 1990; Bogomolov, 1990; Bunich, 1990a, 1990b; Piyasheva, 1990; Smirov, 1990). Many democrats considered privatization through universal giveaways as a way of blocking the nomenclature. Technical problems and the consistency of this approach, including the creation of a real control of owners over management and the decision-making process, were not even discussed.

Criticism of the voucher system appeared. In particular, the rationality of the exchange of up to 110 million coupons for the securities of thousands of enterprises which had not yet been turned into joint-stock companies was questioned (Anulova, 1990; Grigoriev, 1990c; Grigoriev and Yasin, 1991; Kachanov, 1990; Nekipelov, 1990). Through debates, public opinion began to influence the reform process. As in other East European countries, the discussion changed the approach to privatization. But in contrast to Eastern Europe, the emphasis moved to people´s enterprises or to the total redistribution of property while the East European reformers gathered increasing doubts about this approach.

The main lesson of all programmes of transformation to the market economy in 1990 was that the public support was insufficient for any of them. Even the most popular, the 500 days' plan drafted by the Shatalin-Yavlinskii group, was not defended by any massive social and political force or recognized as their own plan (except for the democratic mass media probably). It reflects the absence or weakness of social forces backing the radical market reform. The reform plans came from the top as a rational way to solve practical economic problems. The market was justified by the leaders to the general public as a sort of economic necessity or an instrument to achieve welfare quickly and easily.

Intellectuals and technocrats did not have enough influence in the society, which was characterized by a strong populist and egalitarian mentality. Populists fought the old bureaucracy but lacked a vision of a real market economy. The new entrepreneurial class was too weak to offer significant support to any programme but remained in a defensive position. The lack of consensus on the transition and the resistance of the old bureaucracy to any systemic changes led to the delay of reform. Relative political stability in the centre was reached at the expense of the long-term interests of the society and of radical reform from the top. No fully-fledged programme of privatization or a feasibility study was worked out. From the autumn of 1990 until the summer of 1991 the inevitability of a transition to a market economy did not mean the necessity of real privatization, either to most people or to the nomenclature.

Ulterior private property rights

The economic system of the USSR on the eve of major market reform is often described as being dominated by state ownership and the nomenclature's control over the decision-making process. Central planning caused a complicated system of privileges for the nomenclature. A certain rank in the hierarchy meant certain legal (and illegal) incomes, cheap state services, housing, dachas, etc. It gave a lot of access to expensive health care, recreational facilities and so on, either free or at low subsidized prices.

Rights to make economic decisions carried authority. Control of state property or flows of investments, goods and financial resources may be considered as riskless rents assigned to positions in the bureaucratic pyramid. But in our opinion the high social status, secure jobs and salaries as well as some 'life-time options' for relatives and friends were much more important than any official or invisible privileges.

In legal terms all state property belonged to the people of the country. Thus, privatization could be considered as selling or returning property to the people, as occurred in the East European countries. High-level members of the nomenclature were dismissed, but managers of enterprises mostly stayed. New leaders – technocrats or populists – had nothing to do with the vested interests of the old bureaucracy. In the USSR, on the contrary, all levels of management of the economy are still controlled by the nomenclature. Therefore, the many changes of top managers and staff of ministries and enterprises did not liquidate these rents in 1985-90. Quite the opposite: the proliferation of barter trade, inflation and the total shortage of goods led to more opportunities to receive this kind of managerial income by reallocating resources.

From this perspective, we may look on the collision between the law and the black market as a conflict of rent-seekers of the command economy and profiteers. Here we are talking about a segment of the black market which in a regular market economy is called small enterprises and the wholesale and retail trade. The same type of conflict has arisen between the old command system and new economic agents, such as cooperatives, joint ventures and small enterprises. The contradiction between the command system and the emerging market economy appears to be a conflict between rent-seeking and profit-seeking motivations. But a certain part of the black marketeers made their profits by using opportunities offered by the command system and its distorted prices.

It is a puzzle why the ministry of finance and various authorities repeatedly issue orders or even legal acts against speculation. At first it might be seen as an attempt to prevent the development of new forms of ownership and entrepreneurial stratum, but after a turning point (say by the end of 1990) the purpose was rather to slow the development of this stratum in order to give the nomenclature time to adjust to the coming market.

The domination of the rent-seeking agents was a cause of the stagnation of the economy. The only way to make a career was to become part of the nomenclature. But it meant avoiding entrepreneurial risks. Each level of the bureaucracy had different responsibilities and managerial risks. The higher the position someone held in the bureaucracy, the greater his social safety regardless of the actual results of his activity. Without proposing a theory of nomenclature rent, we may suggest that there were at least three large groups of bureaucrats: managers of industrial and procurement enterprises; officials of district, regional or republican territorial authorities; and officials of central planning, distribution and managerial offices, including ministers. It is necessary to distinguish between clerks (with little influence and legal rent) and decision-makers. Each level of the bureaucracy has different rights and rents. Economic rights are as real as rents, but they are not secured in legal terms. We suggest we call them 'ulterior property rights'. As the system changes, it becomes more or less clear who controls what property by their attempts to secure this control.

The threat to the rent system has become increasingly clear in these years of burgeoning market-oriented reforms. It was undermining the social status and long-term rent perspectives for some branches of the nomenclature: the staff of the central command apparatus of the economic system, clerks at different levels in the procurement system and top enterprise management. Reactions of the ruling substratum to the changing environment in the Soviet economy differed in relation to their options to legitimize their rights to rents. The situation became even more complicated because of the lack of social consensus on the type of reform in 1988-9, the swift changes in economic policy and misleading statements by prominent politicians. For some branches of the nomenclature it was a last-ditch stand; others saw an opportunity to transform their actual rent rights into legal property rights. In many cases it appears to have been a question of unconscious rational behaviour. The most important case concerns industrial enterprises. Ulterior nomenclature rents are the result of the ability of decision-makers in certain key positions to allocate resources, including the supply of raw materials, imported equipment and consumer goods, as well as financial means. Under almost any type of privatization, various elements of the apparatus are supposed to lose their sources of rent. So their basic interest is that legal acts on privatization are uncertain and that destatization and the corporatization of enterprises takes place instead of privatization. In any case, they are trying to control the whole process by other means, especially by regulating procedures.

Additional complications are caused by the internal conflict of interests among different branches of the nomenclature, for example between central and local authorities or ministerial staff and managers of enterprises. A programme of large-scale privatization should take their common or specific interests into account. Probably each branch is able to prevent or adapt any specific type of privatization to its own interest, but each level or branch has its own way of securing its rights. Unlike in East Europe, the old nomenclature has mainly saved its position in the central government. What is most difficult for them, however, is to convert ulterior rights into real ones. Today, advantages of being at the centre are turning out to be disadvantages and they complicate the acquisition of a real hold on property. It is much easier for the territorial branches of the nomenclature which can exploit decentralization or even nationalistic tendencies.

Again, unlike in East Europe, Soviet enterprise managers have not just been appointees of higher ranks of the nomenclature. In most cases they were and are rather competent. Now some of them (regardless of their competence) are trying to find a way to transfer state property to their own small enterprises. A variety of types of spontaneous nomenclature privatizations (Grosfeld, 1990, p. 147) is the result of different mixtures of rights to make decisions. There are many ways and means of transferring state property into private hands.

The gap between the formal state or people's ownership and the real situation has been much wider than has generally been perceived. The existence of the real control of property by certain economic agents concerns not only the industry but all kinds of property. Any attempt to transfer this nominally public property has regularly encountered resistance from previous (ulterior) controllers.

One of the most complicated cases is housing. Flats in urban areas (about half of all dwellings in the country) mostly belong to the state (actually to cities) or enterprises. The other half of the dwellings already belong to individuals. In practice the state was considered obliged to supply cheap or free housing and various services. Inhabitants were basically considered by regulation (and by themselves) as a party with rights to be supplied. In spite of all the restrictions, inhabitants could exercise certain property rights – for example, to take (illegally but almost openly) money for their flats while formally exchanging them. This type of exchange was and is formally illegal but everyday practice is legitimizing it. In some regions the executing of rights to receive free flats from the state has historically been dependent on a certain price paid as a bribe. So a substantial part of the population considers flats as a kind of property. This view is an obstacle to privatization, especially when cities try to receive some funds through privatization. Most people see their flats as a source of rights partly comparable to property rights – not as an object for a buy-out. Another issue in the housing sector is the stock of formal obligations of the state and many enterprises to people without suitable flats who are entitled to receive free new ones. Besides, these obligations may be considered as a hidden part of the state debt.

In retailing and catering, and 'black' wholesale trade, the existence of the illegal rent system is well-known. It may be considered as a system of ulterior property rights. Legal acts have forbidden many forms of trade, which has led to large-scale corruption. The resulting profits or rents actually implied ulterior private property rights. In many cases 'owners' have almost all regular property rights apart from the legal title. These rights are often distributed among different people and informally secured. The state has tried to fight this system as illegal but the result may be considered as 'a tie'. Most attempts to confiscate rights to rents or profits may be considered as small nationalizations. Is it good or bad from a moral point of view that actual owners of shops can exercise their right to the capital value and sometimes even liquidate or relocate their businesses? The rate of profit is very high because of the inefficiency of the market, price distortions, the unequal supply of goods by regions and great legal risks.

This situation complicates the privatization of the distribution system. It is not a two-party game between the state and the people but a three-party game also involving informal owners. In order to execute any law on small privatization it is necessary to nationalize this type of property or to let actual rent-owners secure their rights. But it is impossible because no papers indicate any owners except the criminal reports and the public attitude to the informal owners is highly negative. Even the transfer of the distributive system to employees is not a sufficient solution. There is a contradiction between trying to privatize property against the interest of the existing (illegal or partly illegal) entrepreneurial stratum and at the same time trying to support the emergence of a new one. In certain cases conflicts arise between emerging legal profit-seeking businesses and the two 'old' parties, the rent-seeking bureaucracy and illegal businesses profiting from the old system of distorted prices. The last two groups are potential losers in a competitive market environment (Koroblev, 1991).

Since most property in the country is under the control of different economic agents, the problem of ulterior property rights varies by branch.

A small-scale as well as a large-scale privatization should have on its side one or another branches of the economic nomenclature in order to be successful.

Spontaneous privatization

The major economic problem of privatization in the USSR is the same as in other East European countries – the low level of capital accumulation or the inadequate level of personal savings in relation to the value of the assets of state enterprises. At the end of 1990, the savings of Soviet households were equal to one quarter of the book value of fixed assets. Privatization in the USSR is underway, but, unlike in Poland, Hungary and Czechoslovakia, privatization is a complex mix of the nomenclature and popular forms of privatization.

The central ministerial branch of the nomenclature first became aware of the pressures for privatization for several reasons. First, they perceived a real danger of losing control over the process of the economy. Second, they had seen how their partners in East Europe had lost control. Their conclusions were obvious: to privatize the ulterior control to their own advantage. On the initiative from enterprises or on orders from Prime Minister Nikolai Ryzhkov, a lot of enterprises and ministries started establishing new bodies, concerns, associations and people's enterprises. This wave of nomenclature privatizations meant a basic change in the attitude of this part of the nomenclature: if privatization is inevitable let us enjoy it.

From that moment the nature of the political struggle had changed. It was no longer a battle for or against privatization but a struggle for the control over privatization. Now it looks as if the nomenclature has a good chance of getting its position in society successfully secured. The highest echelons of bureaucrats, however, often need to take intermediate steps in order to gain not ulterior but regular property rights. It is impossible to win against the interests of another group of people with substantial ulterior property rights: enterprise managers. In the autumn of 1990, they joined the opposition against the 500 days' plan because they did not believe in a quick transition and in particular they did not see how their positions could be insured. From that time managers have played an ever more active role in politics and at the same time in privatization. Their activity has partly been disguised as the establishment of 'people's enterprises' with very strong rights of the directors. In many cases, they adopted the practices of their East European colleagues, buying their own enterprises cheaply and creating joint ventures with foreigners. The increasing role of entrepreneurial activity has also been reflected in political and public organizations.

At the same time a widespread spontaneous privatization of flats and shops has taken off in both towns and villages. The largest cities have tried to invent their own systems of the privatization of flats, shops and services. Potentially it may lead to another problem: a great legal muddle. There are too many privatization programmes and ways and means of selling or distributing property. The establishment of a lot of collectively owned people's enterprises may lead to a privatized but non-market economy.

While spontaneous privatization has spread in the country, its real place and scope are unknown. Two thousand commercial banks, numerous 'small' (private) enterprises and different associations are forming a market system, but a good portion of them represents the nomenclature. The evolution of society and the economic crises create an environment conducive to the establishment of new legal entities with very uncertain property rights. A few well-advertised 'model privatizations' of large enterprises are in fact corporatizations, concentrating large bulks of the shares in the hands of ministries. Sometimes they are disguised as people's enterprises, but the statutes of these corporations reveal the strengthening of the managers' control. A privatization programme may mean both nationalization and reprivatization. The complications are obvious, especially in the case of retail shops if existing entrepreneurs are exchanged for new ones while trained human resources are very scarce.

The main problem (leaving the problem of fairness aside) is that nomenclature privatization delays the rise in efficiency, takes more time and prevents new entrepreneurs access to property. It will take time to change the mentality of rent-seekers into profit-seeking. More open privatizations in the interests of enterprise managers (insiders), especially management buy-outs, at least for small enterprises, would be much more fruitful for society.

Social feasibility

This aspect of privatization is particularly complex in the Soviet Union. The social and psychological conditions of privatization in the Soviet Union are quite different from East European countries. No social feasibility study has been prepared so far. Nobody was ready for such quick political and economic changes in the country: until quite recently the question was considered as purely academic. Still, some bits of information are available and provide a certain idea of the limits on speed, forms and the immediate future of privatization in the country.

First of all, in most of the country only a handful of old people have ever lived in a market-economy environment. In many cases the population and even political leaders talk and think about numerous different types of the market economy. Therefore the acceptance of the idea of a market economy by most political movements does not mean a consensus on what should be done or what a future economy should look like. There is a considerable deviation in the interests within the prosperous strata of the population. According to estimates by Aleksandr Zaichenko only about 15 per cent of the population live at a standard of living that may be considered middle class. Half of these 15 per cent earn their living from the state-owned distribution system, while the other half enjoy bureaucratic rent.

The public attitude to private property is still very uncertain. In public polls in the autumn of 1990 and early 1991, we see a deep division in society on the key issue of transformation, the property question. The market economy is generally accepted but cross-checking reveals that just 12 per cent are fully-fledged supporters; 15 per cent are strongly against it; 30 per cent are unstable supporters; and 43 per cent did not define their position. At the same time, other polls show how people see themselves in terms of security; only 10 per cent feel secure; 37 per cent, more or less so; and 18 per cent not at all (Shpilko, 1990, 1991).

The general acceptance of a market economy narrows down when more specific questions are posed. Half the respondents are against the free hiring of 'man by man' or free pricing. The acceptance of private property varies greatly around the country. In one of the polls 44 per cent of respondents supported the idea of having private property in enterprises, varying from 70 per cent in Estonia to 28 per cent in Uzbekistan. The discrepancies between different polls on the crucial issue of market reform and private property are generally great, suggesting swift changes (Rutgaizer and Shpilko, 1990; Shashnov, 1990; Shiller, Boiko and Korobov, 1990; Shpilko, 1991; Urnov, 1991). Many people are still very uncertain. Mainly young, well-educated and prosperous people are backing market reform. Support is growing fast but the situation is complicated by the economic crisis. The longer reform is delayed, the more dangerous any changes look. The vast deviation of opinion on the crucial questions persists. A study of the social feasibility of privatization is still a necessity for any serious programme of system changes. It must take into account not only general political views in society, but the dynamics of the reform process by strata, especially by the branches of the nomenclature, by industries and by republics and regions of Russia. The lack of information both on public attitudes and spontaneous privatization contributes to the great social and political uncertainty.

Concluding remarks

Currently, three simultaneous developments occur at different levels of society. One is the writing of programmes and debates on types of market reform and privatization. The drafting of legal acts is visibly influenced by Western expertise and looks very radical. Another trend is the growing populist threat to any reform, posing a major challenge to economic transformation. A third development is spontaneous commercialization and privatization. A major market reform should take the several ulterior property rights of different strata and the psychological background of the situation into account. Otherwise the resistance to reform and its social costs may become extremely high.

The privatization law of the USSR, approved on 1 July 1991, offers opportunities to corporatize and buy out state enterprises without a clear definition of property rights. The privatization law of Russia, approved on 3 July 1991, is the result of the victory of one wing of populists over another. Formally both groups suggested the free distribution of vouchers to be exchanged for property to all citizens of the republic. The wing that lost intended to give control to work collectives, while the winners wanted to distribute individual property rights to the whole population. These laws have closed the debate for the time being. Now the central problems of privatization will be the distribution of property between the union and the republics and the implementation of both these laws and the laws on privatization of other republics, opening a new page in radical reform.

At the time of the approval of these laws, no detailed programme of privatization was ready. Uncertainty about the goals and methods of privatization will affect the process for a long time. Presumably this situation is rather convenient for the old bureaucracy. It will be in charge of privatization and will try to use its control to preserve its social status and convert ulterior rights into legal property rights.

References

Ahmeduev, A., (1991) 'Razgosudarstvlenie i razvitie form sobstvennosti', *Voprosy ekonomiki*, No. 4, pp. 48-57.

Aleksashenko, S., and Grigoriev, L., (1991) 'Privatization and Capital Market', *Communist Economies and Economic Transformation*, No. 1, pp. 41-56.

Alekseev, S., (1991) 'Dva polusa i magistralnyi put', *Pravda*, 21 June.

Anulova, G., (1990) 'Razdavat' ili prodavat', *Izvestiya*, 1 October.

Åslund, A., (1991) 'Prospects for Economic Reform in the USSR', paper presented to the World Bank Annual Conference on Development Economics, 25-26 April, Washington, DC.

Bauer, T., (1990) 'The Microeconomics of Inflation under Economic Reforms: Enterprises and their Environment', EDI/World Bank – IIASA. Seminar on managing inflation in socialist economies, Laxenburg, Austria, 6-8 March.

Belova, V., (1990) 'Skol'ko stoit sobstvennost'', *Literaturnaya gazeta*, 14 November.

Blanchard, Olivier, Rudiger Dornbusch, Paul Krugman, Richard Layard and Lawrence Summers, (1991) *Reform in Eastern Europe*, MIT Press, Cambridge and London.

Bogomolov, O., (1990) 'Privatizatsiya', *Izvestiya*, 20 September.

Bunich, P., (1990a) 'Kak razdelit' gosudarstvennuyu sobstvennost'', *Izvestiya*, 22 August.

Bunich, P., (1990b) 'Obshchestvennoe bogatstvo i my', *Ekonomika i zhizn'*, No. 37, September.

Dhanji, F. and Milanovic, B., (1990) 'Privatization in East and Central Europe: Objectives, Constraints and Models of Divestiture', EDI-World Bank, 13 June.

Fischer, S., and Gelb, A., (1990) 'Issues in Socialist Economy Reform', draft, (World Bank staff paper), September.

Gomulka, S., (1989) 'How to Create a Capital Market in a Socialist Country and How to Use it for the Purpose of Changing the System of Ownership', (*The proposal to the Government of Poland*).

Gordon, R. H., (1990) 'Privatization: Notes on the Macroeconomic Consequences', draft, the World Bank seminar in Ljubljana, November.

Grigoriev, L., (1990a) 'New Law on Joint-Stock Companies', *Moscow News*, No. 28, July.

Grigoriev, L., (1990b) 'Neizbezhnyi etap reformy – razgosudarstvlenie', *Mirovaya ekonomika i mezhdunarodnye otnoshenia*, No. 6, pp. 77-8.

Grigoriev, L., (1990c) 'Privatization is not easy', *Moscow News*, No. 49, December.

Grigoriev, L., and Korchagina, O., (1991) 'Evolution of the Crisis and Progress of the Reform in USSR', *Most*, No. 1.

Grigoriev, L., and Yasin, E., (1991) 'Vse razdat'?', *Nezavisimaya gazeta*, 1 June.

Grosfeld, I., (1990) 'Prospects for Privatization in Poland', *European Economy*, No. 43, March.

Hanson, Ph., (1990a) 'Soviet Legislation: Ownership Rights in the New Phase of the Soviet Reforms', draft, Birmingham, November.

Hanson, Ph., (1990b) 'Ownership Issues in Perestroika' in *Perestroika and the Private Sector of the Soviet Economy*, John Tedstrom (ed.), Westview Press.

Hanson, Ph., (1991) 'Soviet Economic Reform: Perestroika or "Catastroika"?', *World Policy Journal*, Spring, pp. 289-319.

Hare, Paul, and Grosfeld, Irena, (1991) 'Privatization in Hungary, Poland and Czechoslovakia', *CEPR, Discussion Paper Series*, No. 544.

Hewett, Ed A., (1990) 'The New Soviet Plan', *Foreign Affairs*, Vol. 69, No. 5.

Hinds, M., (1990) 'Issues in the Introduction of Market Forces in Eastern European Socialist Economies', EDI/World Bank – IIASA, seminar on managing inflation in socialist economies, Laxenburg, Austria, 6-8 March.

IMF, IBRD, OECD and EBRD (1991) *A Study of the Soviet Economy*, Vol. 2, February.

Kachanov, O., (1990) 'Nuzhen li blitskrig v privatizatsii', *Rossiiskaya gazeta*, 15 November.

Koroblev, I., (1991) 'Borba elit', *Nezavisimaya gazeta*, 18 June.

Lee, B., and Nellis J., (1991) 'Enterprise Reform and Privatization in Socialist Economies', *World Bank Discussion Papers* No. 104.

Lipton, D., and Sachs, J., (1990) 'Privatization in Eastern Europe: The Case of Poland', Report for the World Bank, seminar in Ljubljana, November.

Maleev, V., (1991) 'Zolotaya seredina: sertifikat sobstvennosti', *Ekonomika i zhizn'*, No. 19, May.

Melikyan, G., (1991) 'Stanovlenie subektov rynochnyh otnoshenii i privatizatsiya sobstvennosti', *Voprosy ekonomiki*, No. 4, pp. 58-67.

Nekipelov, A., (1990) 'Golovolomki privatizatsii', *Pravda*, 6 October.

Nuti, D. M., (1990) 'Stabilization and Sequencing in the Reform of Socialist Economies', EDI/World Bank – IIASA, seminar on managing inflation in socialist economies, Laxenburg, Austria, 6-8 March.

Olshtynskii, A., (1990) 'Puti privatizatsii: nashi problemy i zarubezhnyi opyt', *Voprosy ekonomiki*, No. 9.

Perehod k rynku, (1990), Moscow.

Petrakov, N., (1990) 'Demokratiya bez rynka obrechena', *Izvestiya*, 21 November.

Piyasheva, L., (1990) 'Razdacha', *Literaturnaya gazeta*, 12 December.

Rutgaizer, V., and Shpilko, S., (1990) 'Otnoshenie naselenia k chastnoi sobstvennosti', *Voprosy ekonomiki*, No. 2, pp. 67-72.

Sachs, J., (1991) 'Accelerating Privatization in Eastern Europe', paper presented to the World Bank Annual Conference on Development Economics, 25-26 April, Washington DC.

Shashnov, S., (1990) 'Gotovy li my k peremenam', *Pravitel'stvennnyi vestnik*, No. 44, October.

Shiller, R. J., Boyko, M., and Korobov, V., (1990) 'Popular Attitudes towards Free Markets: the Soviet Union and the United States Compared', *NBER Working Paper*, No. 3453, September.

Shpilko, S., (1991) 'Otnoshenie naseleniya k privatizatsii sobstvennosti', *Voprosy ekonomiki*, No. 4, pp. 108-16.

Smirnov, I. I., (1990) 'Put' k rynku: otkrytaya sistema rynochnoi ekonomiki', Moscow.

'Soyuznyi zakon o privatizatsii: skoro skazka skazyvaetsya', (1991) *Kommersant*, No. 15.

'Stabilization, Liberalization and Devolution (Assessment of the economic situation and reform process in the Soviet Union)', (1990) *European Economy*, No. 45, December.

Tarasov, V., (1990) 'Kak razgosudarstvit' sobstvennost'?', *Ekonomicheskie nauki*, No. 9, pp. 39-46.

Urnov, M., (1991) 'Osvobozhdayas' ot avtoritarizma', *Polis*, No. 1, pp. 122-35.

Vanous, J., (1990) 'Privatization in Eastern Europe: Possibilities, Problems, and the Role of Western Capital', *World Market Focus*, DRI/McGraw Hill, 22 February.

Vanous, J., (1991) 'Near-Term Prospects for Economic Reform in Eastern Europe', paper presented to the World Bank Annual Conference on Development Economics, 25-26 April, Washington DC.

Yarrow, G., (1986) 'Privatization in Theory and Practice', *Economic Policy* (A European Forum), No. 2, April.

Yarrow, G., (1990) 'Privatization: Issues and Problems', World Bank, Washington DC, 13 June.

Yasin, E., (1991) 'Razgosudarstvlenie i Privatizatsiya', *Kommunist*, No. 5, pp. 99-111.

Yavlinskii, G., Mikhailov, A., and Zadornov, M., (1990) *400 dnei doveriya*, Nedra, Moscow.

12

The Grand Bargain

Jeffrey Sachs

In the last couple of weeks, Yavlinskii and I and a few others at Harvard have been talking to the US administration. I want to explain why I want to spend 30 billion dollars, Dr Birman's tax-dollars, for this adventure. My starting point is that I think that:

The successful transformation of the socialist economies, whether in Eastern Europe or in the Soviet Union, has to be based on three fundamental factors. The first is political democratization; the second is truly radical economic reform; and the third is large-scale Western financial assistance. These, I believe, are the three preconditions for a successful (in the sense peaceful) transformation of the Soviet Union and Eastern Europe to a democratic market society.

Stressing the need for financial assistance first I would point out that there are many people who argue in favour of letting the Soviet economy reform itself. They say it is a rich country, and all it has to do is finally to pursue all the right policies and that will be enough for a successful transformation. They think that the only problem is political dictatorship or the role of the communist party and that financial assistance is beside the point.

I reject this argument out of hand as being nonsensical. The transformation of the Soviet Union, even with the best possible government in the world, would be extraordinarily difficult to manage politically and economically without a significant provision of financial assistance from the West. All through history, countries that have reached the level of chaos and crisis that the Soviet Union now has, have required substantial outside help to avoid social calamity. This was true in the inter-war period for countries that reached hyperinflation. This was true after the Second World War with the Marshall plan, and this is true today. The best proof of this is if we leave aside our preconceptions and doubts about Gorbachev, as well as doubts about the reformability of the Soviet Union, and look at the governments of Eastern Europe.

We (the G-24 countries) are putting tens of billions of dollars into Eastern Europe now precisely on the principle that even the very best of governments simply cannot succeed on their own. The G-24 countries have committed up until May 1991 (i.e. between the summer of 1989 and May 1991) 40 billion dollars for the assistance for all of Eastern Europe, not counting another 16.5 billion dollars of debt cancellation that Poland received in April 1991. That is 57 billion dollars committed so far, if the debt cancellation is included. Much more is to come, because this figure does not count all the future flows from the IMF and the World Bank and the EBRD and other government funds that have not yet been committed.

So, as we are speaking of Eastern Europe with a population of about 125 million people, if you think about the roughly equivalent per capita figure for the Soviet Union, you are clearly speaking of a scale of commitment of over 100 billion dollars. I just want to point out that the notion 'reform is its own reward' is wrongheaded. It is not an answer to the question whether aid for the Soviet Union is appropriate now. Keep in mind that if it was ever appropriate, it would have to be extended for a successful transformation, and it does not matter whether you have Lech Walesa as President or Vaclav Havel as President or anyone else. This is such a difficult, excruciating process of transformation right now, that to do it peacefully will require outside help.

If we can put that aside, though, we arrive at a different question: is there a chance now that Western assistance can help to bring about radical and political and economic reform in the Soviet Union, or rather would it serve to do precisely the opposite right now, keep a bunch of incompetents in power? Now, let me also assure you that my strong personal interest in getting involved with this project is not to sustain the monopoly of power of the Communist Party of the Soviet Union, nor to prop up Gorbachev or any particular individual, nor to prop up a dead system. The only justification for aid right now is to support the radical transformation of Soviet society to democratic rule and to lobby for radical reform. I want to make clear that nobody can conceive this discussion of a grand bargain as helping Gorbachev, or as a quid pro quo for Gorbachev's help in freeing Eastern Europe, or anything else. This is purely a forward-looking proposition, that this money could help to make a democratic and economic transformation feasible which otherwise would not be feasible.

Then we come to the question of whether it is possible for assistance actually to serve that role, or is it just naïve to believe that large-scale assistance could do that? Is not talk about this premature, for how could financial assistance just serve this role? The starting point of my assessment is that there is a very deep crisis right now in the Soviet Union; that communism as an economic ideology is dead, although communism as a power bloc has hardly faded from the scene. There are strong forces of democratization that can be built upon, which means that perhaps this is a moment at which influence could play a constructive role. A second point is that any offer of financial assistance at present should be highly conditional. It could be contingent upon democratic reform as well as political reform; financial assistance to the Soviet Union on an unconditional basis at this point would be extremely dangerous and wrongheaded.

The third point is that in the world there is no mechanism for significant financial assistance without conditions: the only way that significant financial assistance can be extended to the Soviet Union is through the multilateral institutions, the IMF and the World Bank, and the European Bank for Reconstruction and Development. These institutions, particularly the two established institutions, the IMF and the World Bank, have 40 years of procedures deeply and fundamentally ingrained to make conditional lending. There is no unconditional lending from these institutions, which is why they are not exactly beloved institutions in the world. They are not fun to work with; they are annoying; and arguments about specific conditions as well as general conditions can be too time-consuming. It should be understood that before a single penny flows from the IMF, for example, the Soviet Union would have to declare in a detailed letter of intent, running probably into a 100-page letter, its commitment to a radical transformation of the economy, to a fully-fledged transformation to a privately owned market-based economy. It would have to propose clear measures, or 'prior conditions' as they are called, such as substantial price liberalization and the devaluation of the rouble to a realistic level. It would also have to elaborate its commitment to a sequence of actions over the course of the following year, down to the level of numerical targets for precisely defined quantities. These numerical targets, from an economic point of view, are somewhat fatuous, because no one can really make a model of such precision that can precisely reach numerical targets, especially in a situation of economic chaos as the Soviet Union is in right now. These, however, serve the specific role of ensuring that no money gets disbursed unless the targets are met. Detailed negotiations are also conducted to show that the government has operated in good faith to meet the targets, so that a waiver of the numerical terms of the specific targets by renegotiation is therefore in order.

Critics of this general idea fear that this may be money that is just going to be handed on the table to prop up a defective system. There is no way that this could come about, at least not significant assistance. Italy may give money without conditions, Germany may give money without conditions, but the concept of large-scale, coordinated, multilateral assistance requires a detailed role to be played by the international financial institutions. It is on these terms that a greater opening of the Soviet system than ever before would come about, which itself would be a pre-condition for any money whatsoever that would flow. This is an important point that needs to be stressed.

Now, Yavlinskii and I and the others are working on the assumption that there may be a moment when such conditions could actually be met during which promises can be made of significant assistance in the future, which in turn could play an important role in mobilizing society, particularly the reformers and the democrats, finally to implement the necessary radical changes. We base our view on this on two facts. First, there are important elements of democratization taking place right now. Today (12

June) is, I think, one of the most historic days in Russian history, and it is not to be downplayed that the Russian people are freely able to choose their leader. This is as fundamental a type of democratization as anything. It is true that the Soviet people are not choosing the leader of the union right now. Mr El´tsin will have enormous leverage in the West, and enormous influence internally, merely by virtue of the fact that he will be the only legitimately and democratically selected leader in the Soviet Union. This will play an important role on which further reforms can proceed.

Second, there is the '9+1' union agreement that was reached on 23 April 1991 which so far is a piece of paper, but it is potentially a document of historic significance if it is not thrown into the dustbin of history. That document says that the Soviet Union will be reconstituted on a voluntary basis from the republics upwards. It states that republics will be able to choose whether to be in or out of the union, which is why there are 9 rather than 15 republics that are signatories to this. It means that the Baltics would be able to choose independence if they want to. It means that a new basis for economic authority will be established by the actions of the republics during 1991, if the terms of the agreement were to go forward. It implies that a new constitution would be elaborated and ratified in the first half of 1992, and, remarkably, that there would be free multiparty elections for the Supreme Soviet of the union in 1992. There is a good chance that none of this will come to pass. This is just a document that was agreed to in the political heat of the moment in specific historical circumstances, even tactical circumstances, so it might not be implemented. However, our argument is to treat it seriously as a basis on which the West can engage the Soviet Union and provide support. If it is not implemented, it is also a basis on which the West can withdraw its support in the future. The Soviets have agreed, and the republics in the union have agreed, to hold free elections in 1992. This is something that should be taken seriously; it is not something to scoff at.

Democracy is of fundamental value for the West. We hope that this does not become a dead letter, but rather one on which a basis of cooperation can be built. One part of the picture is that this is a fragile process of democratization which could be sustained and supported from the outside. Moreover, radical economic reform is more possible at this moment because the Soviet system has reached the end of its tether and is in chaos and will remain in chaos until there is radical economic reform. The pretensions of Prime Minister Valentin Pavlov to use administrative means to control the situation were tried in the first half of 1991; they proved to be as ridiculous and foolhardy as anyone here would have guessed. There is the catastrophic failure of a government and its policies. At the same time there is Eastern Europe, in spite of all its tribulations and difficulties, getting out of the crisis step by step, not easily, but surely in a much more satisfactory way than the Soviet Union. Therefore, a case can be made that there is a way out, and its outlines are perceptible. The idea is that perhaps there is an opportunity for introducing radical economic reform right now, because the failure of the old system is staring everybody in the face, and because the way out might become clear to a meaningful coalition of democrats, reformers and a society generally desperate for some immediate reasonable answers.

Our feeling is that since there is a possibility of moving forward, the West ought to make a highly conditional statement at this point. This would, in effect, signal its preparedness to provide sustained conditional financial assistance over a period of years at a realistic level necessary to make the transformation, but only if the radical reform both in the political and economic sphere proceed. The idea of making that kind of conditional statement is that it might help to clarify the situation inside the Soviet Union. It would at least tell the Soviet people a simple fact of life: there is a plausible way out of the crisis. If that way is not selected, they should understand that this is because the hardliners and the communists are holding and clinging on to power, and others are clinging on to the old system, and refusing to grasp the new opportunities. Such a statement would also show that the West is prepared to cooperate in an open, generous way with those forces that really want to proceed with full-scale transformation. It will give the reformers a political lever, in my view, which they can use to mobilize support for a more radical project inside the Soviet Union. It can show that there is a realistic way forward, which is all that is currently being discussed.

The question arises: why make such a proposal right now, why not a year or two later? Why come in right now, when the system is on its last legs? Why not wait for a democratic government to come forward, declaring its intentions to reform radically, and then respond? The reason is that I believe such a view suffers from a fundamental fallacy that the Soviet Union is going to march in a linear procession behind the developments of Eastern Europe. The question presumes that Eastern Europe went through a passage, first of chaos, then of democratic reform and then of economic reform, and that the Soviet Union will surely follow the same path. I view that, in a sense, as being too optimistic.

Paradoxically, many things can go seriously wrong, as people from the Soviet Union know much better than I do. History tells us not to bank on this kind of chaos, this kind of loss of all social legitimacy, of all order including the administrative order of government functioning, in order somehow to arrive at the right outcome. In a country of 30,000 nuclear warheads and 160 nationalities, with an intense and currently largely unguided political conflict, this is to hope for a great deal. I think it is a kind of determinist fallacy to think that we should stand back and just let the system collapse, because something good is going to follow in its place. I regard that as a dangerous gamble. At least the West can do its best to try to guide events by showing that there is a peaceful way out for the Soviet people: a way that makes sense, that is generous, fair-minded and supportive of the Soviet Union in the global system, and not punitive. I think it could also help answer a lot of questions inside the country and provide the basis for moving forward.

What do we propose concretely? Let me just outline the idea of this programme. The idea is that this general proposition would be put on the table by the West, that there would be meaningful financial assistance in the event of radical political and economic reform. The Soviet Union would respond with the intention to move forward in that direction. That could be the response of Gorbachev. That could be a response from El´tsin and Gorbachev; presumably it would have to be both. The response would have to come in a very concrete form before there is assistance.

The first order of business is to start fulfilling the terms of the 9+1 agreement which stipulated that in the summer of 1991 a new union treaty would be negotiated among the nine or perhaps more republics, that by August or September a basic agreement on economic union would be agreed to, all the time implying that this would be backed by substantial Western assistance when it came into existence.

The economic union would define the central macroeconomic framework for stabilization. The idea is that it would aim to establish a unified market, a monetary system between the participating republics. The fundamental basis of that would be a federal reserve system, a central bank, a single currency within the economic union, a prohibition of republican or lower-level government intervention in the free flow of goods, a kind of interrepublican chamber in the parliament, a European-style economic space or a free flow of goods as in the US, and a common trade policy of the union *vis-à-vis* the rest of the world. The union would also be established as a working entity. Finally, the federal government would have its own designated fiscal system, which means that it will not depend on contributions from the republics, but on its own taxes, which will be agreed to, that it will collect: a corporate income tax, a personal tax and a value-added tax. The centre and the republics would have their own independent tax systems.

A political entity will also be established which we call an interrepublican economic commission. It would be chaired by the Prime Minister of the Soviet Union and have representatives of the republics as its basic members. This would be the negotiating body between the union and the rest of the world, and would particularly be the one to negotiate the terms of the financial loans of the IMF-programme, and so forth. This would be the executive body for the economic union.

Starting in October 1991, within a very short timetable there will be two rounds of negotiations with the International Monetary Fund. The first would be for membership. This stand-by arrangement would be predicated on a programme of radical economic reform, which would be modelled on the radical reforms being undertaken by the East European countries. It would be a basic model for the stabilization of the economy, liberalization, including a quick devaluation of the rouble in the same way that the Czechoslovak crown or the Polish zloty were made internally convertible. As the first step, the radical reform would lead to the liberalization of economic activities, free trade, based on the convertibility of the currency, the limitation of most price controls and so on. This is to be followed by a process of privatization over a period of several years.

At this point there would be an agreement on the IMF programme. There would be an agreement on significant financial assistance from governments to go along with the IMF financial assistance, and this indeed would be conditional on the fulfilment of the IMF programme. So the process would start as it did in Poland, in Czechoslovakia, in Hungary. There would be step-by-step fulfilment of specific targets, which would each release financial assistance on a step-by-step basis. This would be a process spaced over many years. We are envisaging aid in the order of about 30 billion dollars a year in the first two years of the programme, and then something like 20 to 25 billion dollars a year in the third and fourth year. Most of the aid would come in the form of balance-of-payments support and a stabilization fund to support a convertible rouble. Over time, the balance-of-payments support will shrink and be replaced by an increase of support for infrastructure investment and for direct support to the private sector in the Soviet Union along the lines that the US is now providing to the private sector in Hungary and Poland, through the establishment of various venture-capital funds, or what are called private-enterprise funds, which channel money from the West to the Soviet Union. We have tried to project realistic sums for such support, based on the kinds of programmes that are under way in Eastern Europe, and a realistic timetable of measures which basically stretches through until 1997.

Obviously each step of the process remains conditional on a political timetable as well as on an economic timetable. However, the notion that there would be large-scale assistance at the beginning of the programme is not correct. What will be promised at the beginning is the flow of the system over time, assuming that the reforms go forward. That is the rough outline. There may be a 2 per cent chance of something like this happening in fact, but given the possible 2 per cent chance of this actually going forward, given the number of man-hours that went into it, this will still be a very good bargain even if there were a 0.1 per cent chance.

I want to clarify that we are not saying that we must definitely have a bargain right now, or that we must do anything to engage Gorbachev in such a bargain. That is not the point of this proposal. The point is to show the Soviet people that there is a way out and that the West is prepared to extend its support. That is all. If it cannot be accepted now, it might be a tragedy but there is nothing more to it than that. The only point that I am personally worried about is that the reformers in the Soviet Union do not know there is a way out, because they do not understand that this scale of assistance really would be available under the right circumstances. Since they might not understand that they themselves do not have a credible case to present to the Soviet people, they are unable to pinpoint what is being lost by continuing with this failure. They have a realistic opportunity to escape from the system and it is only in making that possibility clear inside the Soviet Union that the real value of this approach lies. The West has an enormously important role to play right now in helping to show a realistic way out of the crisis, and that is the thrust of this project.

Index